The New Grolier

STUDENT
ENCYCLOPEDIA

Munster High School
Resource Center
Munster, Indiana

VOLUME 20

Sweden–United Nations

Munster High School
Media Center
8808 Columbia Ave.
Munster, Indiana 46321

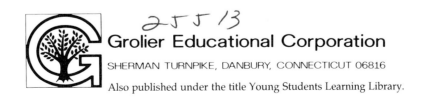 Grolier Educational Corporation

SHERMAN TURNPIKE, DANBURY, CONNECTICUT 06816

Also published under the title Young Students Learning Library.

PHOTO CREDITS

A.T.& T. BELL LABORATORIES page 2447(top right). A-Z BOTANICAL COLLECTION page 2459(bottom left). AEROFILMS page 2437(top right). ALLSPORT page 2366(top right); 2407(top right); 2440(bottom right); 2441(both pics). HEATHER ANGEL page 2460 (top left); 2462(top left). ASSOCIATED PRESS page 2456(bottom left); 2464(top left). BBC HULTON PICTURE LIBRARY page 2398(top left); 2403(top right); 2409(top right); 2467(center right). BIOFOTOS page 2370(top left). BOEING page 2453(top right). BRITISH AIRWAYS page 2454(top left). BRITISH TELECOM page 2388(top right), 2391(center right); 2392(bottom right). ALAN BUNTING page 2470(top left). CENTRAL page 2481(bottom left). BRUCE COLEMAN LTD. page 2478(top left). DAVE COLLINS page 2377(top right). COLORSPORT page 2375(top right); 2442(top left); 2443(top right). THE CONSERVATIVE PARTY page 2419(center right). COURTAULDS page 2416(top left). GENE COX page 2381(bottom left). ARMANDO CURCIO EDITORE SPA page 2365(bottom left); 2366(top left); 2370(bottom left); 2371(top right); 2375(bottom left); 2378(top left); 2380(top left); 2383(both pics); 2390(top left); 2402(top left); 2407(center right); 2416(bottom left); 2419(top right); 2423(top right); 2430(top left); 2433(both pics); 2436(top & center left); 2438(bottom left); 2448(top left); 2452(bottom left); 2463(top right); 2468(top left); 2471(bottom left); 2474(bottom right); 2479(bottom left); 2483(top right). DEFENSE DEPARTMENT page 2471(top right). MARY EVANS PICTURE LIBRARY page 2443(bottom right). F.B.I. page 2463(bottom right). FORD MOTOR COMPANY page 2372(top left). WERNER FORMAN ARCHIVE page 2368(top left). GEORGIA DEPT. OF COMMUNITY DEVELOPMENT page 2415(bottom). GIRL SCOUTS OF THE U.S.A. page 2364(top right). GRANADA T.V. page 2400(top left). PHILIP GRUSHIN page 2365(top right). SONIA HALLIDAY page 2373(top right); 2444(bottom left); 2473(bottom right); 2485(top right). ROBERT HARDING PICTURE LIBRARY page 2385(top right); 2389(bottom); 2392(top left). MICHAEL HOLFORD page 2380(bottom left). JAPANESE TOURIST OFFICE page 2432(bottom right). ROBIN KERROD page 2322(top left). KEYSTONE page 2411(top left). KOBAL COLLECTION page 2303(top right). LIBRARY OF CONGRESS page 2386(top left); 2389(top left & top right); 2472(left). LINOTYPE PAUL page 2480(bottom left); 2481(top right). MAINE DEPT. OF ECONOMIC DEVELOPMENT page 2438(top left). THE MANSELL COLLECTION page 2400(center left). PAT MORRIS page 2458(top left). NHPA page 2426(top right).

NATIONAL ARCHIVES page 2483(bottom right). NATIONAL GALLERY, LONDON page 2382(top right); 2429(bottom right). NATIONAL GALLERY OF ART, WASHINGTON, D.C. page 2429(top right). NATIONAL TOURIST BOARD DAMASCUS page 2372(bottom left). NATIONAL TRUST page 2439(top left). PHOTON page 2438(bottom right). PICTUREPOINT page 2363(top right). POPPERPHOTO page 2426(top left). PORT OF NEW YORK AUTHORITY page 2474(bottom left). SCIENCE MUSEUM, LONDON page 2393(top right). SFP/JEAN CLAUDE PIERDET page 2362; 2399(top right). LISA SIMMONS page 2421(bottom right). SMITHSONIAN INSTITUTE page 2430(center left). SPORT & GENERAL PRESS AGENCY page 2440(top left). SPORTSIMAGE page 2406(top left). STEDELIJK MUSEUM page 2436(top right). SWISS NATIONAL TOURIST OFFICE page 2367(top right). T.V.S. page 2399(bottom right). TAMPA CHAMBER OF COMMERCE page 2431(top right). TENNESSEE TOURIST BOARD page 2405(center right). TEXAS HIGHWAY DEPARTMENT page 2408(top right); 2412(left); 2414(top right). SALLY ANNE THOMPSON page 2449(top right). UNICEF page 2486(bottom left). USDA PHOTO 2434(top left); 2479(top right). UNITED NATIONS page 2485(bottom right). UNITED PRESS INTERNATIONAL page 2423(center right); 2424(top left); 2462(bottom left); 2470(center left). VIRGINIA STATE TRAVEL SERVICE page 2459(top right). ZEFA page 2369(bottom left); 2376(top left); 2384(bottom right); 2402(bottom left); 2404(top left); 2411(bottom right); 2414(bottom left); 2417(top right); 2420(bottom right); 2421(top left); 2424(bottom left); 2426(center left); 2432(top left); 2434(bottom right); 2446(bottom left); 2455(top right); 2456(top left); 2473(top right); 2480(top left); 2484(top left); 2486(top left).

ISBN 0-7172-7137-4

Also published under the title Young Students Learning Library.

CONTENTS

SWEDEN From frozen, lonely fields in the north to meadows and plains in the south, Sweden's landscape is beautiful. Rugged mountains divide Sweden and Norway, the two countries on the Scandinavian Peninsula. Sweden's east coast is on the Baltic Sea and the Gulf of Bothnia. Sweden is about one-tenth larger than California. (See the map with the article on EUROPE.)

Icy rivers and waterfalls spill down the mountains and flow to the coast through the dark forest of northern and central Sweden. There are small farms in clearings in the forest. The only big farms are in southern Sweden, where the soil is more fertile and the climate is warmer.

Sweden's large cities are built along the coast. In the capital city of Stockholm, tall glass and concrete apartment buildings look down on cobblestone streets and ancient churches.

There are no slums in the cities, and few people are very poor. Sweden is a highly industrialized country. It is often described as a socialist state dedicated to assuring material security for all. National health insurance and a pension system are features of Sweden's social welfare state.

Swedes have learned to grow good crops on the small amount of cultivated land. Their main crops are wheat, rye, and potatoes. They have used their timber, iron, and waterpower to build industries. Today,

Sweden is one of the most prosperous countries in the world. Rich mines produce iron for machinery, tools, and shipbuilding. Iron and steel are exported. The forests supply timber for paper. Sweden is noted for high-quality steel products and for well-designed glassware and furniture.

The Evangelical Lutheran Church is the state church. The Swedish language, of Germanic origin, resembles the other Scandinavian languages. Winter sports are popular in cold, snowy Sweden.

The history of Sweden is linked to that of its neighbors. For many centuries, Finland was part of Sweden. Sweden was joined with Denmark and Norway for many years. In the 1500's and 1600's, Sweden was a great Baltic Sea power and ruled over other countries on the coast.

Today, Sweden is a constitutional monarchy. Under the 1975 constitution, King Carl XVI Gustaf of Sweden lost much executive power. The prime minister and a cabinet run the government. A unicameral *Riksdag* (parliament) is the governing body.

Sweden, which was neutral in the two world wars, is still a neutral country. It is not a member of the North Atlantic Treaty Organization (NATO), although its neighbors, Norway and Denmark, are.

ALSO READ: HAMMARSKJOLD, DAG; NOBEL PRIZE; SCANDINAVIA; SCANDINAVIAN LANGUAGES; SOCIALISM.

▲ *Runes, a form of ancient writing, can be seen carved on runic stones all over Sweden.*

◄ *A skillfully designed indoor set and expert camera work can create a realistic scene in a TV drama. (See* TELEVISION BROADCASTING.*)*

SWEDEN

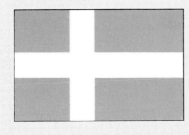

Capital City: Stockholm (660,000 people).

Area: 173,745 square miles (449,964 sq. km).

Population: 8,370,000.

Government: Constitutional monarchy.

Natural Resources: Hydroelectric power, iron ore, lumber.

Export Products: Machinery and transport equipment, metals and metal products, wood and wood pulp.

Unit of Money: Krona.

Official Language: Swedish.

▲ *Jonathan Swift, satirical writer and essayist.*

SWIFT, JONATHAN (1667–1745)

Jonathan Swift was an English writer. His best-known work is his book *Gulliver's Travels*. He was a skilled *satirist* (one who uses writing to make fun of people's stupidity and false pride).

Swift was born in Dublin, Ireland, of English parents. He went to England in 1689 and became a secretary to an English statesman. In 1694, Swift returned to Ireland and became a Protestant minister. But he continued to spend much of his time in England. He wrote many satirical essays and political pamphlets. His opinions influenced the government and people of Great Britain. In 1713, Swift was made dean of Saint Patrick's Cathedral in Dublin.

His book *Gulliver's Travels*, or *Travels into Several Remote Nations of the World*, was published in 1726. It tells about the marvelous adventures of Lemuel Gulliver during four voyages to strange lands. Gulliver is first captured by tiny people called Lilliputians. On his second voyage he discovers the Brobdingnagians, people 12 times larger than himself. His third and fourth voyages take him to many peculiar places. He finally reaches the land of the Houyhnhnms, a tribe of gentle horses that have all the human qualities Swift admired most. The Houyhnhnms are served by unpleasant creatures called Yahoos, who look like people but are stupid and cruel. Most people consider Swift's story to be a delightful and brilliant mockery of human foolishness.

ALSO READ: LITERATURE.

SWIMMING

Fish, water birds, and many four-footed animals are naturally good swimmers. They are either born with the ability to swim, or they swim by making the movements in the water that they use to move on land. Human beings have

▲ *"Blow bubbles in the water and open your eyes," the instructor tells children who are beginners in swimming. By learning to exhale in the water, beginners learn to put their faces in the water comfortably.*

had to learn a complicated system of body movements in order to swim.

Learning to Swim Swimming is a good form of exercise and a popular sport. Everyone should learn how to swim in order to be able to move freely in water. The younger you learn, the better. Once you know how to swim, you can learn other water sports safely.

Learning to swim is easy with proper instruction. Babies have been taught to swim before they can walk. Swimming lessons are offered at summer camps, public swimming pools, and schools throughout the country. One of the best places to learn to swim is at your local branch of the YMCA or YWCA.

The *prone float* is usually the first swimming position beginners learn. In this position, the swimmers lie face down in about 2 feet (60 cm) of water, with their legs extended behind them and their hands on the pool bottom. Slowly, they lift their hands from the bottom and extend them in front of their heads. Some swimming instructors call this position "floating like a log." It helps the swimmers feel the lifting effect of the water and shows them how the water will support the body without any body movements.

After learning the prone float, beginners move on to the *prone glide* by pushing off from the pool bottom or side. By adding a simple up-and-down kick to the prone glide, a swimmer can learn to move across the surface of the water. Some instructors call this move the "motorboat." It is a good idea to practice the up-and-down kick, or the *flutter kick*, while holding onto the side of the pool. The main action in the flutter kick should come from the hips, while the lower legs and ankles remain relaxed.

STROKES. After beginners have learned the basic skills of floating, gliding, and kicking, they are ready to combine them with different swimming strokes. The *crawl* is the fastest stroke. It is a good one for beginners to learn. A learner can begin practicing the arm and breathing actions while standing in chest-deep water. With his or her face in the water, one arm is extended in front of the shoulders. The learner angles the arm, fingers first, down into the water, and then pulls and presses the hand through the water to about the thigh. In a continuous motion, the learner lifts the arm at the shoulder, letting the elbow bend, and repeats the movement. In swimming, the arms are alternated. The swimmer lifts the head and inhales through the mouth on the side that is most comfortable,

just as the opposite arm is entering the water and beginning the press downward. The swimmer exhales through the mouth and nose under the water.

When this arm and breathing action is combined with the flutter kick, the result is the crawl. It is the most commonly used recreational stroke and is often used in racing (where it is called the *freestyle*). The crawl is also used in lifesaving, when it is important to get to a victim quickly.

The *sidestroke* is used when distance, not speed, is the important factor. It is a relaxing stroke that allows the swimmer to breathe freely with the head above the water. The swimmer lies on either side with one arm extended out in the direction he or she wants to go, and the other arm at the side. The swimmer gradually pushes the extended arm downward and backward toward the feet. The leg action is called the *scissors kick*.

The *backstroke* is a fast stroke that permits easy breathing. It is similar to the crawl, except that the swimmers are on their backs. The backstroke is often used in racing.

The *breaststroke* is also used as a racing or recreational stroke. Lying face down on the water, the swimmer uses both arms at the same time to press the water down and back. The swimmer breathes as his or her head

▲ *These children are practicing the prone glide, an important step in learning to swim. The arms are extended to help support the body, and some of the youngsters are doing a flutter kick to help move themselves through the water.*

▼ *This illustration shows the four main methods of swimming: crawl, backstroke, butterfly, and breaststroke. The crawl and breaststroke are the most common swimming strokes.*

▲ *A big step in learning to swim is finding out that you can easily float on your back in a relaxed position.*

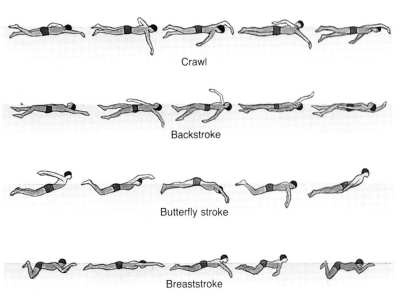

Crawl

Backstroke

Butterfly stroke

Breaststroke

▲ *In 1926, Gertrude Ederle of the United States was the first woman to swim across the English Channel. She is shown entering the water on the French coast. Fourteen hours and 31 minutes later she reached the English side of the Channel.*

No one knows exactly when people first learned to swim, but an Egyptian who lived about 2160 B.C. left a written record that his children were taking swimming lessons.

surfaces on the downward motion of the arms. The *whip kick* is used, which is a sideways thrusting kick made with the legs drawn up and then whipped back and together. You can also swim the breaststroke keeping the head up, which is easier for breathing and more fun as you can look about you and enjoy the surroundings. The stroke should be continuous and even and smooth. The breast stroke is used to a great extent in water ballet.

The *butterfly* is a common stroke used in racing. It is also similar to the crawl, except that both arms and both legs make the stroke at the same time. The butterfly requires great strength and endurance. It is too tiring for long-distance swimming.

History of Swimming Swimming techniques date back thousands of years. Carved stone pictures of the ancient Assyrians show that people were using a crawl-like stroke in about 880 B.C. Evidence also exists that the Greeks and Romans swam in this way. But swimming did not develop into a competitive sport until the late 1800's. When swimming was included in the Olympic Games in 1896, the breast stroke was the only racing stroke used. But in the early 1900's, an Australian swimmer named Richard Cavill introduced the "Australian crawl." It was an instant success, and speed swimmers throughout the world began to work on new and faster strokes. The back crawl was recognized as a competitive stroke in the 1912 Olympic Games. The butterfly was developed in 1934 by an American swimming coach as a kind of breast stroke, but it was not legalized for competition until the late 1950's. The development of these strokes in competitive swimming helped make the activity safer and easier for people everywhere learning how to swim.

Swimming has become one of the most popular summer events in the

▲ *In 1972, Mark Spitz of the United States set a record by winning seven gold medals in one Olympics. They were also all new world records.*

Olympic Games. Among the outstanding American swimmers who have won Olympic gold medals are Don Schollander in 1964, Debbie Meyer in 1968, Melissa Belote in 1972, Mark Spitz in 1968 and 1972 (when he won seven gold medals), Brian Goodell and John Naber in 1976, Steven Lundquist in 1984, and Matt Biondi in 1988. New Olympic record times were set in each year's competition.

ALSO READ: ARTIFICIAL RESPIRATION, DIVING, EXERCISE, LIFESAVING, OLYMPIC GAMES, SCUBA DIVING, SPORTS, SURFING, WATER SKIING, YOUNG PEOPLE'S ASSOCIATIONS.

SWITZERLAND Switzerland is a small, mountainous country in central Europe. It is also a land of lakes and waterfalls. Switzerland is surrounded by France, Germany, Austria, Liechtenstein, and Italy. (See the map with the article on EUROPE.)

The Jura Mountains rise to the northwest of Switzerland. Their low, rounded crests are covered by pine forests and green meadows. To the south are the Alps, which are much higher and more rugged. Few people live in the Alps. Swiss houses, or *chalets*, are clustered in small villages. When roads are closed by snow, young people often ski to school. Sheep, goats, and cows graze on the slopes.

Between the two ranges lie fertile meadows and low hills. Most Swiss live in the villages and cities of this region. The capital is the historic old city of Bern.

Switzerland has little good soil for farming. Most farmers raise cows. The cheese and milk chocolate made from their milk is sold to many countries. Farmers also grow wheat, vegetables, and fruits.

More than half of the Swiss people are factory workers. Their skill and hard work have made Switzerland a wealthy nation, with one of the highest standards of living in Europe, despite its lack of resources and small size. The Swiss make things that take much skill, such as watches, tools, and machinery. Craftworkers make music boxes and other carved wooden objects.

Switzerland is an international banking center and is noted for its hard currency, money that keeps a steady value. It is a favorite tourist area for skiing and mountain climbing. Some climb the majestic peak, the Matterhorn, 14,691 feet (4,478 m) high.

Switzerland is divided into 23 small counties, or *cantons*. The country's history as a free republic began in 1291, when citizens of three cantons

promised to defend each other against invaders. These cantons grew into a strong confederation as more villages from different counties joined.

In each canton, the people still speak the language of their ancestors. As a result, Switzerland has three official languages—German, French and Italian. Some people speak a fourth language, Romansh (also spelled Romansch). It is similar to Latin.

Each canton elects representatives to the Federal Assembly in Bern. The assembly makes the laws and elects seven of its members to run the government. Each year, the assembly elects from these seven a president and vice-president.

▲ *Picturesque villages dot the scenic countryside of Switzerland. This one is in the region of Graubünden.*

SWITZERLAND

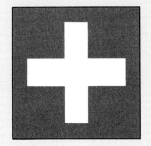

Capital City: Bern (141,000 people).
Area: 15,943 square miles (41,288 sq. km).
Population: 6,500,000.
Government: Federal republic.
Natural Resources: Hydroelectric power, building stone.
Export Products: Machinery, watches, pharmaceutical goods, food.
Unit of Money: Swiss franc.
Official Languages: German, French, Italian.

▲ *A sword was a Viking warrior's most prized possession. The iron hilts were often engraved and richly decorated with silver or gold.*

Switzerland was neutral during both world wars. After World War I, Geneva was chosen as the seat of the League of Nations. The Peace Palace built then is used as the European headquarters of the United Nations. Switzerland is not, however, a member of the United Nations, but it participates in most of the U.N.'s specialized agencies.

ALSO READ: ALPS MOUNTAINS; LEAGUE OF NATIONS; TELL, WILLIAM.

SWORDS AND KNIVES Swords and knives are cutting devices that consist of a metal blade with one end inserted in a handle, or *hilt*. The blade is usually thin and flat, and one edge is usually very sharp. Swords are much larger than knives and are used almost exclusively as weapons in fighting. Knives vary in size from a few inches to about a foot (30 cm). They are frequently used in fighting, too. But knives are also useful tools.

Since people first learned how to work with metals, they have made many types of swords. Early Greek and Roman swords had heavy *two-edged* blades (meaning that both edges

► *Swords changed with fashion and to meet new needs. From left to right: a 16th-century two-handed sword; a 17th-century rapier; a 15th-century cut and thrust sword; and a 19th-century sword.*

were sharp). The *rapier*, which has a long, thin, tapering blade that comes to a sharp point, was designed for piercing rather than slashing the victim. The rapier is still used in fencing. Although most swords were designed to be held in one hand, some, such as the *broadsword*, were so heavy that both hands had to be used. Some swords, such as the Oriental *scimitar* and *katana*, had curved blades. The *saber*, invented during the 1700's, had a rather wide, pointed blade. It was designed for slashing rather than piercing. The *cutlass*—made famous in pirate stories—was a short saber used on ships. A soldier sometimes attaches a short sword called a *bayonet* to the end of a rifle for use in close fighting in battle. But today, military swords are primarily decorative and are worn with dress uniforms.

Knives are still used today because they are more versatile weapons than swords are, since they are smaller and easier to use. One type of knife, the *dagger*, was used as a weapon before the invention of the sword. Daggers were invented during the Stone Age, before people learned to use metals. Many types of daggers and other knives have been designed through the centuries. Early European tribes used the *scramasax*, a big knife that could be used as a weapon and a tool. The *stiletto*, which had a thin blade with a sharp point and no cutting edge, was designed only for stabbing.

In the pioneering days of America, a 15-inch (40-cm) hunting knife became a very popular weapon and tool. The pioneer hero, James Bowie, made this knife popular, so people called it the *bowie knife*. The *switchblade*, a modern invention, is a pocket knife with a blade that springs out when a certain point on the handle is pressed. It is illegal in many states. Other pocket knives, such as the Boy Scout knife, are among the most popular knives in use today.

ALSO READ: DUEL, FENCING.

SYDNEY Sydney is the largest city and the major seaport of Australia. More than three million people live in this modern, growing city. Sydney is located on the southeast coast of Australia. It is the capital of the state of New South Wales.

Sydney, built around Port Jackson, rates as one of the finest harbors in the world. The harbor has an area of about 20 square miles (52 sq. km). It is deep enough for the largest oceangoing ships. Sydney's residents can enjoy swimming, boating, windsurfing, and fishing along the beautiful beaches that line the harbor. Sydney Harbor Bridge, which has a single span of 1,650 feet (503 m), crosses the entrance to Port Jackson. Ships of every major nation visit Sydney harbor to be loaded with Australia's chief exports—meat, wool, and grain. Most of these products are packed and processed in the city. Sydney's workers also manufacture many goods, such as textiles, metals, ships, and automobiles. Sydney is a cultural and educational center. The University of Sydney was founded in 1852. The Sydney Opera House, a striking modern building with roofs

▼ *Some areas of Sydney, such as Paddington, still have beautiful wrought ironwork on balconies and outdoor stairs. The iron was originally carried as ballast by early vessels sailing from England to Australia.*

that look like the sails of a ship, overlooks the harbor.

Sydney was the first European settlement in Australia. In 1788, a British prison colony was founded at Sydney Cove. The British used to send many convicts to their overseas colonies when British jails became overcrowded. Immigrants from Europe later came to Sydney. People began to set up farms on the rich land of New South Wales, and Sydney grew into a thriving trading center.

ALSO READ: AUSTRALIA, BRIDGE.

SYMBIOSIS There is a little bird called an oxpecker that spends much of its time perched on certain types of buffaloes. It eats the ticks and flies it finds on the buffaloes. This is good for the oxpecker—it finds food—but it is also good for the buffaloes, which are freed from their parasites. The oxpecker and the buffaloes are said to be living in mutual symbiosis, because both are gaining benefit from being together.

Animals and plants often live in symbiosis with each other. For example, some bacteria in your intestines help you digest certain types of food. They are your *symbiotic partners*: they could not live without you, and you could not live without them.

Where one partner gets benefit from symbiosis at the expense of the other, the benefiting partner is called a *parasite*. In *commensalism*, one partner gains benefit without harm to the other. In *mutualism*, both partners benefit—as with you and the bacteria.

Another example of mutual symbiosis involves one kind of sea anemone and a hermit crab. The sea anemone lives on the crab's shell and hides it from animals that might eat it. But the sea anemone also is able to eat the bits of food scattered by the crab.

Symbiosis can also exist in a slightly different form, where populations of one type of animal benefit

Australia has an area of about 3 million square miles (8 million sq. km). Sydney has an area of only about 700 square miles (2 thousand sq. km), but almost a fourth of all Australians live in Sydney.

Little cleaner fish have many clients, mostly big fish such as moray eels, surgeon-fish, and wrasses. The big fish know where the cleaner fish work and line up waiting their turn. When the cleaner fish begin working on a client, the big fish floats in the water with fins distended and usually mouth open. The little fish goes inside the gills and mouth of the big fish and cleans them in complete safety.

▲ *Mutual symbiosis benefits both partners. Hermit crabs often carry sea anemones on their borrowed shells. The sea anemone receives free transport and some food while the crab is protected by its passenger's stinging cells.*

from populations of another type, even though some individual animals may suffer. For example, a predator may weed out the weakest of a population of animals, leaving the population as a whole stronger.

ALSO READ: PARASITE, PARASITIC PLANT.

SYMBOLISM Symbolism is the representation of a thing (generally an idea, emotion, or value) by means of a sign. There is always some kind of relationship or similarity between the symbol and the thing symbolized. Symbolism is used in art, language, literature, religion, logic, and even psychology. In literature, symbolism is often used in the fable, allegory, and parable.

Even street and highway signs make use of symbolism. There is now a whole set of international road symbols used to warn drivers of such things as traffic lights, crossroads, men at work, a narrowing road, a bridge, or a tunnel. These signs can be understood by all drivers, whatever language they speak. One well-known modern symbol is the radiation symbol used in hospitals and at nuclear power and research facilities. International airports use symbols so that all travelers can locate baggage

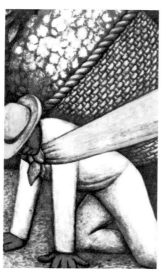

▲ The Flower Vendor *by Diego Rivera.*

check-ins, cafeterias, and restrooms.

In art—particularly in religious art—symbolism has always been very important. For thousands of years, European artists have used the olive branch to stand for peace, the palm branch to stand for triumph, and the anchor to stand for hope. During the early years of Christianity when the penalty for being a Christian was death, the name of Jesus was never written. Symbols were used instead. Christians symbolized Jesus Christ as a lamb, because the lamb was a well-known sacrificial animal. Jesus, called the Lamb of God, was offered as a sacrifice to redeem mankind. The drawing of a fish meant Christ, because the five letters of the Greek word for "fish" are the same as each first letter of the five Greek words meaning "Jesus Christ, Son of God, Savior." The first and last letters of the Greek alphabet also symbolized Christ. These were the letters Alpha and Omega, meaning "the beginning" and "the end."

Symbolism became popular among European writers and artists at the end of the 1800's. Writers wrote about dreams, visions, and mythological tales, using symbolism to make a point. The Belgian author, Maurice Maeterlinck, wrote a play entitled *The Blue Bird.* The blue bird symbolized happiness. One of the painters of the late 1800's who used symbolism was Paul Gauguin of France. Gauguin felt that modern industrial society had made people too aware of material goods. He went off to the South Sea island of Tahiti. There he painted pictures using symbols to represent a simple, freer life. Look at Gauguin's *Tahitian Woman,* shown on the next page. The woman sits in profile with her hair pulled back in a simple style. Her only decoration is a flower tucked into her hair. Gauguin shows the woman sitting relaxed by the water—enjoying the natural life of sun and seashore, unspoiled by modern ways.

A little later, symbolism was used

in North American art by the great artists of the Mexican Revolution. Like the Symbolists of France, the Mexicans used other civilizations to inspire their own art. In the 1920's and 1930's, the art of Mexico's ancient Indian ancestors inspired the works of Diego Rivera, David Siqueiros, and José Clemente Orozco, among other Mexican artists. They studied the beautiful sculptures and temples left by the great pre-Columbian Indian civilizations. They developed a sculptured, rounded way of painting that symbolized the style of ancient Indian art. An example of this is shown on the opposite page in Diego Rivera's painting, *The Flower Vendor*. His figures are rounded and heavy looking, like ancient Indian sculpture. The viewer cannot miss the symbols of Mexico's ancestors, in which the painter felt Mexicans should take pride.

ALSO READ: HIEROGLYPHICS, MODERN ART.

SYMMETRY Symmetry is a similarity or balance between shapes or objects. The letter "A" illustrates one kind of symmetry. Suppose that a line were drawn straight down through the middle of the letter, and the letter were folded along that line. You can see that the two sides of the fold would lie exactly on top of each other. Another way to say this is that the letter "A" has two identical sides. The letter "C" also has this property, only the folding line would go across the letter instead of up and down. Objects with the property of two sides that match when they are folded in this way are said to have *bilateral symmetry*. The folding line—on each side of which the letter is the same—is called the *axis of symmetry*.

■ **LEARN BY DOING**
Many objects in nature have bilateral symmetry. Leaves, many animals, and a person's face are all objects that have bilateral symmetry. Can you find the axis of symmetry for these? ■

A circle has *radial symmetry*. Radial symmetry is more complete than bilateral symmetry. Any line passing through the center of a radially symmetrical object divides the object into two identical halves. A starfish has radial symmetry.

■ **LEARN BY DOING**
Another kind of symmetry is illustrated by the letter "S." If you look closely, you will see that the letter cannot be folded to make the two halves coincide. However, if the center point of the letter "S" is marked, the top and bottom halves are alike. The halves are symmetric about the center point, which is called the *center of symmetry*. What kind of symmetry do some other letters have? ■

ALSO READ: ART, GEOMETRY.

SYNAGOGUE see JUDAISM.

SYNTHESIZER see ELECTRONIC MUSIC.

SYNTHETIC Rubber can be made from *latex*, the sap of a rubber tree. Rubber can also be made synthetically by combining the chemical elements carbon and hydrogen. The

▲ Tahitian Woman *by Paul Gauguin.*

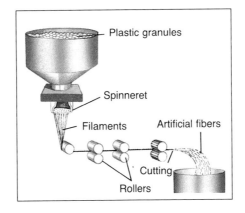

◀ *Artificial fibers are made from plastic granules, which are melted and forced through holes in a spinneret to produce filaments. These are drawn through rollers and then cut to make fibers.*

Plastic granules

Spinneret

Filaments

Artificial fibers

Cutting

Rollers

▲ *Automobile interiors consist largely of synthetic materials—from the dashboard panel with its dials and controls to the seat coverings.*

▼ *Damascus, capital of Syria, is the oldest capital city in the world. It is mentioned in the Bible, and it has been a community for over 4000 years. This is St. Paul's Window and the Ancient Wall.*

latex from the tree is a natural substance (made by nature), while the synthetic rubber is a man-made substance. Synthetic substances are often artificial imitations of natural substances. A synthetic that is exactly like a natural substance is made up of the same elements as the natural substance. For example, a natural diamond is a mineral found in nature. It is made up of carbon atoms arranged in a certain pattern. A synthetic diamond is also made up of carbon atoms, but the atoms are arranged in the pattern by people. Nevertheless, the synthetic diamond is still a *real* diamond. However, there are imitation diamonds made of the chemical compound titanium dioxide. These diamonds are not synthetic. They are fake diamonds because they are not made of the same chemical elements as natural diamonds.

A synthetic product may be better than a natural substance. Synthetic rubber, for example, is better than natural rubber for some uses because it can be made stronger and more rugged.

Dyes were the first synthetic substances ever produced. For thousands of years, dyes had been made from plants, minerals, earth, and parts of animals. In the 1800's, a purple dye was made from coal tar and other chemicals. Now far more synthetic dyes are used than natural dyes. Food flavorings are another group of synthetics made from coal tar.

All plastics are synthetics. They are artificial substitutes for wood, metal, ceramics, and fibers. One important group of plastics are the *resins*. Natural resins occur in the sap of evergreen trees. Resins used to be taken directly from trees, or they were mined from the earth (where they are the fossil remains of trees that died millions of years ago). Synthetic resins are used in varnish, lacquer, medicines, and phonograph records.

Rayon was the first synthetic fiber used in textiles. It is produced from *cellulose*, the substance of which the walls of plant cells are made. *Nylon* was first developed in 1938. When World War II cut off silk imports from Asia, nylon began to be used as a synthetic substitute in such items as parachutes and stockings. Nylon is not a fake silk. It is a synthetic because both nylon and silk are made up of proteins. Other synthetic fibers followed nylon, two of which are *Dacron* and *Orlon*. Glass, spun into threads, produces another synthetic fiber called *fiberglass* or *spun glass*. It is used in making rugs, textiles, glass wool, and many other products.

A sponge is an animal that lives in tropical seas. Sponges have thousands of tiny holes that absorb and hold water. Natural sponges have been gathered and dried for use as a washing aid. Most sponges sold today are synthetic—made by blowing air into plastic materials to make the holes that absorb and hold water.

ALSO READ: CHEMISTRY, DYE, FIBER, GEM, PLASTIC, RUBBER, SILK, SPONGE.

SYRIA One of Earth's most ancient inhabited places is Syria. It is located at the eastern end of the Mediterranean Sea in the heart of the Middle East. Syria is bordered by Turkey, Iraq, Jordan, Israel, and Lebanon. (See the map with the article on the MIDDLE EAST.) In ancient days, the name "Syria" meant all the land on the eastern shores of the Mediterranean, inland to the Arabian Desert.

Grassy, fertile plains make up northern and eastern Syria. The Syrian Desert lies south and west of the Euphrates River, which flows through Syria. Two mountain ranges rise on a narrow western strip along the seacoast. In between is the valley of the Orontes River. Damascus, the capital, is in an oasis.

Syrian people are mainly Arabs, but there are some non-Arab groups, including Kurds and Armenians. Bedouin Arabs herd sheep, goats, and cattle on the plains. Farmers grow wheat, cotton, tobacco, fruits, and sugar beets. Textiles are manufactured, and sugar and fruit are processed. Syrian craftworkers make inlaid metalwork and woodwork, leather and silver goods, brocades and embroideries. Syria has deposits of oil and natural gas.

Ancient Syria was the home of many peoples, including the Phoenicians and Hebrews. It was a part of the empire of Solomon and David. It revolted after 935 B.C. and formed the kingdom of Syria.

Syria was once the center of the caravan trade between East and West. Damascus is one of the oldest continuously inhabited cities in the world. Settlements probably were on its site as early as 2000 B.C. Under Arab control, Syrians learned the Arabic language and became Muslims. The Turks controlled Syria from 1516 until World War I. After that, France ruled until Syria achieved independence in 1946, after World War II.

Between 1958 and 1961, Syria was joined with Egypt as the United Arab Republic. Then Syria withdrew from the partnership. The Socialist Ba'ath party and military leaders seized power in 1963, and Syrian forces attacked Israeli settlements from the Golan Heights in southwest Syria. During the Six-Day, or Arab-Israeli, War of 1967, Syria lost the Golan Heights area to Israel. Syria joined Egypt in a war against Israel in 1973. Beginning in the 1980's, Syria gave military aid to Lebanese Muslims fighting against Lebanese Christians backed by Iraq. Syria remains a radical nation in the Middle East, with close U.S.S.R. ties.

▲ *Under the Romans, Palmyra became a very important city in Syria. But in the late* A.D. *200's Palmyra's queen, Zenobia, declared her country independent. She was captured by the Romans and the city was destroyed. The ruins of the city are shown here.*

SYRIA

Capital City: Damascus (1,200,000 people).
Area: 71,504 square miles (185,180 sq. km).
Population: 12,200,000.
Government: Republic.
Natural Resources: Oil and natural gas, iron ore, phosphates.
Export Products: Oil, cotton and other textiles, phosphates.
Unit of Money: Syrian pound.
Official Language: Arabic.

TABLE TENNIS Table tennis is a fast indoor game that requires skill and coordination. The game is similar to regular tennis, but the table tennis "court" is a table.

The table for the game is 5 feet (1.5 m) wide and 9 feet (2.7 m) long and stands 30 inches (76 cm) high. A net is stretched across the center, just as in a regular tennis game. The table tennis net is about 6 inches (15 cm) high. Each player uses a paddle, or racket, usually made of wood. Some paddles have a surface of ridged rubber. Table tennis balls are made of a lightweight substance called celluloid or a similar plastic.

The object of the game is to score 21 points. A player serves by first hitting the ball down onto the table on his or her side of the net. After the ball has bounced once on the opponent's side of the net, the opponent tries to return the ball by hitting it back over the net. The server must then hit the ball over the net again. This continues back and forth until one player misses—either by not re-turning the ball or by returning it incorrectly. To be a correct return, the ball must cross the net and land in the other "court," just as in regular tennis. A miss gives a point to the other player. The ball may bounce only once—but it must bounce once—on a player's side of the ta-ble—before it is hit. If the ball touches the net or the net posts on the way over, it is still considered good, except in serving. A served ball that touches the net is a *let*, which means that the server must serve again. No matter who wins the point, play begins again with the same server until five points are scored. Then the other player starts serving. The serve changes every five points.

If both players have 20 points, the 21-point rule changes. The winner must have two more points than his or her opponent. In this kind of play-off, the service changes after every point.

Players can be penalized in table tennis. If you lean on the table and make it move, your opponent gets the point. If you touch the net or posts while the ball is in play, your opponent again gets the point. You will also lose the point to your opponent if you touch the surface of the table with your free hand while the ball is in play. Since the ball must bounce before being hit, a player will lose the point if he or she volleys the ball (hits it before it bounces).

Table tennis indirectly helped U.S. relations with the People's Republic of China when, in 1971, American players were invited to participate in matches in China.

ALSO READ: SPORTS, TENNIS.

TAFT, WILLIAM HOWARD

(1857–1930) William Howard Taft's greatest ambition was to become chief justice of the Supreme Court. But even before this ambition was fulfilled (in 1921), Taft served as President of the United States and in several other important government offices.

Taft, one of six children, was born in Cincinnati, Ohio. His father, Alphonso Taft, served as a judge and government official himself and encouraged his children to excel. Young Taft attended Yale University and the Cincinnati Law School. He married Helen Herron, who was influential in his decision to enter political life. Taft practiced law in Ohio for several years until he became a judge in the state

courts in 1887. He was appointed solicitor general of the United States in 1889 and later became a federal judge. President McKinley asked Taft in 1900 to go to the Philippine Islands, which had just been acquired by the United States, and end the harsh military rule there. Taft succeeded in doing this and was appointed civil governor of the islands in 1901. Taft was a remarkably fair, sympathetic governor. He made many improvements for the Filipinos before becoming President Theodore Roosevelt's secretary of war in 1904.

Roosevelt thought highly of Taft and came to depend on him as an adviser. Roosevelt wanted Taft to be his successor as President because he expected Taft to carry on with the business and social reforms begun in Roosevelt's administration. Although Taft preferred the judicial branch of government and did not like politics, Roosevelt and Mrs. Taft persuaded him to run for President in 1908. In the election, Taft received more than a million votes over his Democratic opponent, William Jennings Bryan, who was running for President for the third time.

Taft began his administration under the disadvantage of following a very popular and forceful President. Taft was not as forceful a speaker or politician as President Roosevelt had been. Taft failed to get enough reforms through Congress to please

▲ *The intense concentration is evident on this table tennis player's face as he prepares to serve.*

Members of President Taft's family also were active in political life. His son, Robert Alphonso Taft, was a senator from Ohio from 1939 to 1953. His grandson, Robert Alphonso Taft, Jr., was a senator from Ohio from 1971 to 1977.

WILLIAM HOWARD TAFT
TWENTY-SEVENTH PRESIDENT   MARCH 4, 1909—MARCH 4, 1913

Born: September 15, 1857, Cincinnati, Ohio
Parents: Alphonso and Louisa Torrey Taft
Education: Yale University, New Haven, Connecticut
Religion: Unitarian
Occupation: Lawyer, judge
Political Party: Republican
Married: 1886 to Helen Herron (1862–1943)
Children: Two sons, one daughter
Died: March 8, 1930, Washington, D.C.
Buried: Arlington National Cemetery, Arlington, Virginia

▲ *Though not part of the People's Republic of China, the Taiwanese still keep many of their ancient Chinese traditions, such as opera with its brightly made-up girls in rich costumes.*

Roosevelt and his supporters (or even, to please Taft himself.) Taft's policies and decisions soon split the Republican Party. But Taft was even more effective than Roosevelt in bringing legal action against large businesses, called *trusts*, that controlled certain industries.

Taft used the Sherman Antitrust Act, passed by Congress in 1890, to break up the concentration of power in large businesses. He supported "trust-busting" prosecutions against the Standard Oil trust and the American Tobacco Company in 1911. But Taft's failure to veto the Payne-Aldrich Act, a high-tariff law, caused him to lose favor with many people, including Roosevelt.

When the conservative Republicans renominated Taft in 1912, Roosevelt and other liberal Republicans formed their own party. The new Progressive ("Bull Moose") Party nominated Roosevelt. This action split the Republican vote so widely that the Democratic nominee, Woodrow Wilson, won.

After leaving the White House in 1913, Taft became a professor of law at Yale. President Warren Harding appointed him chief justice of the Supreme Court in 1921. Taft made the administration and operation of the Court much more efficient. He served as chief justice until 1930.

ALSO READ: PRESIDENCY; ROOSEVELT, THEODORE; SUPREME COURT.

TAIWAN Taiwan is an Asian island about 90 miles (145 km) off the coast of the Chinese mainland. Also called Formosa, its official name is the Republic of China. The Chinese Nationalist government is based on Taiwan. (See the map with the article on ASIA.)

The Chinese name, Taiwan, means "terraced bay." Early Portuguese explorers named the island Formosa, meaning "beautiful." It is beautiful, with fields of green rice and steep purple mountains that slope to the sea. Western Taiwan is a long coastal plain. Most of the cities and towns and many farms and fishing villages are located here. The central part of the island gradually rises to high mountains and thick forests. Here Taiwan's first inhabitants, the aborigines, live. They are related to Malaysians, and Indonesians.

The climate is subtropical, which means that crops can grow year-round. Rice is the main crop, but sugar, oranges, bananas, tea, and pineapples are also grown. The Taiwanese have terraced many hills to provide more fields for growing crops. The island's forest products include paper, plywood, and lumber.

Most Taiwanese are Chinese whose ancestors emigrated to the island in the 1600's and 1700's. Others are Chinese who fled from the mainland after the Communist takeover in 1949. Many Taiwanese are Buddhists.

TAIWAN

Capital City: Taipei (2,570,000 people).
Area: 13,886 square miles (35,962 sq. km).
Population: 20,300,000.
Government: Republic.
Natural Resources: Coal, lumber.
Export Products: Textiles, machinery, food, plastics.
Unit of Money: New Taiwan dollar.
Official Language: Chinese.

Dutch traders had a settlement on the island from 1624 to 1661, when Chinese of the Ming dynasty drove them out. The Manchus from China soon took control and held the island until 1895 when the Japanese took over. After 1945, China regained control of Taiwan. Chiang Kai-shek (Jîang Jieshi) moved his Chinese Nationalist government there in 1949. The Chinese Communists threatened to invade Taiwan in the 1950's, but American military and economic aid helped prevent it. Taiwan held the "China seat" in the United Nations until 1971, when Communist China was admitted and Taiwan expelled. Formal diplomatic relations ended between the United States and Taiwan in 1979. Trade and other relations between these two countries, however, were not broken off.

ALSO READ: BUDDHISM, CHIANG KAI-SHEK, CHINA, TAOISM.

TAJ MAHAL The Taj Mahal is a monumental tomb, or mausoleum, in northern India. It is often said to be one of the most beautiful buildings in the world.

The Taj Mahal lies near the ancient Moslem city of Agra. It was built in the 1600's by an Indian emperor named Shah Jahan. He was very much in love with his wife, Mumtaz Mahal, who had borne him 14 children. She died while giving birth to the last child. The Shah then ordered that the Taj Mahal be built as her tomb. More than 20,000 people worked about 22 years to construct the exquisite monument. The Taj Mahal is a square building topped by five rounded, marble domes. At each corner stands a slender tower, or minaret. The white marble walls are set with semiprecious stones, and the carving is like lace. A quiet pool reflects the graceful domes and minarets. A beautiful garden surrounds the building.

Today, the Shah and his queen are both entombed in the "dream in marble." Many people say that the best time to see the Taj Mahal is in the light of the full moon, when the white walls gleam like pearls.

ALSO READ: INDIA.

TANK A tank is a large, armored military vehicle first used by Great Britain during World War I. A tank is powered by a large diesel engine. It moves on a continuous metal track, which is turned by the wheels around which the tracks rotate. This type of

▲ *The Taj Mahal stands in a garden outside the city of Agra, in north-central India.*

▼ *Tanks played a vital role in World War II. The British Valentine (top left) first saw action in 1941. The American Pershing (bottom left) had a speed of 30 mph (50 km/hr). Germany's Tiger (top right) had armor 4 inches (100 mm) thick. The Russian T-34/76 (bottom right) was one of the best tanks of the war.*

▲ *A member of the Masai tribe in Tanzania, covering the roof of a hut with mud.*

continuous belt allows a tank to travel over rough and difficult terrain that soldiers could not otherwise reach.

A tank is basically a huge, movable gun platform. The body of the tank, protected with thick steel, sits above the tractorlike wheels. The tank crew works inside this part of the tank. A rotating turret containing the tank's large gun or cannon is the top part of the body. Other machine guns are also located in the body. A *hatch*, or opening, at the top allows the crew to enter and leave the tank. When in combat, crew members can see out through the *periscopes*—instruments with mirrors that enable a person to see things out of the direct line of vision. Periscopes are also used by submarine crews to see above the water's surface when the submarine is submerged. Tank crews consist of a commander, a driver, and several gunners (depending on the number of guns on the tank). They communicate with other tanks and headquarters by means of two-way radios.

During World War II, some specialized tanks were developed. Guns called flame throwers were attached to tanks, enabling them to set fire to their targets. Tanks that could move through water (called *amphibious* tanks) were important in battles in the Pacific and in landing troops off the coast of Europe.

ALSO READ: ARMOR, WEAPONS, WORLD WAR II.

TANZANIA The Republic of Tanganyika, on the coast of East Africa, and the Republic of Zanzibar, consisting of several islands in the Indian Ocean off the coast of Tanganyika, joined to form the United Republic of Tanzania in 1964. "Tanzania" is a combination of the two names. (See the map with the article on AFRICA.) Tanganyika was a British territory until 1961, while Zanzibar was under British protection until 1963.

Water covers more than 20,000 square miles (50,000 sq. km) of Tanzania's land area. Two of the country's chief lakes are Lake Tanganyika and Lake Victoria, Africa's largest lake. Tanzania's offshore islands, the largest of which are Zanzibar and Pemba, together make up only a small percentage of Tanzania's total area. Mangrove swamps and coconut palm groves line the coastal region of Tanzania, where the climate is almost always hot. Grasslands, called *savannas*, cover the inland plateaus. Several mountains rise above the grasslands, including snowcapped Mount Kilimanjaro, the highest peak in Africa at 19,565 feet (5,963 m). Most of Africa's big game animals can be found in Tanzania. Serengeti National Park is the home of elephants, giraffes, zebras, and antelope. Safaris (expeditions) and mountain climbing are among the country's many attractions.

Diamonds are Tanzania's most

TANZANIA

Capital City: Dar es Salaam (1,400,000).

Area: 364,927 square miles (945,087 sq. km).

Population: 24,740,000.

Government: Republic.

Natural Resources: Diamonds, gold, tin, coal.

Export Products: Coffee, cotton, cashew nuts, diamonds, sisal, cloves, tea.

Unit of Money: Tanzanian shilling.

Official Languages: English, Swahili.

valuable mineral resource. Gold is also mined. The main export crops are coffee, cotton, and cashew nuts. Most of the world's cloves come from the islands of Zanzibar and Pemba.

More than 120 tribes live in Tanzania. The largest are the Sukuma and the Chagga. One of the best known and most colorful tribes is the Masai, a group of tall herders who live partly on a diet of blood and milk from their cattle.

Tanzania's capital and largest city is Dar es Salaam, a port on the Indian Ocean. Dodoma, in the country's center, will become the capital during the 1990s.

ALSO READ: AFRICA.

TAOISM Taoism is a Chinese philosophy and religion. It arose about 500 B.C., during a period when China was torn apart by civil wars. Taoism was, in part, a reaction to the violence of the times. It encouraged people to live simple, quiet lives in harmony with nature and at peace with other human beings.

Tao is a Chinese word meaning "way" or "road." In Taoism, the Tao is the source from which all things spring. It is perfect, unchanging, and complete in itself.

The basic ideas of Taoism are found in the *Tao Te Ching*, a book thought to have been written by the founder of Taoism, Lao-tse. According to the *Tao Te Ching*, a person is born in harmony with nature, but falls out of harmony by acting meanly and selfishly. To return to harmony, the person must act naturally. To act naturally means to act according to the Tao. The Tao supports nature but does nothing to change the course of nature. Similarly, a person must be a part of nature without changing nature.

People should act not only in harmony with nature as a whole, but also in harmony with their own individual nature. They should not try to be any more or less than the persons they naturally are. Even leaders should do no more than they have to do in order to lead. They should leave their followers as free as possible to live according to their own natures.

Taoism began as the philosophy of a few sages (wise counselors). From 200 B.C. to A.D. 200, it changed to a religion with many believers. Certain ancient Chinese gods became Taoist gods. After A.D. 400, Buddhism spread from India into China. Religious Taoism borrowed many gods and ideas from Buddhism, and Buddhism took ideas from Taoism. Different groups, or sects, of Taoists arose. Some worshiped animals and demons, and some believed in magic. Today, most of these unusual sects have died out, and Taoism survives in China as a religion of brotherhood and peace. It is thought to be particularly strong in rural areas.

ALSO READ: BUDDHISM, CHINA, PHILOSOPHY, RELIGION.

TAPE RECORDER see CASSETTE AND CARTRIDGE, RECORDING.

TAPESTRY A tapestry is a woven picture or design. Tapestries have been used for hundreds of years as wall hangings, draperies, or upholstery for furniture.

Most tapestries are designed by artists. The weaver follows the artist's drawing, or *cartoon*, as he or she weaves. Tapestries are woven on a rectangular frame, or *loom*. The weaver first fills the loom lengthwise with threads of strong wool, linen, or cotton to make the *warp*. The cartoon is usually placed under the warp so that the weaver can see it. The weaver then winds different threads, which match each color in the cartoon, onto separate holders, or *bobbins*. Taking one bobbin at a time, he or she

▲ *A detailed Gobelin tapestry called "The Earth."*

▼ *The Bayeux Tapestry is probably the most famous tapestry—but it isn't a tapestry at all but a piece of needlework. It tells the story of the conquest of England by Duke William of Normandy in 1066, and was probably made in England about 1070.*

weaves the colored threads in and out across the warp. The weaver fills each area with the right color to build up the picture. These crosswise threads are called the *weft*. They are usually made of fine wool or silk. The weaver works on the "wrong" side of the tapestry, using a mirror below the loom to check how the weaving is progressing on the "right" side. The weaver "combs" the weft occasionally, pushing it down tightly so that no warp threads show in the finished tapestry.

History of Tapestry Tapestry weaving is an ancient art among many peoples of the world. The Incas of Peru were making elaborate tapestries in the A.D. 700's. Some of the world's finest tapestries were made in Europe during the Middle Ages. Nobles at this time lived in cold, drafty castles. Huge tapestries were used to cover the stone walls. The tapestries kept out the drafts and also were bright and decorative.

During the 1400's, tapestries from the Flemish city of Arras (now in France) were so popular that "arras" became a word for tapestry. After 1600, some of the most beautiful tap-estries were made at the royal Gobelin factory in France. European tapestries often showed religious scenes or pictures from popular stories, woven in jewel-like colors.

The series of tapestries called *The Hunt of the Unicorn* show the capture of this imaginary beast against a background of tiny flowers. The Unicorn Tapestries are now in the Cloisters, part of the Metropolitan Museum of Art in New York City. In modern times, artists such as Pablo Picasso, Joan Miró, and Henri Matisse designed cartoons for tapestries. Modern tapestries are usually hung on walls like pictures.

ALSO READ: NEEDLEWORK, SPINNING AND WEAVING, TEXTILE.

TAPIR The tapir is a heavyset animal with hoofs and short legs. It is closely related to the horse and rhinoceros, but it looks more like a large pig. The tapir's snout and upper lip form a short trunk like that of the elephant. The tapir uses its trunk to pick up the leaves and twigs it eats.

Tapirs are found in tropical areas of Central and South America and in Asia. They live in forested or grassy places near water. Tapirs are good swimmers. They like to splash and play in shallow water and roll around in mud. Tapirs usually live alone or in pairs.

The tapir is a very shy and timid animal. It quickly runs away if it hears, sees, or smells an enemy coming. The tapir's main enemies are members of the cat family, such as tigers and jaguars. Tapirs sleep during the day, hiding under bushes and vines where their enemies cannot see them. They come out at night to hunt for food.

Tapirs are usually dark brown in color, with the exception of the Malay or Asian tapir, which is black and white. Baby tapirs have white stripes and spots, but these disappear when

the animal is about seven months old. Tapirs are easily tamed and usually adjust well to life in zoos.

ALSO READ: HOOFED ANIMALS.

TASMANIA   see AUSTRALIA.

TASTE
Taste is one of your senses. Your organs of taste are called *taste buds*. They are located at different places on your tongue. Substances taken into your mouth cause the taste buds to produce the sensation of taste. This sensation is probably the result of chemical reactions between the taste buds and molecules of the substance being tasted. There are different taste buds for each of the four basic tastes—*sweet*, *salty*, *sour*, and *bitter*.

■ LEARN BY DOING
The taste buds for each basic taste are found in different areas of the tongue. A simple experiment will show you where the different buds are located. You will need a clean, small paintbrush and some sugar, lemon juice, salt, and vanilla. Try putting each substance on different parts of your tongue. Do you taste sugar and

▼ *This highly magnified photo shows the taste buds on the sides of the tiny lumps, or* papillae, *on the tongue.*

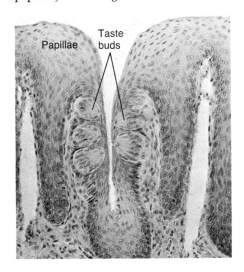

salt on the sides of your tongue? Do you taste them on the front? Where do you taste the lemon juice? How about the vanilla? ■

The flavor of most foods is a mixture of taste and odor. The strong flavor of an onion is mostly odor. If you have a bad cold and cannot smell the onion, you will find that it has a very mild taste.

The temperature and texture (feel) of food also affect the flavor of food. Hot coffee tastes different from cold coffee. Cold foods, such as mustard and pepper, may act on the sense of touch in the tongue to give a sensation of heat. Rough food may taste different from soft food.

We lose taste buds as we grow older. Infants may have more than ten thousand. Adults have fewer. This is why some older people may want more flavoring in their food.

ALSO READ: SENSE ORGAN, SMELL.

TAX
Taxes are the money collected by a government from its citizens. Governments need to levy (charge) taxes in order to pay for government services. The Federal Government must pay and equip the members of armed forces. Employees of other federal agencies must be hired to provide the country with such direct services as welfare, social security, and Medicare payments. The Federal Government also provides indirect services through its aid to states for roads, schools, and other necessities. Local and state governments provide their citizens with roads, schools, water, and sewage facilities, police officers, fire fighters, and welfare services.

Both the Federal Government and most state governments levy *income taxes* on both individuals and corporations. Every working person who earns money—as well as those who receive other income such as interest

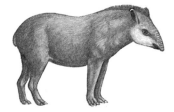

▲ *Tapirs belong to the mammal order* Perissodactyla, *or odd-toed ungulates. Rhinoceroses and horses are the other members of the order.*

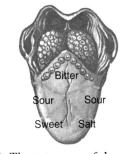

▲ *The taste areas of the tongue: certain areas are more sensitive to particular tastes than others.*

Most people have lost half their taste buds by the time they reach the age of 60.

on savings and dividends on stocks—pay an income tax every year on the money earned that year. Income tax is *progressive*, or *graduated*, which means that the more money a person gets, the more tax he pays on each dollar earned.

State and local governments also levy *property taxes*, through which they get most of their revenue. The U.S. Constitution does not allow the Federal Government to levy these taxes. Property taxes include both real estate tax (on land and buildings) and personal property tax (on cars, jewelry, and other valuable moveable items).

Income and property taxes are placed on *wealth* (what a person has) or on income (what a person earns). Other taxes are levied on *consumption* (what a person uses or buys). Many states levy a *sales tax* on goods that are sold. The person buying the goods pays the tax. Since the sales tax is the same for all people, the less money a person has, the more he or she suffers from this tax. For this reason, food and prescriptions for medicine are usually not taxed. *Excise taxes* are sales taxes placed on specific items. *Tariffs*, or *customs duties*, are taxes levied on goods imported from other countries. These can be increased to make home-produced commodities more attractive to purchasers.

People are often unaware of some of the taxes they pay. These are called *hidden*, or *indirect*, *taxes*. These taxes are not directly charged to consumers although consumers end up paying them. When you buy, for example, two dollars' worth of hamburger meat, you pay for more than the cost of the meat which is rung up on the cash register. The farmer, wholesaler, and retailer all have several taxes to pay, and they include these taxes in the prices they charge for the meat.

ALSO READ: CORPORATION, DEPRESSION, ECONOMICS, MONEY, SOCIAL SECURITY, STOCKS AND BONDS, SUPPLY AND DEMAND.

Only two Presidents had shorter terms in office than Zachary Taylor. They were William Henry Harrison and James Abram Garfield.

▲ *At the time this picture, called the* Tax Gatherers, *was painted, tax collectors often abused their powers and diverted taxes into their own pockets. In most modern countries, taxes are used for the benefit of the whole nation.*

TAYLOR, ZACHARY (1784–1850)

Before Zachary Taylor was elected President at age 64, he had served in the army for 40 years. In his rough brown coat, Taylor did not look like a great war leader. But his military victories in the Mexican War had made him a hero. His soldiers loved him. They nicknamed Taylor "Old Rough and Ready," because he was always ready to meet whatever crisis might occur. American voters were impressed, not only by Taylor's courage, but also by his common sense.

The man who spent most of his life as a soldier was the son of an officer who had served during the American Revolution. Zachary Taylor was born in Orange Country, Virginia. When he was less than a year old, his family moved to the frontier region of Kentucky. His father, Richard Taylor, cleared the land for a farm near the present city of Louisville, and for several years the family lived in fear of Indian attacks. Taylor and his brothers and sisters were tutored for a while but received no other formal education.

Taylor married Margaret Smith of Maryland. He and his wife had six children. Their son, Richard, was a Confederate general during the Civil War. Their daughter, Sarah, married Jefferson Davis, who became President of the Confederacy.

At age 24, Taylor was commissioned a lieutenant in the United States Army. He fought bravely in the War of 1812 against Great Britain and in several wars against the Indians. During the Mexican War, he rose to the rank of major general.

In 1848, the Whig Party nominated Zachary Taylor for the Presidency. He knew very little about government, but his military achievements had made him very popular with the American people.

When Taylor became President in 1849, the nation was passing through a difficult time because of quarrels about slavery. Some Southerners feared that laws then being considered by Congress would be unfair to the South. Some Southern leaders warned that if the laws were passed, their states would secede—that is, leave the Union. The President, a Southerner who owned land and slaves in Louisiana and Mississippi, was expected to agree with them.

Instead, he announced that any attempt at secession would be put down, if necessary, by force.

President Taylor served only one year and four months in office. After attending a Fourth of July celebration at the still unfinished Washington Monument in 1850, he became ill. He died five days later. His Vice-President, Millard Fillmore, succeeded him as President.

ALSO READ: FILLMORE, MILLARD; MEXICAN WAR; WAR OF 1812.

TCHAIKOVSKY, PETER ILYICH (1840–1893) One of the most famous and popular musical composers was Peter Tchaikovsky (spelled also Tschaikovsky or Chaikovsky). Some of his romantic music, such as the *Concerto for Piano and Orchestra No. 1 in B Flat Minor*, is popular throughout the world.

Tchaikovsky was born in Votkinsk (now in the Soviet Union). He studied music at the conservatory (music school) in St. Petersburg (now Leningrad). After graduation, he taught music at the Moscow Conservatory. One of his early compositions was the ballet, *Swan Lake*. Tchaikovsky was eager to spend all his time writing music. When he was 36 years old, a rich widow named Nadezhda von Meck made this possible. For a number of years, she gave him steady

▲ *Peter Ilyich Tchaikovsky, Russian composer.*

Tchaikovsky died from cholera caused by drinking water that had not been boiled. Some people think that the great composer did this deliberately in order to commit suicide.

ZACHARY TAYLOR
TWELFTH PRESIDENT   MARCH 4, 1849—JULY 9, 1850

Born: November 24, 1784, Orange County, Virginia
Parents: Colonel Richard and Sarah Strother Taylor
Education: Did not attend college
Religion: Not a church member
Occupation: Soldier, farmer
Political Party: Whig
Married: 1810 to Margaret Smith (1788–1852)
Children: One son, five daughters (two of whom died in infancy)
Died: July 9, 1850, Washington, D.C.
Buried: Zachary Taylor National Cemetery, near Louisville, Kentucky

▲ *The tea ceremony is a traditional custom in Japan. The Japanese call it* cha-no-yu, *which means simply "hot water tea."*

The people of Ireland are the world's greatest tea drinkers. Their average yearly consumption is well over 1,000 cups of tea per person.

encouragement as well as money. Tchaikovsky never met Madame von Meck, and their friendship depended on letters. During this time, Tchaikovsky wrote some of his greatest music, including the opera, *Eugene Onégin*; the ballet, *Sleeping Beauty*; and the *Violin Concerto in D Major*.

Tchaikovsky conducted his music in a series of concert tours through Europe and the United States. He was the first Russian composer to become popular throughout Europe. Toward the end of his life, Tchaikovsky wrote the popular ballet, *The Nutcracker*, and the *Symphony No. 6*, named the "Pathétique" ("Pathetic") because of its air of sadness and tragedy. The composer died shortly after the first performance of this symphony.

Peter Tchaikovsky wrote the *1812 Overture* in memory of the unsuccessful attack on Moscow by Napoleon Bonaparte in the year 1812. The explosions of guns and strains of the Russian and French national anthems can be heard in the music. Bells at the end of the overture represent the bells of Moscow.

ALSO READ: BALLET, MUSIC.

TEA Tea is a drink made from the leaves of an evergreen plant. The tea plant can grow about 30 feet (9 m) tall. But when it is cultivated, the branches are cut so that it grows as a bush 3 or 4 feet (100 or 120 cm) high. The leaves are usually ready to be picked when the plant is about five years old. It may yield good leaves for 50 years. The tea plant needs rich, light soil, a warm and moist climate, and plenty of rain. Most of the world's tea is grown on plantations in China, Taiwan, India, Bangladesh, Sri Lanka, Indonesia, and Japan. A small amount of tea is also grown in Africa and Latin America.

Tea leaves are picked by hand at the time when the plant is growing fastest. The best leaves are the small ones at the tips of the twigs. After being picked, the leaves are allowed to wither. They are then broken up. Finally, the leaves are roasted, or dried, in hot ovens.

The three main kinds of tea are called *green*, *black*, and *oolong*. For green tea, the leaves are roasted soon after they are picked. For black tea, the leaves are fermented, or left in the air, for about 24 hours before they are roasted. For oolong, the leaves are fermented for a shorter time. Almost all the tea drunk in the United States is black.

Tea contains caffeine and tannin. Caffeine is a *stimulant*, making the drinker feel wide-awake and lively, and tannin provides the color and flavor of tea.

Tea is made into a drink by brewing, or soaking, the leaves in boiling water—usually in a teapot. The liquid is then strained, or poured off, into a cup and drunk, usually hot. Tea can be made "strong" or "weak," depending on how long it is brewed. Most tea in the United States is sold in tea bags, which can be placed directly into a cup of hot water. The American people usually drink their tea with lemon juice or sugar, or both. In Britain, milk is often added in-

▼ *Darjeeling, in northern India, is a renowned tea-growing region.*

stead of lemon. Tea in China is drunk plain.

Tea was first cultivated in China more than 1,500 years ago. In Japan, tea drinking developed into a special ceremony for entertaining guests. A Japanese tea ceremony is held in a special room, and the tea is made according to strict rules.

ALSO READ: FOOD, PLANT PRODUCTS.

TEACHING When you think of teaching, you may think of assigning homework and giving grades. These are things teachers do, but they are not really teaching. Teaching is the process of helping others gain knowledge, giving instruction in skills, and helping others to learn by providing experiences and demonstrations. People teach each other constantly—parents teach children, children teach parents, and friends teach friends. But people are called teachers only when their occupation is teaching.

The primary purpose of teaching is to help students learn what they need to know to live happily and successfully. In order to do this, good teachers should first make their students realize that the subject being taught is useful, interesting, or important in some way. Everyone *wants* to know the things he or she *needs* to know. Good teachers point out to their students the ways learning can help them, so they will want to learn. No one can teach someone who is unwilling to learn. Teaching and learning depend on each other. Both teacher and student must be active participants in order for any teaching or learning to take place.

Methods of teaching a subject vary. The method chosen usually depends on its suitability for the subject and the students, the teacher's personal preference, and the demands of the school system. In the lecture method, the teacher summarizes in speeches the necessary information on a sub-

ject. Students write down notes on what is being said and are usually allowed to ask questions. This method is considered effective only for older students and in subjects covering a great deal of detailed information, such as history. Drills, student repetition of what the teacher says, may be helpful in learning some things, such as the pronunciation of a foreign language, that must be memorized. "Learning by doing" methods are considered quite effective in almost every subject. These methods usually involve laboratory experiments, student projects, and class discussions. Whether a student is learning about frogs or engines or short stories, he or she learns more—and remembers it longer—by actual physical participation and experimentation. You will learn more about a frog if you dissect one than if you simply read about it. You will learn more about engines if you look at—or work on—a real one than if you look at a diagram. Whatever method is used, good teachers make sure their lessons are appropriate for the students' ages and abilities. Students must have enough background knowledge in a subject to understand the new things being taught.

The qualifications for becoming a teacher are different in various states and countries. In most places, however, teachers must have a college

▲ *This teacher is giving English spelling lessons to her pupils of different races.*

▲ *Tecumseh was killed during the Battle of the Thames River near Chatham, Ontario, in 1813.*

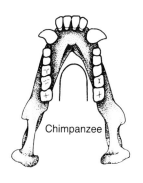

Chimpanzee

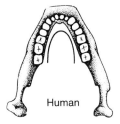

Human

▲ *The shape, size, and arrangement of an animal's teeth show what kind of food the animal eats. As our ancestors changed their diet, their teeth became less apelike. So teeth provide vital clues for anthropologists.*

degree and must have taken certain courses to prepare for teaching. In most countries, teachers must have a government certificate (saying they have fulfilled all requirements) before they can teach in public schools. In the United States, each state issues teaching certificates for its own teachers.

ALSO READ: EDUCATION, LEARNING, SCHOOL, SPECIAL EDUCATION.

TECUMSEH (about 1768–1813) Tecumseh was a Shawnee Indian chief who tried to unite all Indian tribes against the many white settlers moving into Indian lands during the early 1800's. He wanted to preserve the traditional ways of Indian life and stop white settlement beyond the boundary line of the Ohio River.

Tecumseh was born near what is now Springfield, Ohio. His twin brother, Tenskwatawa, was a tribal religious leader called the "Prophet." Together, the two established a village called Prophet's Town on the Tippecanoe River in Indiana. They encouraged the Indians who settled in this village to avoid white people's ways and revive old Indian customs. Prophet's Town became the headquarters of Tecumseh's movement against white settlement.

Tecumseh began to travel around to different Indian tribes to convince them to form a confederacy to defend their land. He argued with General William Henry Harrison, governor of the Indian Territory, about Harrison's efforts to buy land from tribes in Indiana and Illinois. Tecumseh thought that the land belonged to all the Indians and that no individual tribe had the right to sell it. While Tecumseh was visiting southwestern tribes to gain their support in 1811, Harrison, who was later to become President, attacked Prophet's Town. He destroyed the town and killed its people.

Tecumseh joined the British army when the War of 1812 broke out. He was made a brigadier general in charge of Indian forces. He was killed in Canada during the Battle of the Thames River.

ALSO READ: HARRISON, WILLIAM HENRY; INDIANS, AMERICAN; INDIAN WARS; WAR OF 1812.

TEETH Your teeth cut, tear, crush, and grind your food. This breaks the food into small pieces. The bits of food are mixed with saliva so that they become soft and wet, easy to swallow and digest.

Kinds of Teeth An adult human being has 32 teeth, 16 in each jaw. Teeth of different shapes do different kinds of work. The four front teeth in both your upper and lower jaws are *incisors*. Their name comes from the Latin word meaning "to cut." The incisors are shaped like chisels. The edge of a lower incisor moves up behind the upper incisor. This produces a scissorlike cutting action. You use your incisors to bite off pieces of food. Grazing animals, such as horses and cows, cut grass with their incisors.

On each side of the incisors are the pointed teeth called *cuspids*, or *canines*. Cuspid means "point" in Latin and canine means "like a dog" in Latin. The canine teeth of dogs and other meat-eating animals are very large. There is one cuspid on each side of your mouth in both your upper and lower jaw. These teeth are for tearing apart meat.

Next to the cuspids are the *bicuspids*, or *premolars*, which have two points. There are eight in all; two on each side of each of your jaws. Bicuspids both tear and grind.

At the back of each jaw are the *molars*. Their name comes from the Latin word meaning "mill." It is a good name because molars grind food

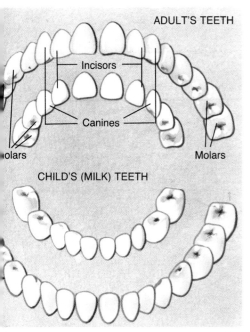

ADULT'S TEETH

Incisors

Canines

Molars

olars

Molars

CHILD'S (MILK) TEETH

▲ *By the time a child is about age 2, he or she usually has 20 milk teeth. These begin to be replaced by permanent teeth when the child is about 6 years old. All the permanent teeth may not appear until the child is 21.*

as mills grind grain. The upper edges of each molar have four or five rounded points. When using your molars to grind food you move your lower jaw in a sideways circular motion. There are three molars on each side of an adult's jaw, making a total of 12. Animals like horses and deer have molars with which they grind grass and leaves. Some meat-eating animals do not have molars because they do not need to chew meat in order to digest it. They swallow it whole.

The Structure of a Tooth The part of a tooth that shows is the *crown*. Next to the crown, and covered by the gum, is the *neck*. Below the neck, and farthest into the jaw, is the *root*. The root rests in a socket in the jawbone and is held firmly in place by a very tough membrane.

The crown of a tooth has a thick covering of *enamel*, the hardest substance in your body. The neck and root are covered by *cementum*, another

very hard substance. These two substances—especially the enamel—must withstand pressures of hundreds of pounds when you bite on hard objects. If the enamel is damaged or broken, it cannot be repaired by your body as a broken bone is repaired.

Inside the enamel and cementum is the main part of the tooth. It is made up of *dentine*. This material looks like bone, but is harder. Within the dentine is a soft core, the *dental pulp*. This consists of blood vessels and nerves.

Milk Teeth and Permanent Teeth Human beings have two sets of teeth. The first teeth, called "milk teeth," are already forming within the gums when an infant is born. The first teeth that grow through the baby's gums are the two lower middle incisors. This usually happens in the second half of a baby's first year. The rest of the teeth grow in quickly. The growth of teeth through the gums, or *teething*, may be painful and may make a baby cry. Usually, by the time a child is about two years old, a complete first set of teeth has grown through the gums. There are only 10 milk teeth in each jaw: four incisors, two cuspids (or canines), and four molarlike premolars.

At about the age of six, a child's milk teeth become loose and fall out, and permanent teeth grow in their places. The first to be replaced are the incisors at the front. Usually, most of the permanent teeth have grown in by the age of 12.

During the teens, one or two molars grow in on each side of each jaw. The second molar may not grow in until about the age of 20. By that time you are supposed to have gained some wisdom, so these last teeth are called "wisdom teeth."

Care of Your Teeth Teeth must have care in order to stay healthy. The best way to keep your teeth

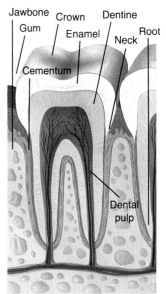

Jawbone Crown Dentine
Gum Enamel Root
Neck
Cementum

Dental pulp

▲ *A tooth consists of a crown above the gum and a root embedded in the bone of the jaw. A layer of hard enamel covers the crown. Under this outer enamel there is a layer of dentine surrounding the core, or pulp.*

We know that bad teeth are one of man's oldest miseries. Two thousand five hundred years ago, Etruscan craftsmen made false teeth of gold and bone. Early false teeth were very difficult to eat with; in fact, they usually had to be taken out before a meal.

Almost 20 percent of all adults in the United States have no natural teeth.

▲ *Copper wires used for carrying telephone and telegraph signals over long distances are being replaced with optical fibers. These carry signals in the form of laser pulses.*

▼ *A teleprinter is a kind of typewriter that is used to send written messages by telephone. The typed message is changed into electric signals, which go along the telephone wires to a teleprinter at the other end. The teleprinter types out the message.*

from decaying is to cut down on candy, cookies, and other sweetened foods. You should also brush your teeth and rinse your mouth after you have eaten. This will get rid of any small bits of food on which the decay bacteria live. You should also see your dentist regularly, twice a year.

ALSO READ: CALCIUM, DENTISTRY, FERMENTATION, HEALTH, HUMAN BODY.

TELECOMMUNICATIONS

Talking to people and sending and receiving messages and information are called communications. Mail and newspapers are traditional forms of communications that depend on the delivery of pieces of paper, which takes some time. Telecommunications—which means communications over a distance—take virtually no time between any two places on Earth. Even to the outer reaches of the solar system, communications take only a few hours.

Pick up a radio and move the tuning controls: you'll hear voices and music coming to you from all over the world. Your television set can bring you live pictures of news and sports that are happening everywhere. Pictures even come from space, bringing us views of planets, moons, and comets throughout the solar system. You can talk to anyone anywhere by telephone or by computer networks, and you can get instant information in these ways, too. Portable telephones and citizen's

band radios keep you in touch with other people when you are on the move. Telex and teletype messages are typed into one terminal and are reproduced in seconds in printed form at the receiving terminal.

The reason why telecommunications are so fast is that all the information, pictures, and sound travel in the form of signals. These signals are either electric currents flowing along wires, radio waves moving through the air or space, or light rays moving along glass fibers. Radio waves and light rays travel at a speed of 186,000 miles (300,000 km) a second. Electric signals move at almost the same speed.

Telephones are mainly connected by a network of metal wires. Computers also use the telephone network. The network of cables used in cable television carries the pictures in the form of electric signals along wires. These services may also use cables containing optical fibers, which are long, thin, glass fibers. They carry signals in the form of light rays fired along each fiber by a laser. Optical fibers can carry more channels of communications and give better quality than metal wires.

Radio communications need no cables and can link any places together. Space communications work by radio. Telephone and television networks also use radio links, including communications satellites orbiting the Earth.

ALSO READ: FACSIMILE, FIBER OPTICS, TELEPHONE, TELEVISION.

TELEGRAPH Through the centuries, people have found many ways to communicate with each other. Drumbeats, smoke signals, and signal flags were some of the early ways used to send messages over long distances. In the 1800's, people found new techniques for sending messages more rapidly. One invention that speeded up communication was the magnetic

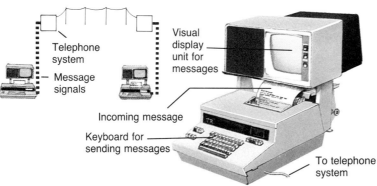

Telephone system

Message signals

Visual display unit for messages

Incoming message

Keyboard for sending messages

To telephone system

▲ *An old telegraph relay station, one of many built after the invention of the telegraph. Signals were relayed between stations.*

telegraph. It could transmit messages by sending an electric current through a wire.

The telegraph was invented by Samuel F. B. Morse in 1837. Morse made the first public demonstration in 1844, sending the message, "What hath God wrought!" from the Capitol in Washington, D.C., to Baltimore, Maryland.

Morse's telegraph consisted of a sending and a receiving apparatus. These were connected by a wire, over which an electric current traveled. At first, battery cells provided the current. Later, the dynamo and storage battery were used.

To operate the telegraph, a key on the sending apparatus (called a *transmitter*) was pressed down and released. This closed and opened an electric circuit. While the circuit was closed, the electric current flowed. When the circuit was opened the current stopped. Morse developed a code (now called *Morse code*) which used two signals—the dot and the dash—in various combinations to represent letters of the alphabet. He could then spell out words by pressing the telegraph key. At the other end of the wire, the receiving apparatus (called a *sounder*) picked up the sounds of the dots and dashes. A telegraph operator would decode the message on hearing it from the sounder.

When the electric current entered the sounder, it flowed through a magnet. This magnet attracted a metal bar on a level (called an *armature*) that

clicked when the two touched. To send messages over very long distances, a relay system was used. Relay stations were placed every 30 miles (38 km) to pick up the signal and pass it on.

The telegraph was used by the railroads to help in running trains. Messages could be sent from station to station ahead of a train to announce its arrival and to get messages to crew and passengers. In 1858, the first successful transatlantic telegraph cable was completed by Cyrus Field. Three years later in 1861, the first transcontinental telegraph line across the United States was completed.

In 1895, the Italian inventor, Guglielmo Marconi, discovered a way to send long-distance messages using radio waves instead of electrical current. His was the first practical system of wireless telegraphy, which led to the use of the voice to send messages over radio.

Today, new forms of telegraphy are employed to send high-speed messages. You can call a telegraph operator on the phone and tell him or her your message. The operator, using a *teleprinter*, types your message on a keyboard similar to that on a typewriter. Signals from the keys are sent out over radio beams. At the destination, the message is printed automatically at a telegraph message center. A

▲ *This rider is steering another horse carrying telegraph wire. During the 1840's and 1850's, thousands of miles of telegraph lines were laid across the United States like this and were then erected onto telegraph poles.*

◀ *The primitive protection of a tent-fly is all these Union soldiers have as they put their commander in touch with his separated brigades during the Civil War. Such field-telegraph stations kept General Grant in touch with his armies on a daily basis and helped him plan for a successful strategy.*

▲ *Alexander Graham Bell at the opening of the New York–Chicago long-distance telephone line in 1892.*

Ninety-five percent of American homes have telephones, and Americans make more than a billion calls a day.

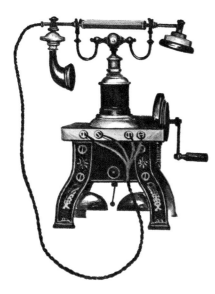

▲ *A telephone of 1892.*

messenger then calls the person to whom it is addressed and reads it over the telephone. The recipient usually receives a written copy of the message either through the mail or by hand delivery.

Radio towers have replaced most of the old telegraph pole lines. These radio towers relay signals from station to station between a nationwide network of ultramodern automatic telegraph switching centers. Using this radio-beam equipment, many thousands of telegrams a minute can be sent in each direction.

The Federal Government, businesses and industries, stock exchanges, and many others make heavy use of modern telegraphic equipment. Millions of messages are sent daily through a network of millions of miles of telegraph lines and beams in the United States and Canada. The telegraph continues to be one of the most important means of world communication.

ALSO READ: COMMUNICATION; ELECTRONICS; MARCONI, GUGLIELMO; MORSE CODE; MORSE, SAMUEL F. B.; RADIO; SIGNAL; TELECOMMUNICATIONS; TELEPHONE.

TELEPHONE All over the world today people can pick up telephones and communicate instantly with others. The telephone is one of the most important means of communication in our modern world. It carries the sound of a human voice over long distances by using electricity. The word telephone comes from two Greek words, *tele*, meaning "far," and *phone*, meaning "sound."

The telephone was invented in 1876 by Alexander Graham Bell, a Scottish-born professor of speech at Boston University. Bell experimented with the harmonic telegraph, a device that sent several messages over a telegraph wire at the same time. During an experiment, Bell learned how to transmit the vibrations of a musical tone over the electric wire. He decided he could transmit a human voice over electric wire in the same way.

He and his assistant, Thomas A. Watson, set to work making an instrument to transmit the human voice. One day Bell spilled some sulfuric acid. He said over his telephone, "Mr. Watson, come here. I want you!" These were the first words spoken over the telephone.

Bell's telephone, like modern telephones, changed the sound waves of the voice into electrical energy. This energy could be sent quickly over electric wires for a distance and then changed back into sound waves at the other end of the wire.

The part of the telephone you talk into is the *transmitter*, or sender of sound. When you speak, the sound waves made by the vibration of your vocal cords hit a thin plate of aluminum, called a *diaphragm*. This plate bends slightly when a sound wave hits it. On the back side of the diaphragm is a small gold-plated brass dome surrounded by a container filled with small grains of carbon. A small amount of electricity flows through the carbon granules as you speak. The diaphragm moves back and forth many hundreds of times a second in patterns that correspond to the sound waves striking it. As the diaphragm moves inwards, it packs the carbon grains more tightly together. This packing makes the carbon a better conductor. More electrical current flows through the carbon. The amount of electricity flowing through the carbon varies with the vibrations of the diaphragm. The variation in electric current is called a signal. This electrical signal is sent through the wire to the *receiver* at the other end.

The receiver takes the electric signals and changes them back to sound waves. In the receiver is another diaphragm fastened to a ring of iron called an *armature*. Outside the ring is a magnet, and on the inside is a coil of wire called a pole piece. When the electricity from the signal passes through this pole piece, the wire is turned into an electromagnet pulling on the armature and the diaphragm. The diaphragm bends back and forth, or vibrates, according to the strength and variation of the signal. These vibrations are duplications of those made at the other end of the line. We hear these vibrations as sounds of the human voice.

Bell introduced his telephone at the Centennial Exposition in Philadelphia in 1876. "My God, it speaks!" the emperor of Brazil is reported to have said when he heard it.

The first commercial telephone was produced by Bell's company in Boston in 1877. The telephone industry developed rapidly from then on. In 1878, the first commercial switchboard opened. Soon a wall set with a crank to summon the operator was invented. In 1886, the long-distance transmitter came into use, and after that the first desk set. In 1907, the magneto wall set appeared with a built-in generator providing current to signal the operator. These telephones were used until the 1930's. In 1919, the first dial phone was used in Sweden.

Modern improvements in the telephone include the home intercom system, the Touch-Tone push-button telephone, and cordless telephones which are increasingly common in homes. Cordless phones enable you to speak to someone from anywhere in the house, or even the garden. They run on rechargeable batteries and have an aerial for reception. More and more homes now have them.

Another modern development is the mobile phone. These are often fitted to automobiles but can also be used for outdoor situations—a building site or a film location setting for example. Cellular mobile phones are so called because they work on a cell system. A city, for example, will be

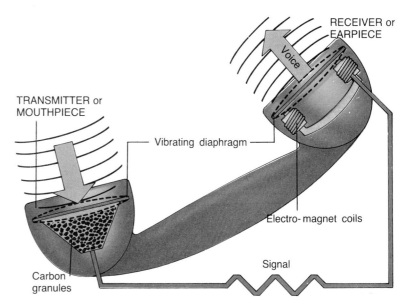

divided into cells. Each cell has a low power transmitter and, as you drive or walk from one cell to the next, a computer hands on your mobile telephone signal to the next transmitter.

Today, the telephone is the basis of an enormous communications network. There are telephones in about 95 out of every 100 American homes. A total of about 135 million phones are used in the United States alone. This is more than one third of the world's telephones. Japan ranks second in telephone use, the U.S.S.R. third, and Germany fourth.

▲ *An engineer examines one of the circuit boards in an electronic telephone exchange.*

The world's largest telephone switchboard is in the Pentagon, in Washington, D.C.

▲ Public telephone booths are found in all shapes and sizes throughout the world. This mobile variety is in downtown Mexico City and provides long distance calls.

■ LEARN BY DOING

You might learn more about the telephone by making a tin-can phone. Take two large empty tin cans opened at one end. Use string or wire to connect the backs of the cans at each end. Pull the string or wire tight and talk into the open end of the can. See how long a wire you can use and still hear a friend over your home-made phone. ■

Telephone Service During the early years of telephone service, anyone who wanted to call someone else first had to call the telephone operator. The telephone operator would then connect the two parties by plugging electric wires into special holes in a large panel, or *switchboard*. It was hard for one telephone operator to take care of many different telephone calls. When the lines were busy, the operator got behind in placing calls and sometimes made mistakes. The telephone company invented electrical equipment that could connect telephones automatically. Today, if you want to call someone, all you have to do is dial or "touch" the person's number on your telephone. The electrical equipment then completes the telephone call automatically.

Other electrical equipment makes it possible for you to call another person almost anywhere in the United States and Canada. Almost 99 percent of the telephones in these two countries are equipped for Direct Distance Dialing (DDD). The United States and Canada are divided into 120 different areas, each of which has its own three-digit area code number. To call someone outside your area, you first dial the person's area code number and then his or her local seven-digit telephone number.

Telephone calls can be dialed automatically between certain parts of Europe and certain parts of the United States. Someone in Europe can call here by dialing a special number, the area code number, and then the local telephone number. It won't be long before you can call any telephone in the world from your home, just by dialing a special telephone number.

There are 2,000 independent telephone companies in the United States. All these companies work together to allow people to make calls easily between areas serviced by different telephone companies.

Special Services Today, recording equipment provides special telephone services in some areas. If you want to find out the exact time, for example, all you have to do is dial a special telephone number. You then hear a recorded voice and a "beep" telling you exactly what time it is.

In some areas, you can find out about the weather by dialing another special telephone number. This number connects you to a recording that tells what the weather will be like in the next few hours. If the forecast changes, the telephone company makes a new recording.

Recording equipment can also be

▼ This telephone has a microprocessor inside it. It can remember ten numbers and will redial the last number called. It also tells the time.

used to take messages when you are out. A tape recorder answers the phone and invites the caller to leave a message. A telephone answering service performs a similar service, but the message is usually taken by an operator rather than a recorder.

Many cities in the United States have had special *electronic* telephone systems installed. These electronic systems let you do many things you cannot do with an electrical telephone system. If you are going to a friend's house, for example, you can dial a special number on your telephone before you leave home. After that, if anyone should telephone your house, the call will be transferred automati-

cally to your friend's house. And if you should then go to someone else's house, you can give the telephone number of that house. No matter where you go, your telephone calls will always reach you.

The new electronic telephone system will also let you call several people at the same time. You and your friends can hold a meeting without any of you leaving home. This is called *teleconferencing*. If you go away on vacation, you can disconnect your telephone automatically just by dialing a special number. When you return from vacation, you can begin receiving telephone calls again just by dialing another special number.

ALSO READ: BELL, ALEXANDER GRAHAM; COMMUNICATIONS SATELLITE; INVENTION; RADIO; SOUND; TELECOMMUNICATIONS; TELEGRAPH; TELEVISION.

▲ *A replica of the reflecting telescope invented by Isaac Newton.*

TELESCOPE An optical telescope is an instrument that makes distant objects appear closer by collecting and focusing the light given off by the objects. A radio telescope collects radio waves, but its operation is very different from that of an optical telescope. When we say "telescope" we usually mean an optical telescope.

The telescope was probably invented by a Dutch spectacle (eyeglass) manufacturer named Hans Lip-

▼ *The McMath Solar Telescope on Kitt Peak in Arizona uses three mirrors to reflect the sun's light to the underground observation room. Most of the structure is buried underground where temperatures are cool and constant. This is important because if there were even a small temperature change, it would upset the delicate measuring instruments.*

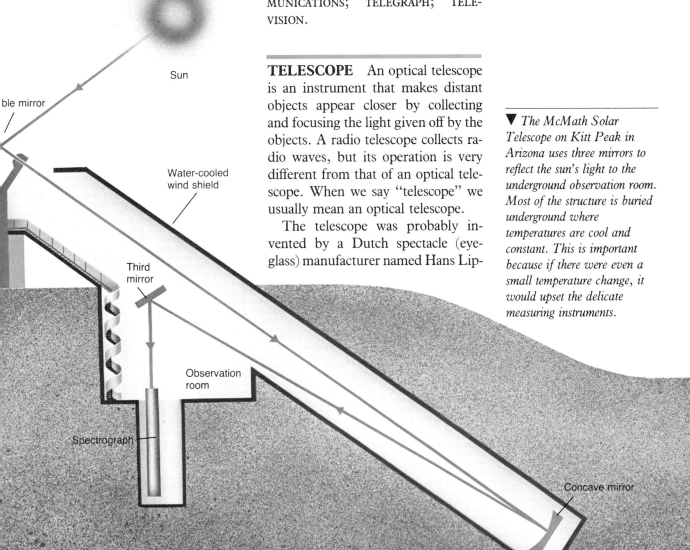

Sun

ble mirror

Water-cooled wind shield

Third mirror

Observation room

Spectrograph

Concave mirror

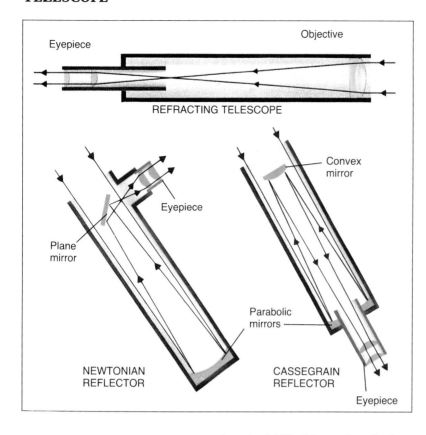

Eyepiece
Objective

REFRACTING TELESCOPE

Convex mirror

Eyepiece

Plane mirror

Parabolic mirrors

NEWTONIAN REFLECTOR

CASSEGRAIN REFLECTOR

Eyepiece

The world's biggest telescope is at Zelenchukskaya in the Soviet Union. It has a mirror 236.2 inches (6 m) across and is so powerful that it could pick up the light of a candle at a distance of 15,000 miles (24,000 km).

pershey in 1608. Lippershey built a *refracting* telescope. In a refracting telescope the light is collected by an objective *lens*. A lens is a piece of clear glass that will bend light to produce an image. The objective lens of a telescope is convex—it curves outward so that it is thicker in the middle. The rays of light striking the objective lens are parallel (side by side and always the same distance apart). The lens *refracts*, or bends, the light so that the rays of light are all directed toward the *focal point*, the point at which parallel rays passing through the lens would come together. The light then passes through a second lens, called the eyepiece. This lens refracts the rays of light so that they are parallel again. An observer looking into the eyepiece can then see an image of the objects giving off the light.

If the eyepiece lens is concave—curves inward so that it is thinner in the middle—the telescope is a *Galilean* refractor. In a Galilean refractor, the eyepiece is located before the focal point of the objective lens. This was

the kind of refractor built by Lippershey and by Galileo, the famous Italian astronomer. In a Galilean refractor, the image appears right side up. In the *Keplerian* refractor, invented by the German astronomer, Johannes Kepler, the eyepiece is convex and is placed beyond the focal point of the objective lens. The image appears *inverted*, or upside-down. The advantage of the Keplerian refractor is that it has a wider field of view than a Galilean refractor has. Galilean refractors, because of their upright image, are often used to observe objects on Earth, while Keplerian refractors are used in astronomy.

Since 1900, most of the major astronomical telescopes built have been *reflectors*. In a reflecting telescope, the light is collected not by a lens but by a concave (inward-curving) mirror. The mirror is shaped so that the light rays bouncing off it are directed at a focal point. The reflected light rays then strike a second mirror that reflects the rays toward an eyepiece. An observer looking through the eyepiece can see an image of the light source.

Telescopes can be measured in different ways. Small telescopes are de-

▼ *A modern reflecting telescope on a tripod.*

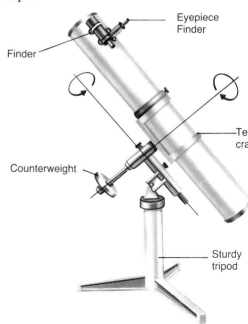

Finder

Eyepiece Finder

Counterweight

Tel crad

Sturdy tripod

scribed by their *power*, the number of times they magnify an object. A 50-power telescope will make an object look 50 times larger than it would appear to the unaided eye. Large astronomical telescopes are usually described by the size of the objective lens, for refractors, or the size of the mirror, for reflectors. The largest refractor, built in 1897 at Yerkes Observatory, Wisconsin, has a 40-inch (100-cm) lens. The largest reflector, completed in 1976 in the Soviet Union, has a 236-inch (600-cm) mirror.

Telescopes have many uses. Surveyors use telescopes to measure distances. Forest rangers use them to spot forest fires. Binoculars are basically two small telescopes joined together. Binoculars often have more than two lenses and may use prisms—pieces of glass that bend and reflect light. Some telescopes also have more than two lenses.

■ LEARN BY DOING

A simple telescope is not hard to make. You will need two cardboard or plastic tubes and two lenses. One tube should slide snugly inside the other. One lens, the objective, should fit tightly into the large tube. The other lens, the eyepiece, should fit inside the small tube. Hold both lenses side by side and look at the printing in a book. The lens that magnifies the *most* should be the eyepiece. Tape or glue the other lens inside one end of the large tube, and the eyepiece inside the open end of the small tube. Look through the eyepiece, and slide the tubes back and forth until you can see an image. ■

ALSO READ: ASTRONOMY; GALILEO, GALILEI; LENS; LIGHT; OBSERVATORY.

TELEVISION The rays of light that enter a photographic camera strike a piece of film in the camera. The film captures the image (picture)

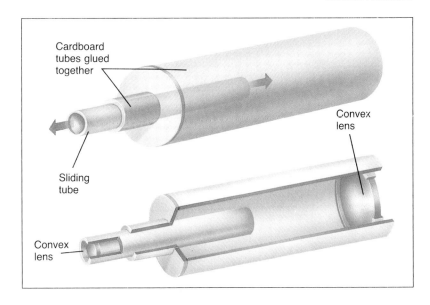

formed by the light rays. A television camera also takes pictures by capturing the rays of light that pass into the camera. But a television camera does not use film to capture the image. Instead, it uses a thin plate of glass or other material that has been made sensitive to light. Whenever a ray of light strikes a spot on the plate, it knocks electrons off the plate. This gives the plate a certain electrical charge at that spot. The amount of charge varies with the number of electrons knocked loose, and the number of electrons varies with the brightness of the light. So the charges at all the different points on the plate capture an electronic image of the pattern of light striking the plate.

The glass plate is inside a long tube. All the air has been taken out of this tube. At the other end of the tube is a small electric wire. When the television camera is turned on, this wire turns white-hot, like the wire inside a light bulb. The hot wire shoots out a beam of electrons.

Magnets can attract and repel electrons and cause them to change direction. Magnets surrounding the beam of electrons direct the beam to the glass plate. The magnets make the beam of electrons *scan*—travel in a line, left to right, across the plate of glass. When the beam gets to the right side, it jumps back to the left side and

John Logie Baird's first television set was made of old cans, bicycle parts, lenses, sealing wax, and string.

▲ *An early television set, with the screen set into the lid. The first public television service was started by the British Broadcasting Corporation (BBC) in 1936.*

down to the next line. The beam of electrons travels across the glass plate 525 times in 1/30 of a second. Then it reaches the bottom of the plate and jumps back to the top to scan the next *frame*, or image, formed on the plate.

The electrons strike the glass plate and bounce back to a *collecting plate*. If the beam of electrons hits a "bright" or highly charged spot on the glass plate, the electrons will be absorbed (soaked up). Very few of the electrons will bounce back to the collecting plate. But if the beam of electrons hits a "dark" or lightly charged spot on the glass plate, most of the electrons will bounce back to the collecting plate.

When the reflected beam of electrons strikes the collecting plate, it creates a current of electricity. This current of electricity carries a signal that tells how light or dark the glass plate is at different spots.

This electric current, or signal, travels from the television camera to the transmitter. The transmitter sends the signal to a television antenna. The current travels through the antenna; this sends the electric signal into the air as a wave of electromagnetic radiation.

When this wave of radiation reaches a home television antenna, the antenna turns the radiation back into an electric signal again. The electric signal travels into the television set or receiver. First, the television set makes the electric signal much stronger. The electric signal then goes to the picture tube on the television set.

At the back of the picture tube is an *electron gun*. A hot wire at the back of the electron gun shoots out a beam of electrons, just as in the television camera. The beam of electrons is aimed by magnets, just as in the television camera. The beam of electrons hits the inside of the glass face of the picture tube. This side of the glass is coated with phosphors—chemicals that glow when light strikes them.

The magnets make the electron beam travel across the screen in a series of lines. The electron beam travels across the screen 525 times in 1/30 of a second, just as in the television camera. Special signals inside the television set make the electron beam move exactly in step with the beam inside the television camera.

Wherever there is a bright spot of light on the glass plate inside the television camera, the electron beam makes a bright spot on the face of the picture tube. Wherever there is a dark spot on the glass plate, the electron beam leaves a dark spot on the picture tube. You cannot see all these spots one by one because the beam moves too fast. But if you look closely at a TV picture, you may see the 525 lines that run across the picture tube. Some countries use a different number of lines.

Color Television Color television cameras and receivers work the same way as black-and-white television sets do. But color television is about three times as complicated as black-and-white.

Mirrors inside the color televison camera divide the light coming into the camera into three parts. There are three filters inside the camera, one for each part of the light. One filter al-

▼ The TV set you have at home is only part of the television system. In the studio, the camera and microphone pick up the pictures and sound and change them into electric signals. The transmitter sends the signals out as radio waves. Your TV antenna is specially shaped to catch these waves and change them back into electric signals. Inside the TV set, the signals are turned back into pictures and sounds.

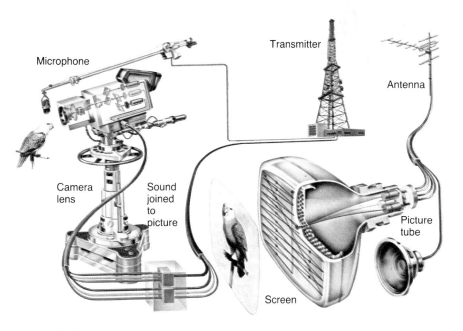

Microphone

Transmitter

Antenna

Camera lens

Sound joined to picture

Picture tube

Screen

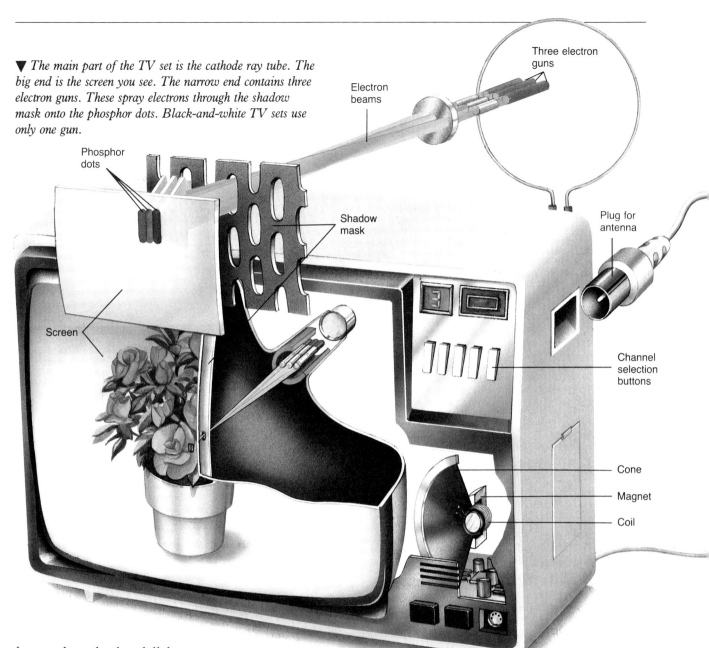

▼ *The main part of the TV set is the cathode ray tube. The big end is the screen you see. The narrow end contains three electron guns. These spray electrons through the shadow mask onto the phosphor dots. Black-and-white TV sets use only one gun.*

Three electron guns

Electron beams

Phosphor dots

Shadow mask

Screen

Plug for antenna

Channel selection buttons

Cone

Magnet

Coil

lows only red-colored light to pass. The second filter allows only blue-colored light to pass. The third filter allows only green-colored light to pass. Each color goes to a different camera tube. Each tube has a separate glass plate and electron beam. From the three tubes, three signals go to the transmitter.

The color television transmitter *multiplexes* the three signals—combines them into one. Then a black-and-white signal is added to the multiplexed signal, and the combined signal is sent to the broadcasting antenna.

The color television set uses three electron beams instead of only one. One electron beam is for red colors,

another is for green colors, and the third is for blue colors. The inside face of the color picture tube is covered with groups of three different kinds of phosphors. One phosphor glows red, one glows green, and one glows blue. Each different color electron beam makes only its own phosphors glow. When everything is working just right inside a color television set, the three colors mix together. You can then see a picture in full color on the screen.

ALSO READ: BAIRD, JOHN LOGIE; COLOR; ELECTRICITY; ELECTRONICS;

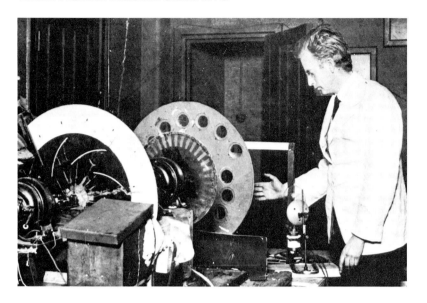

▲ *John Logie Baird, the Scottish television pioneer, experiments with an early TV transmitting system.*

RADIATION; RADIO; TELECOMMUNICATIONS; TELEVISION BROADCASTING; TRANSISTOR.

The average American child between the ages of 2 and 11 watches television for more than 27 hours a week.

TELEVISION BROADCASTING

Television is a relatively recent development in communications. The first public television service was started by the British Broadcasting Corporation (BBC) in 1936. In the United States, commercial television broadcasting began in 1941.

The technical development of television had been going on for some time before that. In 1924, the first crude television system was demonstrated by its inventor, John Logie Baird. The first system could transmit only black-and-white silhouettes. Two years later, an improved system was shown that could transmit halftones (grays). The first license for experimental visual broadcasting in the United States was granted in 1928. Throughout the 1930's, experiments with television continued. In 1939, Franklin D. Roosevelt became the first U.S. President to appear on TV. In the same year, a major league baseball game, a college football game, and a boxing match were also telecast for the first time. In 1940, the Republican and Democratic national political conventions were telecast.

By 1941, commercial telecasting was ready to begin. But World War II interrupted this beginning. Just six commercial stations were in operation at the end of the war. By 1947, there were 17, and the commercial boom started. Many stations applied for licenses, and the Federal Communications Commission (FCC), the government agency that makes regulations for radio and TV, decided to "freeze" the licensing of new stations. No more licenses for new stations would be granted until 1952. But broadcasting improvements continued.

Network TV was born in 1948. The three major U.S. commercial networks are the American Broadcasting Company (ABC), the Columbia Broadcasting System (CBS), and the National Broadcasting Company (NBC). There is also a nonprofit network, the Public Broadcasting Service (PBS). A network is a group of TV stations connected by relay stations. The network provides programs and services to the interconnected group of local stations. Networks grew because TV is a very expensive medium. Large audiences are needed to pay the high programming costs. The networks supply the same programs to many stations, thus spreading out the production costs.

Television has grown rapidly since 1952. In 1960, 501 TV stations were broadcasting to about 46 million homes. In 1980, almost 1,000 TV stations were broadcasting to about 74 million homes. By 1986, more than 87 million homes owned at least one TV set. Ninety-eight percent of all homes in the United States have a television set, which is used in each home for about six hours each day, on the average. When a historic event, such as the Space Shuttle's lift-off, is broadcast, nearly everyone watches.

The function of TV is to present programs. By law, commercial TV stations must broadcast at least 28 hours of programs a week. These programs can be news, special events, sports shows, feature movies, public affairs programs, special educational programs, or games and contests. To finance these programs, stations sell advertising time to sponsors.

The idea for a TV program comes from a writer or producer. The producer and director choose a cast, decide on sets with a designer, and pick music with the help of a music director. The technical department assigns engineers and camera crews. The show is rehearsed until it is ready to go on the air.

In the control room, the director watches a clock for the exact moment to signal the show to begin. The technical director makes cuts from one camera to another. The engineers control the technical quality of the pictures for brightness, contrast, and color. The sound person opens and closes microphones and balances sound. Shows can be produced live, on film, or on videotape.

The videotape room of the station is a beehive of activity. Many TV operations are going on at once there. Taped shows are being sent across the network. Taped news segments are being transmitted to other stations. Incoming programs from other production centers are being taped for later playing. Productions from other studios are being taped and edited. A commercial is being recorded. Many people work in the tape room, controlling, recording, and editing the tapes.

Other people work outside the studio on "remote operations." They may be covering sports events, such as football or hockey games; special events, such as political conventions or parades; or disasters, such as fires, floods, or riots. Mobile units—remote trucks fitted out as control rooms—are sent to take pictures. Hand-held cameras that can be carried around are often used by TV crews to cover large areas. These cameras relay signals to the mobile unit, which has facilities to send TV signals to the transmitter. Signals are relayed by microwave or coaxial cable.

Sometimes sports programs are televised by a remote truck. But most major sports stadiums have a regular TV control room. From this room, a show can be broadcast live or recorded on videotape.

News programs are another important part of television. Almost every TV station has a news department. The networks and major stations have large staffs of producers, editors, film editors, directors, writers, and commentators.

Educational TV, closed-circuit TV, and pay and cable TV are special kinds of television. The educational TV stations show programs devoted to education and public service on a non-profit basis. Closed-circuit TV is used to send particular programs to selected receivers by means of a coaxial cable or relay. It is used in schools, hospitals, factories, spaceflights, traffic control, and railroad freight operations. Pay TV enables viewers to pay for the programs they want. With cable TV, the signal is transmitted through a cable rather than

▲ *Cameramen wear headphones so that they can receive instructions from the director in the control room.*

▼ *The director works from the control room. The bottom row of monitors shows the picture from each camera. The vision mixer cuts to each picture as the director asks for it.*

▲ *A film crew prepares an outdoor scene for the television series* Jewel In The Crown. *Production and behind-the-scenes organization can take a whole day just to film a few seconds for television broadcasting.*

▲ *William Tell, with his famous crossbow, from an engraving by Thevet.*

through space. By 1990 another system was becoming popular—the satellite TV station. In this, signals are beamed from a ground studio to a satellite in fixed orbit, which relays them back to earth. Viewers pay to unscramble the signals.

Video recorders and players enable viewers to record programs, or play their own or rented videotapes.

ALSO READ: COMMUNICATIONS SATELLITE, JOURNALISM, RADIO BROADCASTING, TELECOMMUNICATIONS, TELEVISION, TRANSISTOR, VIDEO.

TELL, WILLIAM William Tell is a legendary Swiss hero. His story was first told in a ballad during the 1400's. According to legend, Tell lived in the canton (district) of Uri, Switzerland, in the 1300's. The Swiss were trying to win their independence from the Austrians, who ruled them at that time.

The regional Austrian governor, Gessler, put his hat on a pole in the town square at Altdorf and ordered everyone to bow to it. William Tell, an expert archer, refused. Gessler

sentenced Tell to shoot an apple on the head of his own son with a bow and arrow. Tell aimed and successfully hit the apple. But he defiantly claimed that if his son had been harmed he would have shot Gessler.

In a fury, Gessler had Tell chained and sent off across a lake to be imprisoned in his castle dungeon. But a great storm blew up on the way, and Tell escaped in the excitement. He killed Gessler and, the story says, led the Swiss people in an uprising for freedom. A play by dramatist Friedrich von Schiller and an opera by composer Gioacchino Rossini were written about the story of William Tell.

ALSO READ: SWITZERLAND.

TEMPERATURE SCALE It is usually easy for us to tell when something is hot and when something is cold without bothering to take the temperature of these things. But sometimes it is important to know exactly what the temperature is. For example, a doctor must know your exact temperature when you are sick. This helps the doctor diagnose what is wrong with you. When you bake a pie or a cake, you must know exactly what the temperature is inside the oven.

Scientists often study the behavior of matter at very high or very low temperatures. At such temperatures, some substances change their characteristics. The study of occurrences at very low temperatures is called *cryogenics.*

When you want to know a temperature exactly, you use a thermometer. You then read the temperature on the scale of the thermometer. A temperature scale is marked off in *degrees.* A weather report may say, for example, that the temperature today is 65 degrees Fahrenheit. The temperature is printed in a newspaper as 65° F. The ° mark, or symbol, means "degrees."

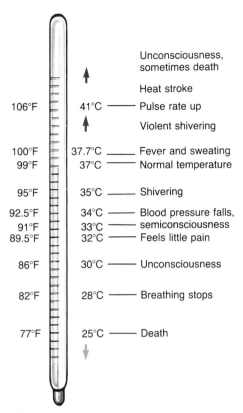

106°F	41°C	Unconsciousness, sometimes death
		Heat stroke
		Pulse rate up
		Violent shivering
100°F	37.7°C	Fever and sweating
99°F	37°C	Normal temperature
95°F	35°C	Shivering
92.5°F	34°C	Blood pressure falls,
91°F	33°C	semiconsciousness
89.5°F	32°C	Feels little pain
86°F	30°C	Unconsciousness
82°F	28°C	Breathing stops
77°F	25°C	Death

▲ *Normal human body temperature is 98.6°F (37°C). The human body can deal with different temperatures but cannot adjust easily to extremes.*

F is another symbol that means "Fahrenheit."

The Fahrenheit temperature scale, which is still commonly used in the United States and Canada today, was devised by a German physicist, Gabriel Daniel Fahrenheit, in the early 1700's. Fahrenheit set the temperature of a normal human body at 96 degrees on his scale. (Later calculations showed that the normal temperature was actually 98.6 degrees.) He then put his thermometer in the coldest mixture he could make of water, ice, and salt. He let this temperature be zero degrees (0°). On Fahrenheit's scale, plain water (water without any salt in it) freezes at 32° F. Water boils at 212° F.

The Celsius temperature scale, also called the centigrade scale, was devised by a Swedish astronomer, Anders Celsius, in 1742. It is commonly used in most countries of the world. On the Celsius scale, plain water

freezes at zero degrees (0° C). The C stands for "Celsius" or "centigrade." Plain tap water boils at 100° C. The normal temperature of the human body is 37° C. This scale is used by scientists all over the world. If you want to be a scientist some day, you must learn the Celsius scale. When you study chemistry, you will use it.

Scientists also use the Kelvin temperature scale, devised by a British mathematician, Lord William Thomson Kelvin, in 1848. This scale uses the same units as the Celsius scale, but it starts at a different point. 0° K equals minus 273° C, and 273° K equals 0° C. 0° K is absolute zero, the temperature at which all motion would stop and there would be absolutely no heat at all. This is the lowest possible temperature that can be imagined, and it is theoretically impossible to achieve.

ALSO READ: HEAT AND COLD, MEASUREMENT, THERMOMETER.

The lowest temperature ever recorded on earth was −459.6699991 degrees Fahrenheit—about one millionth of a degree above absolute zero (the lowest temperature possible). It was obtained by scientists at Saclay in France.

The average human being gives out 104 calories of heat an hour. This is about the same as a 120-watt light bulb. You can see, therefore, why it can become very hot if a lot of people are gathered in a room!

TEMPERATURE CONVERSION TABLE

	Celsius (Centigrade)	Fahrenheit	Kelvin
	−273	−459	0
	−40	−40	233
Freezing Point	0	32	273
	10	50	283
	20	68	293
	30	86	303
	40	104	313
	50	122	323
	60	140	333
	70	158	343
	80	176	353
	90	194	363
Boiling Point	100	212	373
	110	230	383
	120	248	393
	130	266	403
	140	284	413
	150	302	423
	200	392	473
	250	482	523
	300	572	573

To convert Fahrenheit to centigrade—subtract 32, multiply by 5, and divide by 9. To convert centigrade to Fahrenheit, multiply by 9, divide by 5, and add 32. To convert centigrade to Kelvin, add 273 degrees.

▲ *The people of ancient Rome kept a sacred fire burning inside this temple, which was dedicated to Vesta, the Roman goddess of the hearth.*

▼ *This is the Grand Palace in Bangkok, Thailand, which has a square mile of impressive statues, sloping roofs, and richly decorated temples.*

TEMPLE   A temple is a building or other area reserved for religious worship. Temples were an important part of most early religions, especially those in Egypt, Israel, Greece, Rome, and the Orient. Even today, houses of worship in the Mormon, Jewish, Hindu, and Buddhist religions are called temples. Because of their importance, temples have usually been elaborately decorated. They often represent the best of the society's architecture.

One of the best-known temples in the world was the Temple of Solomon in Jerusalem. It was built during the reign of King Solomon (about 3,000 years ago). The Ark of the Covenant, a holy object in the Jewish religion, was kept there. The Temple of Solomon was destroyed in 586 B.C. by King Nebuchadnezzar of Babylonia, but it was later rebuilt. Beginning in 20 B.C., King Herod rebuilt the temple even more beautifully, using marble in place of the original wood. Much of the original arrangement was kept, but magnificent carved decorations in the Roman architectural style were added. This was the temple from which, according to the Bible, Jesus threw out the money-changers

and merchants. The Romans destroyed the temple in about A.D. 70. It was never rebuilt. A portion of the ruined temple, called the Wailing Wall, still stands in Jerusalem.

The early Greeks and Romans believed that their gods lived within natural objects and forces and made their wishes known through natural occurrences, such as wind and lightning. Because of this belief, their earliest temples were special groves of trees, streams, or rocky areas.

As the Greek and Roman civilizations became more stable and more advanced, people built enclosed shelters for their gods. As years passed, these shelters became increasingly elaborate. Greek temples often consisted of several buildings—the temple itself, housing for the priests, and shelters for animals to be sacrificed to the gods. Since religion was supremely important in Greek and Roman life, the best of their architecture and art was lavished on the temples they built. The Parthenon in Athens and the Pantheon in Rome are two outstanding examples of the kinds of temples the Greeks and Romans built.

ALSO READ: ABU SIMBEL, ACROPOLIS, ARCHITECTURE, GREEK ART, PAGODA, ROMAN ART.

TENG HSIAO-P'ING (born 1904)
If Mao Tse-tung created modern China, then Teng Hsiao-p'ing reshaped its outlook, following the upheaval of Mao's Cultural Revolution.

Teng was born in Szechwan province. He studied in France and joined the Communist party. During the 1930's and 1940's, he was a colleague of Mao Tse-tung in the Communist campaign that defeated the Japanese and the Nationalist forces of Chiang Kai-shek.

Teng was prominent in foreign policy and Communist party organization. In the 1960's, he led Chinese delegations to the U.S.S.R. But in the 1970's he fell from power, possibly because he was seen as a likely rival by Mao and Mao's associates. But after Mao's death in 1976, Teng moved toward power and was quickly acknowledged as China's most dominant leader. In 1979, his visit to the United States restored relations between the two countries. Teng criticized mistakes made during Mao's rule, and he began the process by which China relaxed its rigid communism and opened its doors to more Western contacts. His name is also spelled *Deng Xiaoping*.

ALSO READ: CHINA, COMMUNISM, MAO TSE-TUNG.

TENNESSEE The nickname for Tennessee is "Volunteer State." It is called that because of the large number of persons from Tennessee who volunteered to serve their country in the American Revolution.

Tennessee was the home state of several well-known leaders. Sam Houston and Davy Crockett, heroes of the Texas war for independence, came from Tennessee. John Sevier, a leader in the American Revolution, was Tennessee's first governor. The *Hermitage* near Nashville, the state capital, was the home of Andrew Jackson, seventh President of the United States. Two other Presidents, James Knox Polk and Andrew Johnson, also grew up in Tennessee.

One of the greatest accomplishments in providing hydroelectric power has taken place in Tennessee. The Tennessee River valley has been transformed by the work and funds from the Tennessee Valley Authority (TVA), an agency of the Federal Government that was established in 1933. Never before had a whole river valley been developed at one time. Dams were built to keep the river from flooding. The dams created long lakes. These lakes formed a waterway

that boats could use even in the dry season. The lakes offer water for manufacturing, and water flowing from the dams provides power for generating electricity. In addition to harnessing the river, the TVA planted trees to protect the soil on steep hillsides. It taught farmers how to prevent erosion of the soil and how to rotate their crops in order to make better use of their land.

During World War II, a government scientific laboratory was established at Oak Ridge, Tennessee. Scientists working there produced materials for atomic bombs. Today, materials for atomic power plants are produced at Oak Ridge. Exhibits in the Oak Ridge museum show examples of the scientific work done at the laboratory.

The Land and Climate This state is a part of the South. It lies south of Kentucky and Virginia. It is north of Mississippi, Alabama, and Georgia. The Mississippi River flows past it on the west. North Carolina is on its eastern side.

The state may be divided into three sections. In West Tennessee, a strip of floodplain called the "Mississippi Bottoms" lies along the Mississippi River. Whenever the river flooded this strip, it dropped silt there. Centuries of floods built up a deep, rich topsoil. The rest of West Tennessee is a broad plain. Rivers wind among its low hills.

The Nashville Basin, which has fertile land, lies in Middle Tennessee. On either side of the basin is higher ground, the Highland Rim. Middle Tennessee is the largest of the state's three sections. It extends from the Tennessee River in the west to the Cumberland Plateau in the east.

From the Cumberland Plateau eastward, the land is quite high and usually rough. All of this section is in the Appalachian Highland. Mountains rise along the eastern boundary of the state. The place to see them is

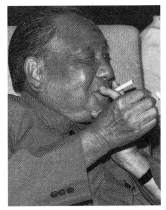

▲ *Teng Hsiao-P'ing, leader of China, who has pushed the country closer to the Western world in economic, industrial, commercial, and cultural ties in the 1980's.*

Cherokee Indians called the Great Smoky Mountains the "Land of the Great Smoke" because a blue, smokelike mist often hangs over them. The mist is caused by hydrocarbon released by the many conifers growing on the mountains.

▲ *The Norris Dam was the first to be built by the Tennessee Valley Authority, which was set up in 1933.*

the Great Smoky Mountains National Park. This big park crosses the Tennessee–North Carolina border and is popular with vacationers.

Summer weather is hot and moist in West and Middle Tennessee. Winters are mild, and the cold season doesn't last long. East Tennessee is higher and has cooler summers and colder winters. The whole state receives ample rain. The most rain falls in winter and early spring.

History The first white people in Tennessee were Spaniards. Hernando de Soto's little force arrived in 1541. De Soto first saw the Mississippi from a bluff about where Memphis is today. Villages of Chickasaw Indians were there. Farther east lived the Creeks, Cherokees, and other Indians. The Spaniards did not stay long. For the next 130 years, the Tennessee Indians were left to themselves. Then French explorers came down the Mississippi. Later, English fur traders arrived. Very few French settlers came to Tennessee. The settlements were mostly English. They were started in the mountains of East Tennessee. During the American Revolution, Colonel Evan Shelby and Colonel John Sevier led Tennessee settlers against British forces.

The area that is now Tennessee was a part of North Carolina. When North Carolina ceded its western lands to the Federal Government in 1784, Tennessee people formed their own "state" of Franklin. It lasted four years. Tennessee was then organized as a territory. It became a state in 1796.

Settlers from the East poured in. They came by wagon or by riverboat. Cotton and wheat were the big crops. Many farmers of West and Middle Tennessee had slaves to work their fields. East Tennessee did not have as many slaves.

In 1861, Tennesseans voted to leave the Union. East Tennessee was against leaving, but it was outvoted by the other two sections. Many Civil War battles, including Shiloh, Chickamauga, and Chattanooga, were fought in Tennessee.

All slaves were freed in 1865. As in other Southern states, a struggle for power followed. At first, blacks and their white friends seemed to be winning. But many white people joined groups like the Ku Klux Klan. These groups used violence to gain control. For a long time, most black Tennesseans were kept from voting and from obtaining good jobs. Black and white youngsters were segregated in the state's public schools until 1956. Since the 1960's, conditions have greatly improved for the blacks.

Tennesseans at Work Farming is no longer the state's main business, since electric power for industry is plentiful. Textiles, metals, chemicals, and chemical products (among them plastics and rubber) are manufactured. Kingsport in East Tennessee is a printing and chemicals center. Memphis, a Mississippi River port in western Tennessee, is a cotton market. Nashville is the national center for country, folk, and western music. The city has about 40 studio complexes for recording music.

Mining is also an important business in Tennessee, which has large deposits of zinc, ball clay, coal, and phosphate rock. Much of the zinc that is mined is used in the manufacture of electric batteries. High-grade ball clays are used in the ceramics industry.

There are Civil War battlefields, stately mansions, and many parks to visit in Tennessee. The Great Smoky Mountains National Park with its scenic beauty is located about 40 miles (65 km) southeast of Knoxville, site of the 1982 World's Fair.

ALSO READ: CROCKETT, DAVY; HOUSTON, SAMUEL; JACKSON, ANDREW; JOHNSON, ANDREW; POLK, JAMES KNOX; SEQUOYAH.

TENNESSEE

Capital
Nashville (462,000 people)

Area
42,244 square miles (109,404 sq. km)
Rank: 34th

Population
4,895,000 people. Rank: 16th

Statehood
June 1, 1796 (16th state admitted)

Principal river
Tennessee River

Highest point
Clingman's Dome 6,642 feet (2,025 m)

Largest city
Memphis (648,000 people)

Motto
"Agriculture and Commerce"

Song
"The Tennessee Waltz"

Famous people
Davy Crockett, David Farragut

▲ *A Civil War cannon commands this impressive view across Chattanooga, at the Moccasin Bend of the Tennessee River.*

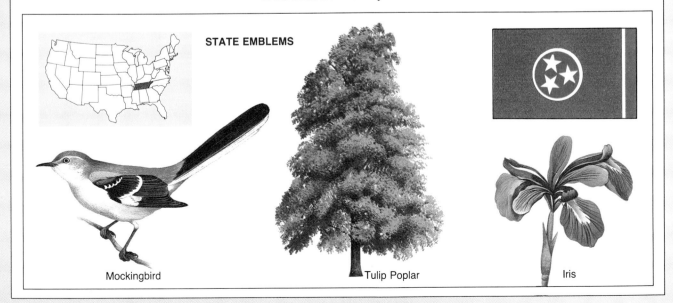

STATE EMBLEMS

Mockingbird

Tulip Poplar

Iris

▲ *John McEnroe, of the United States, was a versatile and powerful tennis champion in the early 1980's. He was better known, however, for his temperamental fits and unruly behavior on court than for his brilliant tennis playing. In the mid-1980's, after a long break from tournament playing, he attempted a comeback.*

A tennis ball can leave the racket at a terrific speed. Serves at speeds exceeding 130 mph (210 km/hr) have been timed electronically.

TENNIS   Tennis is an active sport for all ages. The game, which involves hitting a small ball with a racket, requires speed and physical coordination.

Tennis is played on a special flat rectangular area called a *court*. The court is 27 feet (8.2 m) wide for a singles game, in which one person is on each side of the net. For a doubles game, in which two players are on each side, the court is 9 feet (2.7 m) wider. It is 78 feet (23.8 m) long for both singles and doubles games. The court is marked by white lines. Each half of the court is divided (parallel to the net) into a *backcourt* and a *forecourt*. At right angles to the net, the forecourt is divided in the middle into a *right service court* and *left service court*. The lines marking two opposite ends of the court are called *base lines*. The lines showing the widths for singles and doubles courts are called *sidelines*. The area between the singles and doubles sidelines is called the *alley*. Most outdoor courts are built to lie north and south so that the sun will come in from the sides and not blind either player. The court surface may be clay, grass, asphalt, or concrete. Indoor courts usually have wood floors. Most indoor and some outdoor courts are surfaced with a carpetlike or synthetic material.

Tennis balls are rubber covered with fuzzy cloth. Each ball is about 2½ inches (6 cm) in diameter and weighs about 2 ounces (57 g).

The racket used to hit the ball consists of a handle and an oval frame containing tightly woven strings. Many rackets have a wooden handle and frame. Wooden rackets are stored in a tight frame called a *press* to keep them from warping. Inside the frame, nylon or gut is woven into a tight net. (Gut strings are made from the intestines of animals.) In recent years, tennis rackets with metal frames have become far more popular.

The game of tennis starts with one player standing behind the baseline on the right side of his or her court. To serve, the player throws the ball straight up into the air and hits it with the racket as it starts to come down. To be a good serve, the ball must go into the diagonally opposite service court. If the ball hits the net before landing inside the proper service court, the service is called a *let* and must be retaken.

If the first serve is no good, it is called a *fault*. The server then hits a second serve. If this is also no good, the server has a *double fault* and loses the point. On a serve, the ball must bounce once before it is returned. On all following returns, the ball may be hit before it bounces (a *volley*) or after one bounce.

The exchange of balls in the return is called the *rally*. When one player fails to return the ball or returns it into the net or out of bounds, the other player earns the point. The player who served then serves again, but this time from behind the baseline on the left side. In the following game, the other player will serve. Scoring points in tennis is not so difficult as it sounds. Four points win a game, and six winning games for one player make a set. Two out of three, or three out of five, sets make a match. The points in a game are scored 15, 30, 40, and game point. If a player has no points, his or her score

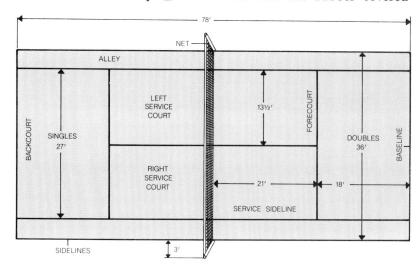

is called *love*. A tie score of three points each, 40 to 40, is called *deuce*. To win a tie game, a player must score two consecutive points. The first point won after deuce is called *advantage* or *ad*. If a player with the advantage loses the next point, the game returns to deuce. If the game score is five to five (deuce set), play goes on until a player has won a two game margin. Often, a *tie breaker*, consisting of a play-off of a number of points, is played if the game score is six to six. In announcing the score, the server's score is always given first.

Tennis players use different strokes to hit the ball. In the forehand for righthanders, the racket is held on the right side of the body to return the ball. When righthanders use the backhand, the body is turned so the racket is held on the left side of the body. It is just the reverse for lefthanded players. When players have the opportunity, they use the *smash*, a hard overhand stroke that is difficult to return. A *lob* is a ball that is hit over the net in a slow, high arch.

Some tennis players, called professionals or pros, earn a living by playing tennis in tournaments. The tournaments may be in their own countries or in other countries. Many countries hold their own national championship tournaments every year. The tournament at Wimbledon, England, is the oldest and probably the best known. The courts at Wimbledon are grass. The tournament for the Davis Cup is one of the most famous. Each year, men's teams from all of the tennis-playing nations hold an elimination competition. Until 1972, the previous year's Davis Cup winner did not compete but defended the title against the winner of the eliminations rounds. Today, under new rules, the Davis Cup winner must play through the elimination rounds. The winner of the final match becomes the new Davis Cup champion. Each year, the Wightman Cup matches are played between British and American women's teams.

ALSO READ: RACQUETBALL, SPORTS, SQUASH, TABLE TENNIS.

▲ *Chris Evert of the United States who, with her rival Martina Navratilova, dominated women's tennis in the 1970's and 1980's.*

TENNYSON ALFRED (1809–1892) Alfred, Lord Tennyson, was one of the greatest of all English poets. He was born in Somersby, Lincolnshire. Encouraged by his father, who was a clergyman, Tennyson began writing when in his teens. At only 12 years of age, he had already written a poem of several thousand lines. Tennyson later attended Cambridge University but left before completing his studies. With one of his college friends, Arthur Henry Hallam, Tennyson spent several months in Spain fighting in a rebellion.

His first book, *Poems, Chiefly Lyrical*, was published in 1830. In 1833, his friend, Hallam, died suddenly, and Tennyson was crushed with sadness. He spent the next ten years studying, thinking, and writing, and then began to publish more poems. His work was widely praised, and he became England's most distinguished poet. In 1850, he published "In Memoriam," a poem written in memory of Arthur Hallam. That same year, Queen Victoria appointed Tennyson poet laureate, or royal poet, of England. He was made a baron and member of the House of Lords in 1883. Tennyson was a master of imaginative verse, as in "The Mermaid":

Who would be a mermaid fair,
Singing alone, combing her hair
Under the sea, in a golden curl
With a comb of pearl, on a throne?

Some of Tennyson's best-known poems are "The Lady of Shalott," "The Charge of the Light Brigade," "Maud," and a collection of poems about King Arthur, *Idylls of the King*.

ALSO READ: POETRY.

▲ *Alfred, Lord Tennyson, English poet.*

TENT Tents are shelters made of cloth or animal skins stretched over a pole framework. These portable, easily constructed shelters were among the earliest human homes. Nomads, or wandering shepherds, have used tents as homes for thousands of years. They need homes they can take down and pack on animals' backs as they move with their herds. Arab invaders from Africa and Asia probably brought tents into Europe in the A.D. 700's. Feudal lords then built tents to house their hunting parties and armies. North American Indians also lived in tents. Some were tipis and some were wigwams.

Some of the biggest tents were once used by circuses. The largest circus tent, called the "big top," could shelter thousands of people. Perhaps the smallest kind of tent is the pup tent. It is made of two canvas rectangles, buttoned together at the top and supported by two poles. Pup tents are big

▼ Bedouin nomads of Arabia live in long, low tents made of cloth woven from black goat hair. The Kazaks and Mongolians of Central Asia use another kind of tent—the ger, or yurt. Yurts look more like portable huts than tents. Made of thick layers of felt laid over a wooden frame, they have an outer covering of hide or canvas.

▲ A family has pitched a wall tent on the shore of a lake in a state park near Burnet, Texas.

▲ Bedouin tent   ▼ Mongolian yurts

enough to sleep two people, side by side. They are often used by Boy and Girl Scout troops, armies on the march, and other overnight hikers. Another commonly used army tent is the pyramid tent. It has a pointed roof formed by four triangular sides. Rectangular flaps hang down to the ground from each of the triangular sides. The flaps may be rolled up or pegged to the ground.

Today, most tents are used for vacations. A variety of tents can be seen during the summer in national parks and campgrounds. Some are large canvas structures built over raised wooden floors. Others, of lightweight nylon, fold into small backpacks. One common tent is the wall tent, shaped rather like a house, with upright sides for more head room. The umbrella tent is also popular. New versions of the umbrella tent have frames that pop up when a latch is released.

ALSO READ: CAMPING; INDIANS, AMERICAN; NOMAD; SHELTER.

TERESA, MOTHER (born 1910) A few people are famous simply for doing good. A modern example is Mother Teresa. She was awarded the

Nobel Peace Prize in 1979 for her work for the poor and sick people of India.

Mother Teresa was born Agnes Gonxha Bojaxhiu. She lived in Skopje, a town in what is now Yugoslavia, where her father kept a grocery store. At age 18 she left home to become a nun and to train as a teacher. She went first to Ireland but soon sailed for India. There she went to work in the slums of the overcrowded city of Calcutta.

Later, she asked permission to set up her own religious order, the Missionaries of Charity. She was now known as Mother Teresa, and she and her Indian nuns wore saris (Indian dress). She started medical clinics and schools for the poor. She cared for the old, the young, and the incurable. When the pope visited India in 1964, he gave her his limousine. Mother Teresa raffled it off, to raise money for a leper colony she had founded.

TERMITE A termite is a small, antlike insect. Like ants, termites live in large colonies. Termites that live in the tropics surround their nests with large mounds of earth that look like huge anthills. Some termites have soft, white bodies. For these reasons, termites are sometimes called "white ants." But termites are not ants. One major difference is that ants have thin, threadlike "waists," while termites have thick ones.

A termite colony has several *castes*, or classes. There are workers, soldiers, and reproductives. The soldiers' job is to defend the colony against enemies. The workers' job is to build and tend the nest and search for food. Although the workers and soldiers may be either male or female, they cannot reproduce themselves. That is the job of the reproductives, or the kings and queens. The primary king and queen are the founders of the colony and the parents of all the other termites in the colony. Lesser

kings and queens often found colonies of their own. The primary queen becomes an egg-laying machine that produces millions of eggs during her lifetime. Her abdomen may swell until she is several hundred times as large as a worker. She becomes so large that she cannot move. The workers feed and take care of her.

There are about 2,000 different species of termites. Most of them live in the tropics, but some live in the temperate regions of North and South America and in Europe. The workers build claylike tubes through which the termites travel from the ground to wooden parts of buildings. Those that live in the United States build their nests underground. If a termite is exposed to air, its soft body dries out and it dies.

Termites eat wood, but they cannot digest it. The digestion is done for the termite by one-celled animals that live in their intestines. Termites that live in the forest serve a useful function by clearing away dead wood. But termites that live near people cause much damage. They destroy buildings, furniture, telephone and power poles, and timber supplies. Termites have even been known to burrow straight through concrete.

ALSO READ: ANT, INSECT, PARASITE.

▲ *Mother Teresa, whose ceaseless work for the poor and needy in India earned her the Nobel Peace Prize in 1979.*

▼ *Many termites build their nests inside huge mounds. Inside the nest is a network of tunnels and chambers where the workers look after the young. The large queen is at the center. Soldier termites defend the nest against intruders.*

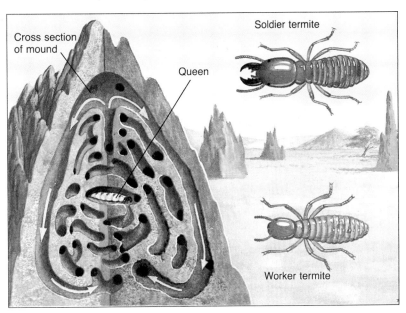

TERRARIUM A terrarium is a glass-enclosed container used for raising small land animals and plants. A terrarium may hold just plants or a combination of plants and animals. If a combination is used, the plants and animals should be kinds that would naturally live together in the same environment.

■ LEARN BY DOING

It can be interesting and fun to build your own terrarium. A fish tank makes the best container, but you can also use a large glass jar with a top. Cover the bottom of the container with gravel or sand and add a layer of soil. If you are building a desert terrarium, mix equal parts of sand and soil. (It would be a good idea to take your soil from the same place you take the plants and animals for the terrarium.) Then moisten the soil. If you want to raise plants that need a lot of moisture, such as mosses, or animals that live in humid climates, add a lot of water (without making mud) and cover the container tightly with glass or metal. This will increase the humidity inside the terrarium. (If the walls get foggy, remove the lid until they become clear again.) If you are building a desert terrarium, little moisture will be needed. In this case, you should add very little water and

leave the top off the terrarium. Put a lamp above the container to provide extra light and heat. If you put in animals that might climb out, you can cover the terrarium with a wire mesh screen.

After you add the plants and animals, you will have to take care of the terrarium. The soil around most plants (except, for example, cacti in a desert terrarium) should be kept moist. Your animals must be fed and given water regularly. ■

A desert terrarium may house horned lizards, snakes, gerbils, or other desert animals living on warm sand alongside cacti or other desert plants. Woodland and swamp terrariums can hold frogs, salamanders, or turtles, along with mosses, ferns, and other small plants. Ivy grows well in woodland terrariums. Swamp terrariums survive best with soil from the animals' and plants' original homes. Frogs, turtles, and salamanders eat bits of meat, worms, and insects, especially flies. Frogs and toads spend some time in water, and tadpoles must live in water until they grow into adults. Therefore, terrariums containing these creatures should include a pool of water.

Snakes are sometimes difficult to keep in terrariums because of their diet. Most snakes eat live prey, such as mice, lizards, and other snakes, so feeding may be a problem.

Whatever type of terrarium you choose to make, you can learn a great deal about animal life from these "environments in a bottle."

ALSO READ: ANIMAL, ANIMAL HOMES, AQUARIUM, ECOLOGY, FERN, FROGS AND TOADS, HOBBY, MOSSES AND LIVERWORTS, NATURE STUDY, PLANT, PLANT BREEDING, REPTILE, SALAMANDER, SNAKE, TURTLE.

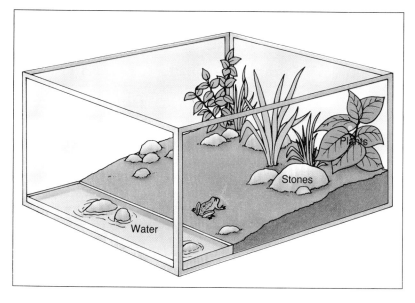

Plants

Stones

Water

TERRITORY see COLONY.

A truck burns in a street in Belfast, Northern Ireland, a result of the bitter conflict between Roman Catholics and Protestants. Both groups use terrorist organizations to intimidate and murder one another. The British forces stationed in Northern Ireland are often the target for these terrorists.

TERRORISM Violence is frightening, and the use of violence to achieve a political goal is especially frightening. The use of terror to achieve political ends has become a persistent feature of the world since World War II.

Opponents of a lawful government can use lawful democratic methods of opposition. But others may instead turn to terrorism. Terrorists murder by shooting and bombing, sabotage transportation, kidnap business leaders and other people and hold them as hostages, rob banks, and take part in drug trafficking. Even a small group of violent terrorists can do great damage and prove difficult to catch.

Innocent air travelers have sometimes been hijacked by terrorists. Gunmen disguised as passengers have seized airliners in midair and forced the pilot to fly them to a friendly country. Whole planeloads of people have been held hostage by terrorists

seeking to gain the release of fellow-terrorists held in jail.

Terrorism is a worldwide problem, but it is most violent in South America and the Middle East. In 1986, United States jets bombed Libya because the U.S. government believed the Libyan regime was supporting terrorism around the world.

TEXAS In what state is the largest cattle ranch in the United States? You will have no trouble guessing. It is in Texas. The ranch is the famous King Ranch, which lies southwest of Corpus Christi. It covers 823,403 acres (333,231 hectares), an area about the size of Rhode Island, the smallest state. At one time, the ranch covered 1,250,000 acres (505,875 hectares).

The main gate is on Highway 141 near Kingsville. A person at the gatehouse gives each visitor a folder that carries the King "Running W" brand. By following a map, visitors can drive through the ranch for about 12 miles (20 km). They see cattle feeding in pastures and large pens. The breed called *Santa Gertrudis* was developed on the King Ranch. Fine horses are also raised here.

The Land and Climate Texas has other big ranches, too. And it has big farms. It has big oil fields and big

Six flags have flown over Texas during its history—the flags of Spain, France, Mexico, the Republic of Texas, the Confederate States of America, and the United States.

▼ The preserved mission of "The Alamo" in San Antonio, Texas, where Texans valiantly fought for independence against Mexican forces under General Santa Anna. It is the "cradle of Texas liberty."

The Texan state capitol in Austin is the nation's largest capitol. Its dome is almost 310 feet (94 m) high.

▲ *Autumn comes to McKittrick Canyon, part of the scenic sanctuary that is Guadalupe Mountains National Park in west Texas.*

manufacturing centers. Almost everything in Texas is big!

This state is the largest of the 48 contiguous (touching along boundaries) states of the United States. Only Alaska is larger. Texas has a land area larger than New England, New York, New Jersey, Pennsylvania, Ohio, and Indiana combined. The state has many very different sections. There are four main regions.

COASTAL PLAIN. This plain lies beside the Gulf of Mexico. It stretches from the Rio Grande to the border of Louisiana. The land is flat and is crossed by many rivers. The northern part of the plain is the Pine Belt. Nearly all the timber cut for sale in Texas comes from this belt. South of it are the coastal prairies. Their grass feeds great herds of cattle. (The King Ranch is here.) Rice, cotton, and vegetables grow in wide, level fields. The southern point of Texas is the Rio Grande Plain. Cattle, sheep, and goats are raised here. So are irrigated crops, such as oranges and grapefruits.

LOWER WESTERN PLAINS. Texans call these the "North Central Plains." They are part of the Great Plains that lie all along the Rocky Mountains. This region is partly hilly and partly rolling. It is livestock country, but fruits and vegetables are raised where the land is fairly level.

HIGH PLAINS. This region also belongs to the Great Plains, but it is higher than the plains east of it. The High Plains are nearer the Rockies. The land here is cut by deep river gorges. There are few trees, except along the rivers. Wheat and the grain called *sorghum* are grown in the north. On the Edwards Plateau in the southeast, there is rough grazing. Texans say, "Grass for cattle. Weeds for sheep. Brush for goats."

TRANS-PECOS. This name means "across, or beyond, the Pecos River." West of that river, Texas is mountainous. Here is the Diablo (Devil) Plateau where salt flats glisten in the sun.

High mountain ranges tower over it and over the Stockton Plateau. Between the ranges are dry plains.

In the Pecos Valley and on the Stockton Plateau, cotton and alfalfa are raised by irrigation. There are irrigated cotton fields in the Rio Grande Valley, too.

An area as large as Texas is bound to have great differences in climate. Near the Louisiana border, there is plenty of rain. But it is drier as you go west. All Texas is hot in summer, but winter temperatures differ from one part of the state to another. Winters are very cold in northern and western Texas. They are mild on the Gulf of Mexico.

History Spaniards were the first Europeans in Texas. At the time they arrived, the Caddo were the most numerous Indians. The first Spanish settlement was Ysleta, which is near El Paso in the Trans-Pecos. But the area that the Spaniards most wanted to settle was eastern Texas. They wanted to hold back the French of Louisiana. So they founded towns and started missions in the east. These were church settlements. Indians were gathered together at the missions, and they were taught Christianity and European trades.

In 1821, Mexico won independence from Spain. Texas was then part of Mexico. The Mexican government wanted to increase the white population of Texas and gave land to Americans who would settle there. Stephen F. Austin, for whom the Texas capital is named, started an American colony on the Brazos River. After some years, the Spanish-speaking Mexican government and the English-speaking Texans quarreled. Fighting broke out. It became a war.

On March 1, 1836, Texan leaders met at the little town of Washington-on-the-Brazos. The next day they declared Texas independent. Five days later, several thousand Mexican

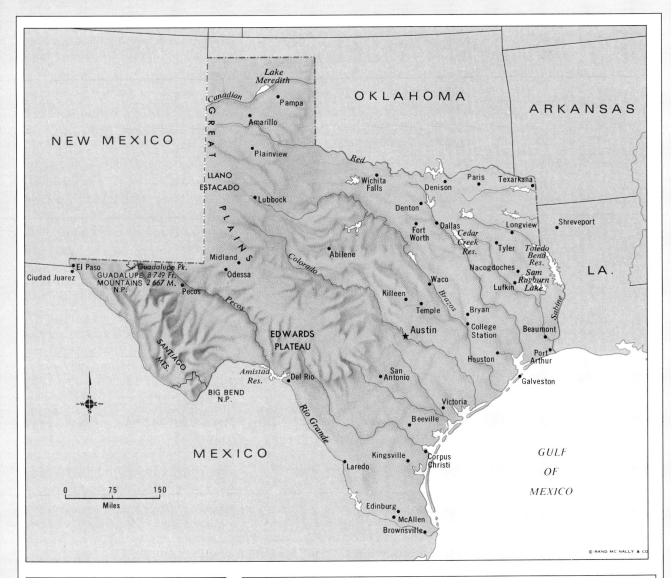

Map labels

NEW MEXICO

OKLAHOMA

ARKANSAS

GREAT PLAINS

LLANO ESTACADO

LA.

MEXICO

GULF OF MEXICO

Lake Meredith
Canadian
Pampa
Amarillo
Plainview
Lubbock
Red
Wichita Falls
Denison
Paris
Texarkana
Denton
Fort Worth
Dallas
Longview
Shreveport
Cedar Creek Res.
Tyler
Toledo Bend Res.
Midland
Colorado
Abilene
Nacogdoches
Sam Rayburn Lake
El Paso
Guadalupe Pk.
GUADALUPE 8 749 Ft.
MOUNTAINS 2 667 M.
N.P.
Ciudad Juarez
Odessa
Waco
Killeen
Brazos
Lufkin
Sabine
Pecos
Temple
Bryan
Beaumont
EDWARDS PLATEAU
Austin
College Station
Port Arthur
SANTIAGO MTS.
Amistad Res.
Del Rio
Houston
Galveston
BIG BEND N.P.
San Antonio
Victoria
Rio Grande
Beeville
Kingsville
Corpus Christi
Laredo
Edinburg
McAllen
Brownsville

0 75 150
Miles

© RAND MC NALLY & CO

TEXAS

Capital
Austin (397,000 people)

Area
267,339 square miles (692,355 sq. km). Rank: 2nd

Population
16,841,000 people. Rank: 3rd

Statehood
December 29, 1845 (28th state)

Principal rivers
Red River, Brazos River, Rio Grande

Highest point
Guadalupe Peak 8,751 feet (2,667 m)

Largest city
Houston (1,706,000 people)

Motto
"Friendship"

Song
"Texas, Our Texas"

Famous people
Stephen Austin, James Bowie, Chester Nimitz, Sam Rayburn

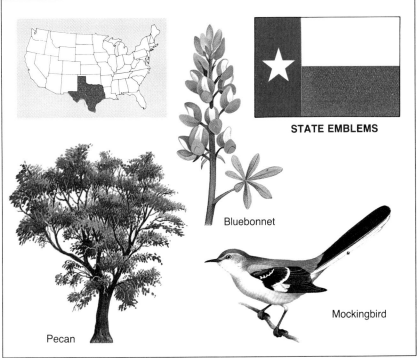

STATE EMBLEMS

Bluebonnet

Pecan

Mockingbird

troops besieged a force of about 180 Americans, who fought to the last person at a fort called the Alamo in San Antonio. "Remember the Alamo" became a Texan battle slogan. The next month, General Sam Houston attacked a force at San Jacinto under the Mexican president, General Antonio López de Santa Anna. The Mexicans were defeated, and Santa Anna was captured. Texas had won its independence. It became the Republic of Texas and adopted a flag with one star ·on it. A nickname for Texas is the "Lone Star State."

The new republic joined the United States in December 1845. War between Mexico and the United States followed.

In 1861, Texans voted to leave the Union. Texas became one of the Confederate States of America. There was not much fighting in Texas, but the defeat of the Confederacy brought great changes. The main one was the end of farming by slave labor.

However, agriculture continued to be the state's leading business. But in 1901, oil was discovered near Beaumont in eastern Texas. Oil helped greatly to develop a big manufacturing industry in the state.

In the 1960's, the United States Manned Spacecraft Center was set up near Houston. It controlled the spacecraft that carried the astronauts to the moon.

▲ *Youngsters take the Runaway Mine Train Ride at Six Flags Over Texas, a family entertainment center in Arlington, Texas.*

Texans at Work Texas is one of the busiest and richest states in the Union. Texan cities have grown to be big and prosperous. The state's oil refining industry is concentrated in the area of the port of Houston. Dallas is a financial, fashion, and cultural center. Grain markets and meatpacking plants are a part of Fort Worth. El Paso, on the border across from Juárez, Mexico, is the trading center of western Texas. It is a city with a Spanish flavor. San Antonio has one of the country's largest medical centers.

Manufacturing is the most important business in Texas. Chemicals, food products, machinery, and aircraft are the leading manufactured items. Mining is a major business, too. Enormous amounts of petroleum (oil) and natural gas are pumped from underground reserves. Pipelines carry the oil and natural gas to other parts of the United States. Texas also has large, valuable deposits of sulfur, salt, asphalt, graphite, and other minerals.

Texas receives much money from agriculture. The state has more than 200,000 farms and ranches. Beef and dairy cattle, hogs, sheep, and poultry

▼ *Dallas is a wealthy city with money from oil, cattle, and electronics. This is reflected in its futuristic architecture.*

are raised in large numbers. Cotton (the main crop), sorghum grain, rice, wheat, pecans, and peanuts are the most valuable crops grown. Many fish, including shrimp, menhaden, and red snapper, are caught by Texans in the waters of the Gulf of Mexico.

Tourists enjoy Texas's many sandy beaches, state and national parks and forests, and other recreational areas. Houston's giant indoor stadium, the Astrodome, and nearby large entertainment center, Astroworld, are popular places to visit.

ALSO READ: ALAMO; BOWIE, JIM; CROCKETT, DAVY; GULF OF MEXICO; HOUSTON, SAMUEL; MEXICAN WAR; RIO GRANDE.

TEXTILE Any woven fabric made from threads or yarn is a textile. The making of textiles was one of the earliest human crafts. In ancient Egypt, linen textiles were woven from the fibers of the flax plant. Ancient people of eastern Europe spun and wove woolen fabrics from the fleece of sheep. According to Chinese legend, the art of weaving silk from the threads of the silkworm cocoon was discovered in 700 B.C. Although cotton is the most common natural textile used today, it was the last to be widely produced. The invention of the cotton gin by Eli Whitney in 1794 made it possible to clean and prepare a lot of cotton fibers in a short time.

Textiles are grouped by the kind of fiber from which they are made. Wool, cotton, linen, and silk are the most important *natural* fibers. *Synthetic* fibers include rayon, nylon, polyesters, polyvinyls, polyethylenes, and fibers made from glass. To change these materials into fabric, each must be made into thread.

Textiles are also grouped according to the pattern of weave. Weaves can be smooth or rough, thick or sheer, loose or tight, plain or fancy. The way

the weave looks has nothing to do with the kind of fiber used. The weave depends on how fine (thin) the thread is, and the number of threads it takes to weave an inch of fabric. The three basic weaves are called plain, twill, and satin.

In the *plain weave*, the threads are evenly woven over and under in both directions. Fabrics in the plain weave group include broadcloth, calico, crepe, cheesecloth, muslin, percale, flannel, tweed, and others. The plain weave forms the tightest, sturdiest type of cloth. Threads in a finished plain-weave fabric form a checkerboard pattern. Sheets, tablecloths, typewriter ribbons, and men's shirts are usually made with the plain weave.

The threads of a finished *twill weave* form a diagonal pattern. Twills are looser than plain weaves, but they are very rugged and are used in suits, coats, and other heavy pieces of clothing. Twills also hold their shape well. Herringbone, serge, worsted gabardine, ticking cloth, and denim are a few common twill-weave fabrics.

Satin weaves are shiny, smooth weaves. The smooth, flat surface is made by running one set of threads over a large number of crossing threads before weaving them in. The reflection of light on these threads gives the satin weave its sheen. Satin is the weakest weave, and the threads snag easily.

Other types of weave include the dobby, jacquard, and pile weaves. The *dobby weave* is used to make

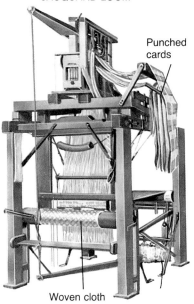

JACQUARD LOOM

Punched cards

Woven cloth

▲ *The first automatic loom was invented by Joseph Marie Jacquard in France in 1801. Cards punched with holes were fed into the loom to make it weave a particular pattern.*

◄ *Power-driven looms in the modern textile mill make inexpensive cloth available worldwide.*

▲ *Raw viscose being prepared. Today viscose, a synthetic fabric that looks like silk, is second only to cotton in fabric manufacture.*

▲ *William Makepeace Thackeray, English author.*

fancy raised patterns in a fabric. The *jacquard* is done on a special loom to weave tapestries, brocades, and other very fancy and very complicated designs. *Pile weaves* are made by drawing threads up above the surface of the cloth as it is woven. These raised threads form loops. If the loops are cut, the fabric is called *cut pile*. Toweling, corduroys, velvets, and woven pile rugs are examples of pile-weave fabrics.

Not all textiles are made by weaving. Some are *knitted* and others are *felted*. Felting is done by pressing fibers together under heat and pressure. Plastic fabrics that are felted tend to melt into a more solid mass. They are stronger than regular felt, made from wool, which does not melt under heat and pressure.

A textile may be all of one fiber, such as wool, or of a combination of fibers, such as wool and Orlon (a synthetic fiber). American colonists wove a fabric called linsey-woolsey, made from linen and wool. U.S. government regulations require that many fabrics be labeled with the exact fiber content. This is done to protect the customer from buying a cheaper synthetic "wool" for the price of more expensive natural wool. Synthetic fibers are so well-made that it is often impossible to tell a synthetic from a natural fiber simply by looking at it.

The color patterns on textiles are produced in a number of ways. Some are made by weaving the fabric with threads of different colors. Woolen plaids are a good example of this. Solid-color fabrics can be dyed after weaving or can be woven with pre-dyed threads.

Many fabrics have printed patterns or designs. Textile printing is usually done with large *rollers* on which the design has been etched. A separate roller is used for each color in the design. *Screen printing* is done with a stencil on which the design is cut out. When the stencil is placed on the fabric, the dye colors only the cut-out areas. Screen prints are usually used for designs of one color.

Once a textile has been printed, it may go through one or more finishing processes. Some fabrics are treated to keep them from creasing or fading or the colors from running. Some are coated with resins to give a shiny appearance, while others are bonded with a thin foam-rubber backing to help them keep their shape. Other treatments protect fabrics from shrinking, staining, soiling, and being damaged by mildew and moths. Some fabrics are *laminated* (coated) with plastic or rubber to make such waterproof, easy-care items as place mats and boots.

ALSO READ: CLOTHING; COTTON; DYE; FIBER; KNITTING; PLASTIC; SEWING; SILK; SPINNING AND WEAVING; SYNTHETIC; WHITNEY, ELI.

THACKERAY, WILLIAM MAKEPEACE (1811–1863) William Makepeace Thackeray was a popular English writer of stories and novels. Thackeray was born in Calcutta, India. He was sent to school in England and attended Cambridge University. He later studied art in Paris. Thackeray's first attempts at writing were made only to earn money. His wife, whom he married in 1836, became mentally ill after the birth of their third daughter. She never recovered, and Thackeray was forced to rear his children alone.

He wrote many articles and stories for magazines. He sometimes illustrated his work with sketches. Thackeray's greatest novel, *Vanity Fair*, first appeared in monthly sections in a magazine. The novel is set in the early 1800's. It is about the lives of Amelia Sedley and Becky Sharp, two very different types of women. Amelia is wealthy and sweet-natured. Becky is a poor and charming schemer, constantly striving to get ahead by every available means. Thackeray's writing is always vivid and humorous, and often bitterly satirical. In his works, he often attacks snobbish people and foolish social rules.

Among Thackeray's other novels are *Pendennis*, *Henry Esmond*, and the *Newcomes*. During the 1850's, Thackeray made two lecture tours of the United States. He used his experiences in the United States to write *The Virginians*, which continues the story of *Henry Esmond*.

ALSO READ: LITERATURE.

THAILAND Thailand, which once was called Siam, is in the center of mainland southeast Asia. Burma is to the west, and Kampuchea and Laos are to the east. Southern Thailand is on the Malaysian peninsula, north of Malaysia. (See the map with the article on ASIA.)

Thailand is about three-fourths the size of Texas. Forested mountains and fertile valleys fill the northern land. The northeast is a large plateau, and the central plain is a rich agricultural area. In the south, the long sliver of land is covered mostly by rain forest, where tigers, gibbons, and beautiful birds may be found. The climate is hot, damp, and tropical. Monsoons control the weather.

The country is one of the world's leading rice exporters. Most of the rice is grown in the central plain, where water is plentiful. Overflow water from the Chao Phraya River is stored in reservoirs and canals during the rainy season. Elephants are trained to haul teak logs to the rivers, and the logs are floated downstream. Corn, cassava, sugarcane, and cattle are raised. There are rubber plantations, tin and tungsten mines, and small fishing villages.

Bangkok, the capital, is a busy city with lovely palaces and temples. It also has a "floating market" where shopkeepers pole their flat-bottomed boats, or *sampans*, along the canals and sell fruits and vegetables.

Thailand has often been called the "land of smiles" because of the easygoing nature of the people. Most Thais are Buddhists. Every Thai man is expected to spend a few months of his life in a Buddhist monastery. Ornate Buddhist temples are called *wats*.

Thailand (Muang Thai) means "land of the free." It is the only southeast Asian country that has never been a colony of a European nation. In the 1400's, it was a strong country in its area. Merchants and missionaries came from France and England in the 1800's, but Thailand was strong enough to keep its independence. However, it gave up some of its land. In 1932, a revolt changed the monarchy from an absolute one (completely powerful) to a constitutional monarchy. It has a king and a prime minister. Military leaders took over the government in 1976, but general elections followed this.

ALSO READ: ASIA, BUDDHISM, RICE.

▲ *Boats crowd the busy* klongs, *or canals, of Bangkok, the capital of Thailand. Much of the food and timber from Thailand's farms and forests still reaches Bangkok by canal.*

THAILAND

Capital City: Bangkok (5,018,000 people).
Area: 198,471 square miles (514,000 sq. km).
Population: 55,000,000.
Government: Constitutional monarchy.
Natural Resources: Tin, wolfram and other minerals.
Export Products: Rice, tapioca products, rubber, corn, machinery, sugar, tin, silk.
Unit of Money: Baht.
Official Language: Thai.

In 1939, President Roosevelt decided that Thanksgiving Day should be one week earlier than it had been—the next to the last Thursday in November. He wanted to help business by lengthening the shopping period before Christmas. In 1941, Congress finally ruled that the holiday would be held on the fourth Thursday in November.

▼ *The Thames in London, with the dome of St. Paul's Cathedral visible in the background.*

THAMES RIVER The Thames is one of the two longest rivers in Great Britain. It is about the same length as the River Severn. The Thames rises in the Cotswold Hills of southwest England and flows southeastward for about 210 miles (340 km). After winding through the city of London, the river widens into an estuary (bay) at the North Sea.

The upper Thames runs through rich farmlands and small towns, including the university town of Oxford, where the river is called the Isis. A series of *locks* (mechanisms for raising and lowering ships) allows small boats to travel almost to the source of the river. Flat-bottomed boats called *punts* are popular pleasure craft here.

The Thames once made London one of the busiest ports in Europe because this section of the river rises and falls with the tides of the North Sea. In the "Pool," just below Tower Bridge, large ships were berthed in special docks shut off by gates that kept the water at a constant level within the docks. Today, with the

worldwide decline in shipping, most of London's docks lie empty.

Sightseeing boats on the Thames take visitors past some of London's best-known landmarks. At Westminster, the Houses of Parliament and the clock tower of Big Ben stand on the north bank of the river. Below Westminster, the river flows under a number of bridges, including London Bridge, which replaced the old London Bridge. The old bridge has now been rebuilt in the state of Arizona. Farther downstream, the familiar Tower Bridge leads to the Tower of London, where many well-known figures in English history were imprisoned and some were beheaded.

In 1984, the Thames Barrier was officially opened at Woolwich Reach to prevent the river from flooding. It is the largest river barrier in the world and is made up of ten gates that lie horizontally to allow ships to go through. If floods threaten, the gates can be raised in about 30 minutes.

The Thames freezes over in exceptionally cold winters. The ice was so thick in the winter of 1894 that Londoners were able to skate across the river. Rowing is a popular sport on the Thames. The universities of Oxford and Cambridge hold their famous boat race on the river every spring.

ALSO READ: ENGLAND, LONDON, TOWER OF LONDON.

THANKSGIVING Thanksgiving is a national holiday in the United States. It is celebrated each year on the fourth Thursday in November. On this day, families gather together, and many people say prayers of thanks for the year's blessings. In many homes, a big dinner of roast turkey and stuffing is served. Thanksgiving is traditionally a harvest festival. Similar festivals are celebrated in many parts of the world to give thanks after the year's crops have

been safely harvested. Canada celebrates its Thanksgiving the second Monday in October.

The first American Thanksgiving probably took place in New England. It was celebrated by the Pilgrim settlers, who established Plymouth Colony in Massachusetts in 1620. The Pilgrims had struggled bravely through a grim first winter with much sickness and little food. Only about half of the original group who had sailed across the Atlantic in the *Mayflower* managed to survive. The following spring, friendly Indians helped the settlers to plant corn, and in the autumn, the first crop was harvested. Governor William Bradford proclaimed three days of prayer and thanksgiving. The Pilgrims gave a huge feast and invited the Indian chief, Massasoit, and 90 of his people.

The custom of observing a special harvest thanksgiving day spread throughout the other colonies in the following years. After the American Revolution, the various American states continued the custom, each one naming its own day for giving thanks. In 1863, President Abraham Lincoln proclaimed the first national Thanksgiving Day on the last Thursday in November. The present date was established by Congress in 1941.

ALSO READ: MASSASOIT, PILGRIM SETTLERS.

THATCHER, MARGARET (born 1925) In 1979, Margaret Thatcher became the first woman to head the government of a Western nation, Great Britain. She was born Margaret Hilda Roberts in the town of Grantham, Lincolnshire, England. Her father kept a grocery store. She was a capable student, studying first chemistry and then law. In 1951, she married Denis Thatcher, a businessman.

Margaret Thatcher joined the Conservative party and, in 1959 she was elected to the British Parliament. She

was promoted to ministerial rank in the government, but few people saw her as a future leader. No woman had ever led the Conservatives.

In 1975, following two election defeats, the Conservative party sought a new leader. Margaret Thatcher challenged former prime minister Edward Heath and won. In 1979, the Conservatives won the parliamentary general election, and Margaret Thatcher became Britain's prime minister.

As prime minister, she led the Conservatives to a second term in 1983. Her overriding policy was to give Britain a sound economic base from which it could compete internationally. Her determination not to be swayed by opposition to her policies earned her the nickname of "The Iron Lady." In 1987, she won her third term. Thatcher resigned in 1990 after losing her party's support and John Major was chosen to lead the party.

ALSO READ: BRITISH ISLES, PARLIAMENT, PRIME MINISTER.

THEATER The lights dim. The busy chattering of the audience falls to a hushed murmur and then to expectant stillness. The curtain slowly rises and the play begins. The audience is experiencing "theater," the art of staging a play, or drama. The word "theater" also means a building designed to hold dramatic performances, especially plays. Theaters have changed in shape and size many times throughout their history.

▲ *The first New England Thanksgiving was celebrated to give thanks to God for the harvest. A number of Indians joined in the feast. They brought turkeys and venison.*

▲ *Margaret Thatcher, Prime Minister of Britain from 1979–1990.*

The first theater in the American colonies was opened in Williamsburg, Virginia, in 1716.

THEATER

▲ *A Greek theater, called an amphitheater, with its stage and circular orchestra for the chorus. The actors were men who wore masks to show the part they were playing.*

These changes have reflected the changes and the growth of drama. All of the arts come together in the theater—acting, music, singing, the dance, painting, and the literature of drama.

Theater of the Ancient Greeks
Ancient Greece was the birthplace of the theater, about 2,500 years ago. The Greek word *theatron* meant a "viewing place." Most of the early theaters were outdoors. Some held as many as 20,000 people. A Greek theater was usually constructed in a hollowed-out area of a hillside. The audience sat on tiers of stone or wooden benches that rose in a huge semicircle up the side of the hill. At the foot of the slope was a round stone area called the *orchestra*. At the back of the orchestra stood the *stage*—a narrow, raised platform. The *chorus*, or speakers in Greek drama, stood in the orchestra. The actors performed on the stage. Behind the stage was the *skene*, or scene building. It held crude dressing rooms for the actors. The front wall of the skene was used as background scenery for the play. This wall and the stage were together called the *proskenion* ("proscenium"). Side walls, or wings, projected forward from each side of the skene.

The Romans to the Renaissance
The Romans copied the design of their theaters from the Greeks. But the tiers of seats in Roman theaters were usually supported by brick walls instead of being built against a hillside. The chorus was seldom used in Roman drama, and the whole play took place on the stage. Part of the audience sat in the orchestra. A large archway was built in the center of the skene wall. The area where the audience sat became known as the *auditorium*, from the Latin word *audire* ("to hear"). The Romans also held entertainments in gigantic oval arenas called *amphitheaters*. These had seats all around the performing area. The Colosseum in Rome was said to have seated about 50,000 people.

After the fall of the Roman Empire in the A.D. 400's, the Christian Church ruled that playacting was sinful. Very few theaters were built in Europe for several hundred years. Then, in the A.D. 900's, the Christian Church began to allow performances of religious dramas called *mystery* or *miracle plays*. At first, these plays were acted inside the cathedrals and churches. They were later performed

▼ *The Colosseum in Rome, completed in A.D. 80, was the scene of gladiatorial and wild beast shows. Men and animals were kept in quarters below the arena.*

▲ *A beautiful example of the German baroque style in the Cuvilliers Theater in Munich. It has a proscenium arch and tiers of boxes.*

on movable stages in the town squares.

During the 1500's, there was a great renewal of interest in the arts of ancient Greece and Rome. This movement was called the Renaissance. Theaters were built in Italy in a style similar to those of ancient Rome. But the Italian theaters were roofed over. One of the best-known Italian Renaissance theaters was the Teatro Olimpico at Vicenza.

Theaters in England For many years, actors in England performed their plays in the courtyards of inns. When the first English theaters were built in the 1500's, they had the same design as the courtyards. The Rose, Globe, and Swan were well-known theaters of this type. These theaters had a large, raised stage. It was surrounded on three sides by a *pit*, or yard, where the poorest people in the audience stood. The stage was sometimes roofed over, but the pit was open to the sky. The back of the stage was made to look like a three-story building. This building usually had a *gallery*, or balcony, where some of the acting took place. Around the other three sides of the theater were three or four stories of galleries containing wooden seats. The wealthy members of the audience sat in the galleries.

There was no real scenery. Instead, someone would hold up a sign that told the audience where the action was taking place. William Shakespeare wrote plays that were performed in such theaters.

At the end of the 1700's, the English began to copy the style of the Italian Renaissance theaters, which had become popular throughout most of Europe. By now, these theaters had begun to look much like our theaters today. A curtain had been added, which could be lowered in front of the stage. The old Roman arch in the center of the background wall had become so large that it framed the whole *proscenium* (background and stage) like a picture. This archway was called the *proscenium arch*. The sides of the arch hid the wings, from which the actors entered and left the stage.

During the 1800's, the apron stage became smaller. Special galleries, or *boxes*, for the audience were built into the sides of the proscenium arch.

Theaters in the United States
American theaters were built in the English style for many years. Today, many theaters still have the proscenium arch. Part of the audience sits in one or more balconies above the main floor, or orchestra. The first motion picture theaters in the early 1900's were built in this style.

A theatrical revue called **The Golden Horseshoe Revue** played continually for 31 years at **Disneyland in Anaheim, California.** This presentation holds the record for the highest number of performances—more than 47,000 by the time it closed in 1986.

▼ *Outdoor theaters can provide ideal natural settings for many plays. This performance of* Bartholomew Fair *by Ben Johnson is taking place in the center of London, England, at Regent's Park.*

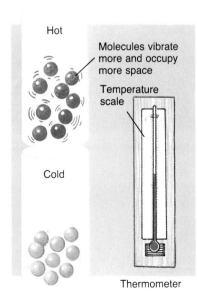

▲ *Reading the thermometer is a regular task for the weather watcher. This one is a maximum and minimum thermometer. It contains pointers that register the highest and lowest temperatures reached over a period.*

Hot

Molecules vibrate more and occupy more space

Temperature scale

Cold

Thermometer

In recent years, many changes have come to the theater. Plays are often performed in small playhouses called *little theaters*. Some of these theaters are combined with dining areas and are called "theater restaurants." Others have an *arena stage* and are called "theater-in-the-round," in which the audience sits in a circle all around the stage.

ALSO READ: ACTORS AND ACTING; COLOSSEUM; DRAMA; MAKEUP; OPERA; SHAKESPEARE, WILLIAM.

THEORY   see SCIENCE.

THERMOMETER   Almost everything in the world expands, or swells up, when it gets hot. When it cools off again, it contracts, or shrinks back to its former size. Liquids like water, alcohol, and mercury expand when they get hot. (However, ice shrinks as it melts to form water.)

Instruments called thermometers measure heat by measuring how much liquids expand when they become hot and how much they contract when they become colder.

A thermometer is a tube of glass with very thick walls. A small hole runs through the center of the glass tube. One end of the glass tube is closed by melting the glass in a fire. The other end of the glass tube is made a bit larger. The large end of the thermometer is called the *bulb* of the thermometer. A small amount of liquid, usually mercury or alcohol, is put in the bulb. Alcohol, which is colored red, is used in areas where the temperature will drop below the freezing point of mercury: $-39°C$ ($-38°F$).

Whenever the liquid in the bulb

◀ *Inside a thermometer is a thin glass tube with a bulb containing a liquid. The liquid expands and contracts as the vibration of its atoms or molecules increases and decreases.*

becomes warm, it must expand. As the liquid expands, it moves up the narrow opening running through the middle of the thermometer. The hotter the liquid becomes, the more it rises in the tubing. The temperature is read by noting the level of the liquid against marks showing the degrees.

Mercury is used in the thermometers that doctors use to take your temperature. Chemists also use mercury thermometers in their laboratories because they often have to measure very hot temperatures. Other thermometers use gases instead of liquids. Gas thermometers are more accurate than liquid ones are, but they are also more delicate. Some thermometers use liquid crystals which respond to your inner body temperature and produce a color-coded display reading. They are placed on the forehead.

ALSO READ: TEMPERATURE SCALE.

THOREAU, HENRY DAVID (1817–1862)   Henry David Thoreau was a U.S. writer and student of nature. He was born in Concord, Massachusetts, and spent most of his life in that area. Thoreau attended Harvard University and taught school for some years. He became a friend of the writer, Ralph Waldo Emerson.

In 1845, Thoreau built a tiny hut on the shores of Walden Pond near Concord and lived there for two years. He wanted to try living as simply as possible, growing his own food and watching the day-to-day changes in nature. The journal he kept of his daily life and surroundings was later published as the book, *Walden, or Life in the Woods*. In *Walden*, he wrote, "Simplify, simplify." The only other book by Thoreau published during his lifetime was *A Week on the Concord and Merrimack Rivers*. After he died, his friends put many of his letters and notebooks into book form.

Thoreau's *Walden* is delightful to read because Thoreau's personality and wit are very apparent. He took great pleasure in small things, such as the shifting colors of a lake, or watching an owl blink. Thoreau felt that a person ought to be an individual and follow his or her own beliefs. In *Walden*, he wrote, "If a man does not keep pace with his companions, perhaps it is because he hears a different drummer. Let him step to the music which he hears, however measured or far away."

Thoreau is also well remembered for his famous essay, "Civil Disobedience," in which he stated his ideas about government and civil law. While at Walden Pond in 1846, Thoreau refused to pay a poll tax and spent a night in jail. He said he could not support a government fighting a war (the Mexican War) that would, he believed, extend slavery. He advocated passive resistance to any government law that a person believes is unjust. This is an individual act of conscience. Thoreau said that a higher law than the civil law justified his action. "Civil Disobedience" greatly influenced Mahatma Gandhi of India, as well as leaders of the U.S. civil rights movement.

ALSO READ: CIVIL RIGHTS MOVEMENT; EMERSON, RALPH WALDO; GANDHI, MAHATMA; LITERATURE.

THORPE, JIM (1886–1953) One of the most outstanding all-around athletes in history was an American Indian named Jim Thorpe. In 1950, he was selected by U.S. sportswriters and broadcasters as the greatest American athlete and best football player of the first half of the 1900's.

James Francis Thorpe was born on an Indian reservation near Prague, Oklahoma. He was primarily of Fox and Sauk Indian descent. At the Carlisle Indian School in Pennsylvania, Thorpe became a sensational halfback and helped make the school's football team one of the best in the country. He won all-American honors in 1911 and 1912.

Thorpe took part in the 1912 Olympic Games in Stockholm, Sweden, as a member of the United States track and field team. He became the first athlete to win both the pentathlon and decathlon. However, it was discovered later that Thorpe had once played baseball for money. He was then forced to return his Olympic gold medals. The International Olympic Committee restored Thorpe's gold medals in 1982.

From 1913 to 1919, Thorpe was an outfielder on three major league baseball teams. He was also a professional football player until 1926. Lacrosse, swimming, boxing, and hockey were other sports in which he excelled. In 1963, Thorpe was elected a charter member of the Professional Football Hall of Fame. The town of Jim Thorpe, Pennsylvania, is named in his honor.

ALSO READ: OLYMPIC GAMES, SPORTS.

THUNDER see LIGHTNING AND THUNDER.

THURBER, JAMES (1894–1961) James Thurber was an American cartoonist and writer. He was born in Columbus, Ohio, and became blind in one eye when he was a child. In his last years, he was almost completely sightless. Thurber attended Ohio State University. He took a job with the Department of State as a code clerk and later worked as a newspaper reporter. He became a regular contributor of cartoons to *The New Yorker* magazine.

Thurber wrote and illustrated many books, including *The Owl in the Attic*, *The Seal in the Bedroom*, *Fables for Our Time*, and *My World—and Welcome To It*. He also wrote the

THURBER, JAMES

▲ *Henry David Thoreau, American author.*

▲ *American Indian athlete, Jim Thorpe.*

2423

▲ *American humorist, James Thurber.*

▼ *This Tibetan community is perched some 13,000 feet (4,000 m) high, but is still towered over by the Himalayan mountain summits behind it. Notice the Buddhist shrine to the left.*

short story "The Secret Life of Walter Mitty," in which a timid man who leads a dull life dreams he is an adventurous hero. Thurber wrote two plays, *The Male Animal* and *A Thurber Carnival*, and three delightful books for children, *The White Deer*, *The Wonderful O*, and *The Thirteen Clocks. My World—and Welcome To It* was the basis of a television series.

He drew his cartoons rapidly, using simple, undetailed lines. He usually pictured grumpy human beings and animals facing up to impossible situations. Thurber's humor was sometimes sour, often strange and off beat, and always wickedly funny.

ALSO READ: CARTOONING.

TIBET At the "top of the world" on a high mountain plateau in central Asia is the windswept and little-known region of Tibet. Tibet is larger than Texas, Oklahoma, and New Mexico combined. It has been part of China since 1959, although it had been independent for many years. It is separated from India, Nepal, and Bhutan to the south by the great Himalayan Mountains. Tibet and Nepal share some Himalayan peaks, including Everest. In the east are the valleys of the Brahamaputra, Salween, Mekong, and Yangtze rivers. (See the map with the article on ASIA).

Tibet has stayed isolated for many centuries because of its remoteness and the lack of roads. Mountain peaks reach higher than 25,000 feet (7,600 m). The average elevation of the region is 17,000 feet (5,200 m), about 3,000 feet (900 m) higher than Pike's Peak, Colorado. Strong, dry winds sweep across Tibet. Much of the region has less than 10 inches (250 mm) of rain per year.

Most of the people live in southern Tibet in an area near the Tsangpo River. Here is located Lhasa, the capital city, which was forbidden to foreigners until the early 1900's. Almost all Tibetan people engage in trade, whether they are nomads, farmers, shepherds, or monks. Wool, hides, and salt are exported. Barley is the main food product. Rice, wheat, vegetables, and fruits are also grown. A wealthy person might own large herds of sheep, goats, and yaks (oxen).

Buddhism was introduced into the region in the A.D. 600's. Today, Tibetans practice a form of Buddhism called *Lamaism*. Some people are *lamas* (monks) who live in *lamaseries* (monasteries). For more than 300 years, the Dalai (High) Lama was the country's ruler and the Panchen Lama was its spiritual head. In 1959, the Chinese Communists took control of Tibet and ended the rule of Dalai Lama, who fled with many followers to India. The Panchen Lama was removed from power in 1964. The Chinese Communists then made Tibet an autonomous (independent) region, though it remains strictly under the control of China. Riots flared up against Chinese control in 1987.

ALSO READ: BUDDHISM, CHINA, HIMALAYA MOUNTAINS, NEPAL.

TIDE For centuries, people have been fascinated by the motion of the tides. Poets have written verses about it. Sailors and scientists have studied the tides for centuries.

Tides are classified according to the distance of their flow onto the shore. *High tide* and *low tide* are the points of highest and lowest water. They are called periods of *slack water* because they are between the *flood tide* (rising water) and *ebb tide* (falling water). They are times when the water does not move. High tides usually occur about 12 hours and 25 minutes apart, with low tides following six hours later. *Tide tables* allow mariners to predict high and low tides in any place.

Tides are caused by the gravitational pull of the moon and sun upon the Earth. The pull from the moon is greater, even though it is a smaller body than the sun. The sun is farther away from the Earth, and so its gravitational pull is much less. The moon's gravitational force exerts a powerful pull on the part of Earth nearest to the moon. This pull causes the ocean to rise above its normal level, forming a "dome" of water. This dome of high water raises the waterline along the shore, causing high tide. On the other side of the Earth farthest from the moon, another dome of water forms. This happens because the Earth and moon are both orbiting around a point between their centers. There is a tendency for the water to move outwards away from this point because of its *inertia*. This inertia is the tendency of anything to keep moving at the same speed in a straight line unless some other force acts on it. Sometimes we say that there is a *centrifugal force* acting outwards away from the center of the orbit. On the far side of the Earth, the moon's gravitational pull still attracts the water, but the attraction is weaker because the distance is greater. The overall effect is for water to flow and form a second dome on the far side. This means that high tide is always occurring in two places—at the point on Earth nearest the moon and at the point on Earth farthest from the moon.

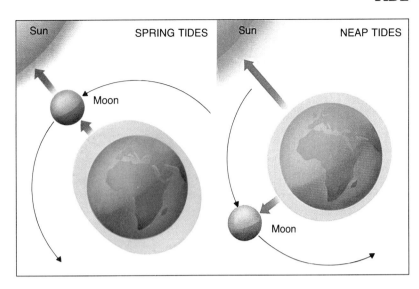

The range of the tides (distance they travel between their high and low points) varies according to the time of month and according to the shape of the coastline. Tides travel their greatest distances twice a month—during the time of the full moon and again during the new moon. At these times, the gravitational forces of both the sun and the moon are working together. These tides that have reached their greatest range of flow are called *spring tides*.

A tide's smallest range of flow occurs during *neap tide*—twice a month, when the moon is in its first and third quarters. During neap tide, the sun and the moon are at right angles to each other. Their gravitational forces do not pull together, and so the tides do not move so far onto and off the shore.

The shape of the coastline greatly affects the behavior of tides. Tides that must flow through narrow channels build up great speed. They are called *tidal races*. They race along at speed of 10 miles (16 km) an hour or more.

When a tide is moving out from shore, the water beneath the surface exerts a tremendous pull out to sea. This pull is called the *undertow*. The force of the undertow is often strong enough to pull great boulders or tons of sand out to sea. If you go swimming in the ocean, be sure to learn

▲ *Spring tides are caused when the sun and moon pull together. Neap tides result when they pull in different directions.*

Because the Mediterranean Sea has almost no tides, the ancient Romans knew nothing about them. When Julius Caesar went to Britain in 55 B.C. he lost many ships because his men didn't haul them high enough on the beaches. The tides came in and floated them away.

The moon pulls the oceans into tides as it circles the Earth. But the land, too, is affected by the moon's pull. The whole land mass of the United States may rise 6 inches (14 cm) when the moon is overhead.

▲ *This high quay side indicates how great is the rise and fall of the tide in the Bay of Fundy, off the eastern Canadian coast. The average spring tide range is 48 feet (14.5 m), though tidal ranges of up to 54 feet (16.3 m) are recorded. This is the highest in the world.*

▲ *The tiger's hunting weapons in the wild are its long, sharp teeth and powerful claws, as well as its tremendous speed.*

about the undertow. It is not unusual for people to get trapped in the undertow, pulled under the water, and swept out to sea.

ALSO READ: GRAVITY AND GRAVITATION, MOON, OCEAN.

TIGER The tiger is the largest member of the cat family, and now one of the rarest. The male tiger is larger than the female. A full-grown male may be 9 feet (2.7 m) long, including its tail, and may weigh more than 500 pounds (225 kg).

Tigers have bodies similar to those of lions, but they are different in color. The tiger's fur ranges from orange-red to brownish yellow and is marked with black stripes. The stripes may differ in length and width. A ruff of hair, shorter than a lion's mane, may be around the side of the tiger's head.

Wild tigers are found in the tall grasslands, jungles, and forests of Asia. The largest tigers live in the cold forests of Siberia, where it is thought all tigers originated. Siberian tigers have longer, thicker, and paler fur than the tigers of southern Asia.

Tigers are meat-eaters, usually feeding on deer, antelope, cattle, and other animals. They often hunt at night, stalking their prey or lying in wait for it. Tigers depend on their sharp eyes, ears, and sense of smell while hunting. They rush at their prey in a series of bounds. An old, sick, or wounded tiger may find human beings easier prey and become a man-eater. But most tigers avoid people and other animals that are capable of harming them. Packs of smaller

▲ *The Indian tiger's stripes imitate the shadows of jungle vegetation.*

animals, such as India's fierce wild dogs, the *dholes*, sometimes attack and kill a solitary tiger.

Tigers usually live alone. The male tiger claims an area that he may share with one or several females. A female tiger, or tigress, usually gives birth to two or three (occasionally four, five, or six) cubs at a time. The cubs, blind at birth, stay with the mother until about the second year, when they can hunt for themselves. Tigers normally live from 10 to 20 years.

ALSO READ: CAT, WILD; LION.

TIGRIS AND EUPHRATES RIVERS The Tigris and Euphrates are two historic rivers in the Middle East. Some of the earliest human civilizations came into being along the plains of these rivers.

The region between the Tigris and Euphrates rivers in Iraq was named Mesopotamia by the ancient Greeks. Mesopotamia was part of the *Fertile Crescent*, an area stretching westward to the Mediterranean Sea. In this area, people learned to raise animals and grow crops. The Sumerians and Babylonians built civilizations along the Tigris and Euphrates rivers. They channeled water from the rivers into networks of irrigation canals. Rain is scarce in the region, but the soil is rich if it is watered.

Both of these rivers begin in the mountains of Turkey. The Tigris, about 1,150 miles (1,850 km) long, flows through part of Syria before entering Iraq. The Euphrates, about 1,700 miles (2,735 km) long, flows the entire length of Iraq. The rivers run southeastward on a parallel course through the central valley of Iraq. They finally join at Al Qurna to form a broad waterway called the Shatt al Arab. This waterway continues for 120 miles (193 km) before it empties into the Persian Gulf. The Tigris is deeper and swifter than the Euphrates and has more commerical traffic, although sandbars make river navigation tricky. Both rivers carry large amounts of *silt*, or mud, which is gradually filling in the Persian Gulf. The *delta*, where the rivers meet the gulf, has moved farther to the east.

ALSO READ: ANCIENT CIVILIZATIONS, IRAQ, MESOPOTAMIA, MIDDLE EAST.

TIMBERLINE   see PLANT DISTRIBUTION.

▼ *The Fertile Crescent, around the Tigris and Euphrates rivers (and Nile River), where farming first developed, about 8000 B.C.*

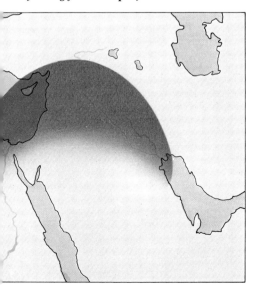

TIME   Time is a way of marking the moment when an event occurs and marking the intervals between different events. Although even simple plants and animals display a sense of time, only human beings have developed ways of measuring time. We use our measurements of time to put the past in order, to plan for the future, and to know the present.

Early people measured days by the sun's movement across the sky from sunrise to sunset. They measured months by the changes in the moon. Later, they marked parts of the day by the movement of a shadow on a sundial, or by the sand running through an hourglass. Nowadays, accurate clocks and watches are used to measure time. Atomic clocks are the most accurate. They measure time using lasers and are regulated by the vibrations of atoms. An atomic clock operates at a frequency of about 9,000 million cycles per second, and it is accurate to 10 million millionths of a second.

Standard Time   The sun seems to move across the sky from east to west, because the Earth turns on its axis from west to east. As the sun moves, the hour moves. The hour of the day is later to the east, and earlier to the west. If every city, town, and village set its clocks exactly by the sun, few

Modern clocks and watches are more accurate than those of days gone by. But the early chronometers were more accurate than many people think. The chronometer that Captain Cook took on his voyage to Australia in 1772 was only 7 minutes 45 seconds slow after three years at sea.

▼ *Sundials and water clocks were invented in Egypt about 1500 B.C. The first sundials were simply sticks placed in the ground. The water clock showed the time as water dripped at a steady rate from one container into another. The side of the container was marked with a scale, and the level of the water on the scale indicated the time.*

Sundial

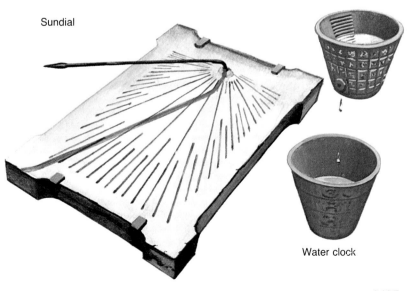

Water clock

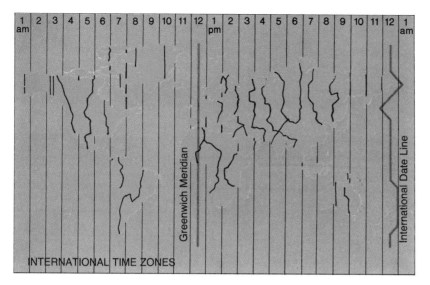

INTERNATIONAL TIME ZONES

Greenwich Meridian

International Date Line

▲ *This illustration shows how time differs around the world. So, when it is 6 a.m. in Chicago it is already noon in London, England, and 6 p.m. in Calcutta, India.*

Astronomers have a measure of time they call the "cosmic year." This is the time it takes for the sun and its planets to rotate once around the center of the Milky Way galaxy—225 million years.

A *leap second* was added to the last minute before midnight of June 30, 1972. That minute had 61 seconds instead of 60 to correct the clocks of the world.

places would be on the same time. If you wanted to meet a friend in a town east or west of your town, which town's time would you use? To overcome this confusing situation, *standard time zones* were decided upon.

At a conference held in 1884 in Washington, D.C., scientists from many countries divided the Earth's surface into 24 time zones. Each zone is bounded by the *meridians of longitude*, imaginary lines 15 degrees apart that run from the North Pole to the South Pole. The meridian that runs through Greenwich, England, is the zero degree line. Standard time zones are measured from *Greenwich time*. All the clocks in a time zone are set at the same time. All the clocks in the time zone to the east are one hour later. All those in the time zone to the west are one hour earlier. Time within a zone is *standard time*. There are four standard time zones in the mainland United States—Eastern, Central, Mountain, and Pacific.

Measuring a Year A year is measured by one complete journey of the Earth in its orbit around the sun. This takes about 365¼ days. This means that in the time it takes the Earth to circle the sun once, the Earth makes 365¼ turns on its axis. Since we cannot have one-fourth of a day that stands alone, we say that there are 365 days in a year. We ignore the extra

one-fourth day for three years in every four. After four years, the extra one-fourth days add up to one full day. We add this day to the fourth year at the end of February. We call the fourth year *leap year*.

Time and Space Albert Einstein's theory of relativity showed that the rate at which time passes varies according to the speed at which the observer is traveling. Thus, on a supersonic jet all clocks or watches move just slightly slower than they do on the ground. The difference would only be noticeable in a spacecraft moving close to the speed of light. This gives rise to the possibility that future space travelers may age less than those they leave behind on Earth.

ALSO READ: INTERNATIONAL DATE LINE, LATITUDE AND LONGITUDE, RELATIVITY.

TIRE A tire is a covering for the outside of a wheel. A tire grips the road surface and protects the wheel from wear. Tires are used on all outdoor vehicles, such as cars and airplanes, and many indoor vehicles and appliances, such as vacuum cleaners and shopping carts. Until the mid-1800's, tires were made of steel or iron.

In 1839, Charles Goodyear discovered that rubber could be softened and strengthened with heat, a process called *vulcanization*. Then people began making tires of solid rubber, which made the ride a little more comfortable. The *pneumatic* (air-filled) tire was invented in 1845 and became widely used in the 1890's, when bicycles became popular. When air is pumped into a pneumatic tire, the air pressure makes the edges of the tire grip the rim of the wheel.

When the automobile was invented, it was discovered that ordinary pneumatic tires could not withstand the weight and speed of a car.

The tires would come loose from the wheel rim and let air escape. So the inner tube was invented. This was a tube that was placed inside the tire and pumped full of air.

But the tires and inner tubes were easily punctured, causing frequent blowouts. A tubeless pneumatic tire that could be used on cars, trucks, and other heavy vehicles was developed in the early 1950's.

A modern pneumatic tire is made in several layers. The outside layer of rubber, the part that comes in contact with the road, is called the *tread*. The tread has deep grooves to help the tire grip the road. Snow tires have especially deep treads that resist skidding even in snow and ice. The body of the tire (which lies inside the tread, out of view) is made up of several layers, called *plies*. Each ply consists of fabric—often nylon or rayon—dipped in natural and synthetic (man-made)

▼ *Most modern cars have radial tires, so called because their internal cords run radially. Tractors have tires with huge treads for traveling over rough ground. Racing cars have smooth tires that permit very high speeds.*

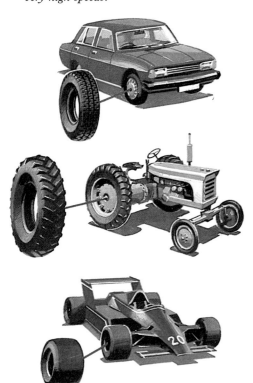

rubber. These are reinforced with steel wire. The plies give a tire its shape and its strength. The more plies that are used, the stronger the tire will be. Most automobile tires have two or four plies. A tire is held in place by two strips, called *beads*, of wire covered with fabric and rubber on its edges. The beads hold the tire tight against the rim of the wheel and keep the air from escaping. Steel-belted tires have extra steel wires in the body and around the sidewall to give them greater durability.

ALSO READ: AIRPLANE, AUTOMOBILE, RUBBER, TRANSPORTATION, TRUCKS AND TRUCKING.

TITIAN (1487–1576) The handsome, 12-year-old Ranuccio Farnese in the picture shown here is dressed up to have his portrait painted. This was a special occasion, as he was sitting for the greatest portraitist of the Italian Renaissance—Tiziano Vecelli Titian.

Titian was 65 when he did this portrait of Ranuccio for the boy's mother. He had a difficult subject here. Painting portraits of children is harder than painting adults, but Titian painted children well. At this time, Titian (who married late) had children about Ranuccio's age.

The use of glowing and vivid color was one of Titian's great talents. It shows here in the boy's satin doublet. The soft, feathery brushstrokes suggest light playing on the glossy satin and on the rows of decorative tucks. The light on the boy's face gives a glowing softness to his flesh. Contrasting with the colorful pink doublet is a black robe slashed with the white Maltese cross. The robe marks the importance of this boy, who at age 12 was already prior of the Knights of Malta.

Soon after Titian did this painting, he was invited to Rome by the pope. He created many paintings there and

▲ Ranuccio Farnese, *a portrait by Titian. National Gallery of Art, Washington, D.C., the Samuel H. Kress Collection.*

▲ *Titian's* Portrait of a Man with a Blue Sleeve, *1511. Like other Venetian painters, Titian was famous for his use of light and color.*

▲ *Marshall Tito, leader of Yugoslavia.*

▲ *Two shamans' (medicine men's) masks used by the Tlingit Indians.*

changed to a somewhat freer style of painting. He also changed the main colors he used—from red and green to tones of yellow and blue. Titian's sweeping use of the brush revolutionized painting. He began a new, free way of showing form, light, and shade that found many followers.

ALSO READ: PAINTING, RENAISSANCE.

TITO (1892–1980) Tito was the leader who set up a Communist government in Yugoslavia in 1945, after World War II. In 1963, he was elected president of Yugoslavia for life.

Tito was born in the region of Croatia, now part of Yugoslavia. His original name was Josip Broz. He fought with the Austrian army during World War I and was captured by the Russians. After the Russian Revolution of 1917, Broz joined the Russian Bolshevik (or Communist) party. He later returned to his country and joined the Yugoslavian Communist party. He was arrested for plotting against the government and imprisoned for several years. During this time, he adopted "Tito" as his Communist code name.

Yugoslavia was occupied by the Germans during World War II. Tito organized a *resistance movement* that worked secretly to defeat the Germans. By the end of the war, the resistance forces had liberated (freed) Yugoslavia from the Germans. Unlike most other East European countries, Yugoslavia has no borders with the Soviet Union, and the nation was liberated without the help of the Soviet army. In 1948, Tito announced that he would keep his new government independent of Soviet control. He developed agriculture and industry in Yugoslavia and set up trade relations with countries in the Americas and Asia. Tito allowed Yugoslavians greater freedom than exists in most other Communist countries.

TLINGIT INDIANS The Tlingit Indians were a group of tribes that lived in Alaska and northwestern Canada, along the coast of the Pacific Ocean. They were skilled craftworkers and were noted for their weaving and woodcarving ability. The remains of their huge totem poles, carved with the figures of symbolic animals and people, can still be seen in the area.

The Tlingit were fishermen and traders. They ate salmon and traded the products of the seals and whales they caught for other goods. Tlingit society was divided into chiefs, nobles, common people, and slaves. The nobles were constantly trying to improve their social status by holding feasts call *potlatches*. At a potlatch, a rich Tlingit would give a big party, provide food for everyone, and give away much wealth in the form of blankets or other valuable goods. In this way, nobles would gain respect for themselves and their clan and make other Tlingits indebted to them for their hospitality.

Russian fur traders invaded Tlingit land in the early 1800's. Gradually they gained control of the area. The Tlingits tried to resist Russian rule, but they were unsuccessful. Fighting and disease reduced their numbers. Old customs were lost. Today, about 15,000 Tlingit live along the Alaskan coast. Many of them work in the fishing industry.

ALSO READ: ALASKA, TOTEM.

TOBACCO Tobacco is the name of a group of plants grown for their leaves. The leaves are used in making cigarettes, cigars, pipe tobacco, snuff, and chewing tobacco. Nicotine, a chemical obtained from tobacco leaves, is used in making insecticides.

Tobacco has been grown in America for about 2,000 years. When European explorers first came to North America, they took tobacco back to

Europe, where it became very popular. Tobacco has been widely used ever since. The nicotine in tobacco, although poisonous in large quantities, is habit-forming in small quantities and seems to calm the nerves. In recent years, the use of tobacco has decreased because of the discovery that smoking may cause lung cancer and heart disease.

Tobacco plants grow from 2 to 6 feet (0.6 to 1.8 m) high, depending on the type of plant. The leaves of most tobacco plants are wide and long, sometimes as long as 3 feet (1 m). Tobacco can be grown in differnt kinds of soil in a variety of climates, but the leaves will differ in quality. Climate affects the aroma, or smell, of the tobacco. Soil affects its texture.

After the tobacco leaves are harvested, they are *cured*, or dried, in special barns. They may be cured with air, smoke (fire-cured), or piped-in artificial heat (flue-cured). Tobacco is classified according to the method of curing and the tobacco product it will be used for. After curing, the tobacco leaves are sold, usually at auctions held in large warehouses.

China is the world's leading producer of tobacco, followed by the United States, India, and Russia. Tobacco grown in Cuba, Sumatra, and Turkey is prized for its quality. Cuban and Sumatran tobaccos make especially fine cigars.

ALSO READ: SMOKING.

TOBOGGAN   see SLED.

TOGO   The Republic of Togo is a thin strip of land on the southern edge of West Africa. It is bounded by Ghana on the west, Benin on the east, and Burkina Faso on the north. (See the map with the article on AFRICA.)

Togo has two main geographical regions. The southern coastal region is a flat, low plain covered with grasslands, forests, and swamps. The Togo Mountains separate this region from the higher northern plain. Togo has a hot, humid climate. The northern area receives more rainfall than the southern area and is the chief farming region.

Most of the people in Togo are farmers. They raise coffee, cacao (from which cocoa is made), and cot-

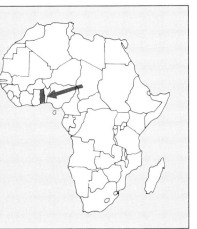

▲ *Cigars must be stored at special temperatures to keep their flavor and prevent them from drying out.*

Sir Walter Raleigh is usually named as the first person who brought tobacco to Europe after his return from Virginia in 1586. But some years before this, a Frenchman named Jean Nicot had introduced tobacco to France. It is from Nicot's name that we have the word "nicotine."

TOGO

Capital City: Lomé (300,000 people).
Area: 21,623 square miles (56,000 sq. km).
Population: 3,400,000.
Government: Republic.
Natural Resources: Phosphates, bauxite, iron ore.
Export Products: Phosphates, coffee, cacao, cotton.
Unit of Money: Franc of the African Financial Community.
Official Language: French.

▲ *The modern city of Tokyo. Tokyo was rebuilt after the 1923 earthquake and again after heavy bombing in World War II. It still suffers regular earth tremors.*

ton for export. The country has little industry, apart from an important mining operation in one of the world's largest deposits of phosphates.

Between the 1100's and the 1300's, the Ewe people came to southern Togo and to neighboring Ghana from the Niger River valley. The Ewe are now the largest tribal group in Togo. Germany declared a protectorate over the area (then called Togoland) in the 1880's and ruled the territory until World War I. After Germany's defeat in 1918, Togo was governed by France under a League of Nations mandate. This changed to a U.N. trusteeship after World War II. The country gained its independence on April 27, 1960.

Lomé, on the southern coast, is Togo's capital and chief port. Lomé is also the country's transportation center. Rail lines and roads connect it with other parts of the country, and an international airport links it with other countries.

ALSO READ: AFRICA, UNITED NATIONS.

Two big problems for Tokyo are high property prices and lack of open spaces. The Ginza district is considered the most expensive real estate in the world, with values of $18,000 per square foot. Tokyo is overcrowded, with only ten percent of the city having any open space or parks for the people.

TOKYO Japan's capital and largest city is Tokyo. With its suburbs, Tokyo's population is almost 12 million people. This city is also the country's most important industrial, commercial, and financial center, as well as its main educational and cultural center. Tokyo is on Honshu, the largest island of Japan.

Flowering azaleas and cherry and plum blossoms brighten the city's gardens and parks in the spring, while chrysanthemums bloom there in the fall. Traditional Japanese architecture has been preserved in the city's many Buddhist temples.

Tokyo is one of the newer cities of Japan. Before the 1600's, a tiny fishing port called Edo stood on the site of the present city. The capital of Japan was in Kyoto, where the emperor had his palace. During the 1600's, army dictators called shoguns

gradually took power away from the emperors. The shoguns made their headquarters at Edo. They forced the lords and large landowners of Japan to make their homes at Edo. In 1868, the shoguns were overthrown by the emperor, Meiji. The emperor moved his capital to Edo and renamed it Tokyo.

In 1923, a terrible earthquake and a fire destroyed more than half the city. The Japanese took advantage of the destruction to rebuild Tokyo with wide, modern streets, parks, and handsome steel and glass buildings. During World War II, the city was heavily bombed. Rebuilding took place after the war and increased just before the 1964 summer Olympic Games, held in Japan.

The city has many universities, including the University of Tokyo. A landmark, Tokyo Tower (1,092 feet or 333 m high), is one of the tallest television towers in the world. An observation platform on the tower gives a bird's-eye view of the city.

ALSO READ: JAPAN.

TOLKIEN, J.R.R. see CHILDREN'S LITERATURE.

▼ *Ginza Street in Tokyo is the Japanese capital's great shopping center.*

TOLSTOY, LEO (1828–1910)

Leo Tolstoy was a Russian writer and author of one of the world's greatest novels, *War and Peace*. He was born on his family's estate in Tula, a province of Russia near Moscow. After studying at the University of Kazan, Tolstoy joined the Russian army and fought in the Crimean War. He resigned from the army in 1856 and traveled through Europe. On his return to Russia, he married and started a school for peasant children on his country estate. He kept a journal describing his experiences.

Tolstoy hated the greed and ruthlessness he had found on his travels and began to reject his own wealthy, aimless way of life. He turned away from the Russian Orthodox Church and developed a new kind of Christianity. He tried to create for himself the simplest kind of life and gave all of his property and possessions to his wife and children. At the age of 82, Tolstoy left home completely, but he soon became ill and died in a small railroad station.

Tolstoy's novel, *War and Peace*, takes place in the early 1800's, during Napoleon's invasion of Russia. Tolstoy shows how war touches the lives of many different people. He vividly describes the details of these lives and recreates the immense and colorful battles of the time. Tolstoy also wrote *Anna Karenina*, the tragic story of a married woman's love for a man who is not her husband.

ALSO READ: RUSSIAN HISTORY.

TOMB OF THE UNKNOWNS

Buried under a white marble memorial in the Arlington National Cemetery in Arlington, Virginia, are four American soldiers. No one knows their names, their ages, or where they were from. These unknown soldiers represent all Americans killed in World War I, World War II, the Korean War, and the Vietnam War. Their resting place is called the Tomb of the Unknowns.

After World War I, an unknown soldier was selected from the American war dead in France. The body was brought back to the United States and buried in Arlington Cemetery on November 11, 1921. The memorial was called the Tomb of the Unknown Soldier and was later built into a shrine. On one side, the tomb is decorated with three symbolic figures of Peace, Valor (bravery), and Victory. The opposite side bears the inscription, "Here rests in honored glory an American soldier known but to God."

On Memorial Day, 1958, two more unknown soldiers were buried at the tomb—one from World War II and one from the Korean War. It was then renamed the Tomb of the Unknowns. The Vietnam War unknown soldier was buried in the tomb during a Memorial Day ceremony in 1984.

Most of the other countries that fought in World War I and World War II have also erected memorials to their unknown soldiers, including Germany and the Soviet Union. The French Unknown Soldier is buried beneath the *Arc de Triomphe* (Arch of Triumph) in Paris. Great Britain's Unknown Warrior is buried in Westminster Abbey in London.

ALSO READ: MEMORIAL DAY.

TONGA   see PACIFIC ISLANDS AND POLYNESIA.

TONSILS   see BREATHING.

TOOL   see CARPENTRY, CONSTRUCTION, HUMAN BEINGS, INDUSTRIAL REVOLUTION, IRON AND STEEL, AND STONE AGE.

TOPOLOGY   see MATHEMATICS.

▲ *Leo Tolstoy, Russian author of* War and Peace *and other classic novels.*

▲ *An honor guard stands at attention before the Tomb of the Unknowns in Arlington, Virginia.*

TORNADO

▲ *The funnel-shaped cloud of a tornado (sometimes called a twister) twists its destructive path through a Kansas town.*

The worst tornado in U.S. history took place on March 18, 1925. It tore through a 125-mile-long (200-km-long) belt in Missouri, Illinois, and Indiana and killed 689 people.

TORNADO A tornado is a violently whirling wind storm. The winds of a tornado are the most powerful winds on Earth. They may whirl around at speeds of 300 miles (500 km) an hour or more. The width of a tornado varies from several feet (about a meter) to a mile (1.6 km) or more. Its path ranges from a few miles to 50 miles (80 km) or more. Tornadoes usually have forward speeds of between 30 and 40 miles (50 and 60 km) an hour.

Tornadoes start in muggy thunderstorm weather, usually in late spring and summer. Hot, moist air begins to rise rapidly from the ground. Temperature conditions higher up cause the rising air to begin to whirl. This forms a long, funnel-shaped cloud that reaches from low-hanging clouds to the ground. Within the funnel, the rising air reaches very high speeds. The updraft picks up much dust. This dust and the water droplets in the tornado cloud give the tornado its dark appearance. The lower end of the tornado funnel may rise from the ground and descend again several times before it finally disappears upward into the clouds.

The great speed and force of tornado winds can pick up things as heavy as automobiles and hurl them hundreds of yards. The updraft causes a very low air pressure within the funnel. If the funnel passes over a building, air pressure outside the building is suddenly lower than inside. As a result, the building may explode outward.

There are about 700 tornadoes in the United States every year. Most are in the Midwest, but tornadoes also occur as far north and east as New England. Australia and the Soviet Union also have tornadoes. *Waterspouts* are tornadoes over the ocean. Tornadoes cause millions of dollars in damage. Today the National Weather Service can send tornado warnings via radio and television and so save lives.

ALSO READ: AIR PRESSURE, CLOUD, HUMIDITY, HURRICANE, LIGHTNING AND THUNDER.

TORONTO is the capital of the Canadian province of Ontario. Lying on the north shore of Lake Ontario, it is a major port. It is reached by ocean-going ships that get there by sailing up the St. Lawrence Seaway. Toronto is Canada's leading financial and industrial city. Industries employ about a third of Toronto's workers. Industries include food processing, printing and publishing, and the manufacture of clothing, electronic and electrical equipment, and wood products.

The city is a major cultural and educational center, with a symphony orchestra and many facilities for the other performing arts. The Royal Ontario Museum is Canada's largest museum, and the University of Toronto was founded in 1827. Downtown Toronto contains an unusual example of modern architecture in its City Hall and many tall buildings. The CN Tower, completed in 1976, is the world's tallest self-supporting structure. It is 1,822 feet (555.3 m) high.

In the early 1700's, the French established a mission and later a trad-

▼ *An impressive array of architectural styles greets the visitor to Toronto. The CN Tower dominates the city from both the lakeside and from inland.*

2434

ing post and fort on the site of Toronto. They named the settlement after a Huron Indian word for "meeting place." The British renamed the town York in 1793, but they restored the original name in 1834 when Toronto became a city. It became the capital of Ontario in 1867. With its suburbs, Toronto now has 3,430,000 people. This is the largest metropolitan area population in Canada. But the actual city of Toronto has fewer people than Montreal.

ALSO READ: ONTARIO.

TOTEM A totem is an animal, plant, or object in nature that a particular family group or clan holds in high regard. People who revere totems often believe that they are descended from the totem. They may use the name of the totem to designate their clan or use a symbol of the totem to decorate their property.

Totems are revered in Australia, Africa, Asia, and North and South America. Indians in the Pacific Northwest carved and painted the images of their totems on totem poles. The poles told the history of a family or clan. They were erected in front of the owner's house or over his grave.

These huge poles represent some of the most accomplished art of the American Indian. Some of them soar 30 feet (9 m) in the air. Entire poles may reflect the totems of their owners and the achievements of their lives.

ALSO READ: INDIAN ART, AMERICAN; INDIANS, AMERICAN; RELIGION; TLINGIT INDIANS.

TOUCH Touch, or feeling, is one of the five senses. The organs that register touch are nerve endings in the cells of the skin. The nerve endings, or *end organs*, are found in the *dermis*, the bottom layer of skin. They are not distributed evenly throughout the body. The fingertips and tongue have the most end organs. These parts of

the body are the most sensitive to touch. The back has the fewest end organs, so it is the least sensitive.

■ LEARN BY DOING

Blindfold yourself with a handkerchief. Ask a friend to press a pencil point lightly on the top of a finger of your upturned hand. Have him or her repeat this action, using two pencil points held about a quarter of an inch apart. Let your friend continue to press the pencil points on your fingertips, sometimes using one point and sometimes two. You probably will have no trouble telling whether the friend is using one or two. Have him or her repeat this action on the skin of your back, between your shoulder blades. Now you probably will not be able to tell how many pencil points are being used. Touch the back of your hand with the point of a pencil. At some points the pencil will feel cold. Why? ■

Touch is usually thought of as a single sense, but the sensation of touch is really a combination of five different kinds of feelings—pressure, pain, contact, heat, and cold. The different kinds of end organs for pressure, pain, contact, heat, and cold are distributed unevenly over the body. Because of this, some areas of the body may be more sensitive to a feeling, such as heat, than others.

ALSO READ: NERVOUS SYSTEM, SENSE ORGAN, SKIN.

▲ *Part of a totem pole carved by the Kwakiutl, an American Indian tribe of Canada.*

▼ *The area of the brain that receives and analyzes the sensations of touch is divided unequally among the various parts of the body. Hands, feet, and mouth have large areas; arms and face smaller ones.*

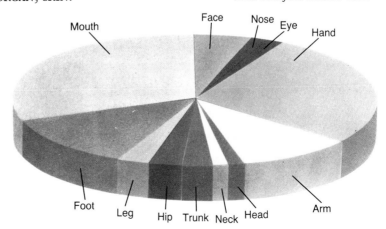

Mouth Face Nose Eye Hand

Foot Leg Hip Trunk Neck Head Arm

▲ *A painting of Jane Avril by Henri de Toulouse-Lautrec.*

▲ *A poster of Jane Avril by Henri de Toulouse-Lautrec.*

TOULOUSE-LAUTREC, HENRI DE (1864–1901) Henri de Toulouse-Lautrec was the son of a French count. At the age of 13, Toulouse-Lautrec slipped on a hardwood floor and broke one leg. The next year, he fell into a dry creek bed and broke the other one. Neither break mended properly, and his legs stopped growing. In spite of this handicap, Toulouse-Lautrec became one of the leading French artists of the late 1800's.

In his early years, Toulouse-Lautrec studied painting with various well-known teachers. His family was wealthy, so he did not have to depend on painting for a living. This gave him a greater choice of subjects than some artists have, and he painted what he wanted to.

He was fascinated by the world of nightclubs, cafés, and dance halls. Toulouse-Lautrec spent long hours in Paris nightclubs sketching the people and trying to capture the drama of their lives on paper. This lonely little man loved the company of these colorful people.

Look at Toulouse-Lautrec's oil painting (shown here) of a dancer named Jane Avril. His skillful brushwork captures a feeling of movement and action. Yet he also tries to show the pert dancer's character. This is not a painting of just anyone dancing. This is Jane Avril—a very definite, frail, elegant person.

Toulouse-Lautrec created beautiful advertising posters. He and a few other artists of his time made the printed poster a new art form. He used a style similar to that of the Japanese—simple lines and flat colors to create a strong feeling. The one here advertises the dancer, Jane Avril, at the Jardin de Paris. Compare the painting and poster, both showing her.

In spite of the greatness of his art, Toulouse-Lautrec remained a lonely man. He thought that everyone

▲ *Toulouse-Lautrec did this portrait of his fellow artist, Vincent Van Gogh, in 1887. It skillfully captures the Dutch painter's intensity.*

laughed at his short, crippled body, and he felt left out of the world of normal people. He eventually became an alcoholic. His death at the age of 37 cut short the life and career of a kind, gentle man and a great artist.

ALSO READ: DEGAS, EDGAR; MODERN ART; PAINTING.

TOURISM see TRAVEL.

TOWER OF LONDON The Tower of London is an ancient fortress in the heart of London, England. It was first built by King William I, "the Conqueror." The tower was a royal palace during the Middle Ages. After about 1450, it was used as a prison by the kings and queens of England. Today, the crown jewels of the royal family are kept in the tower. The guards at the tower are called "beefeaters."

The oldest part of the tower is the massive White Tower at the center. It is surrounded by two walls and a *moat*, or ditch. Several smaller towers were added at a later date. Tower Bridge, built in the 1800's leads across the Thames River to the tower.

During the 1500's, the Tudor monarchs sent many important people to the Tower of London. Princess Elizabeth (later Queen Elizabeth I) was imprisoned there for a short time. The statesman, Sir Thomas More, and two wives of King Henry VIII were executed in the tower. Sir Walter Raleigh was imprisoned there for 13 years before he was beheaded.

ALSO READ: CROWN JEWELS, ENGLISH HISTORY, LONDON.

TOYS Dolls, wagons, balls, toy soldiers, puppets, and miniature objects have been favorite playthings of youngsters for thousands of years. Toys may be very simple (such as a rattle or a game of marbles) or very complex (such as a model ship or a chemistry set). Many toys, such as cards, dice, board games, and electric train sets are enjoyed by adults as well as youngsters. Some people keep their teddy bears for years after the usual teddy bear age. Toys are any playthings that provide fun and amusement to people.

Toys and Children The simplest toys are made for babies and very young children. Rattles, pull toys, stuffed animals, and blocks have few or no moving parts, are usually unbreakable, and give small children practice in learning to handle objects with skill.

As youngsters grow older, they are able to handle and take care of more complex toys with more parts and pieces. Young people push their dolls in baby carriages. They build things with sets of blocks, logs, metal girders, and Tinker Toys. They create things with clay, paint, and crayons. They can put jigsaw puzzles together and use sports equipment.

History of Toys Early people probably had few real toys. Their whole lives were taken up with getting food and protecting themselves. Small youngsters may have played with gourd rattles or toy hunting tools. But in a nomadic hunting tribe, people had little time to make toys and even less time to play with them.

Some simple toys were made as long as 6,000 years ago. Archeologists have found rough-hewn, flutelike musical instruments, and balls made from animal skins and stuffed with

▼ *Toys through the ages: (1) Greek terracotta doll and horse, 400's B.C.; (2) pre-Columbian clay dog on wheels from an early Mexican culture; (3) hoop made of twisted reeds, from ancient times; (4) cup and ball game, 1800's; (5) toy soldier, 1800; (6) picture blocks, 1890's; (7) teddy bear, 1910; (8) toy Mercedes 28/32, 1908.*

▲ *The White Tower is the only standing part of the Tower of London, which was built by William the Conqueror.*

▲ *It is great fun to complete pictures. See if you can match the figures on the border of this picture with the blanked-out spaces.*

▲ *A hobbyhorse is a toy to delight and enchant any small child. The model shown here was popular in the late 1800's.*

dried reeds. Young people in ancient Egypt, Greece, and Rome pulled little wheeled carts and also played games using wooden balls. They played with dolls that had movable arms and legs and with toy animals whose jaws could open and close. Puppets, toy chariots, little metal soldiers, and miniature weapons were toys from ancient civilizations. All over the world, youngsters and adults have played early versions of dice, jacks, marbles, chess, and other types of board games. In Asia, people have enjoyed flying kites for thousands of years. In Alexandria, Egypt, about 100 B.C., a scientist named Hero created very complicated *animated toys* (toys that can be made to move when wound up or cranked.) Among Hero's toys were an animated blacksmith shop, a bird that could move and sing, and movable figures of temple priests.

Toys have often been miniature copies of things used by adults. For this reason, toys provide a miniature record of human civilization. Just as Roman youngsters played with chariots, those of the European Middle Ages played with tiny horses, knights in armor, toy lances, spears, and bows and arrows. Dolls were dressed in long, flowing robes in the same styles

as adult clothing of those times. Toy making became a skilled profession, and craftworkers traveled from town to town selling their toys.

In the early 1900's, the United States, Great Britain, and Japan began making toys for export all over the world. Many old-style toys were made with wind-up mechanisms and electrical motors inside to make them move. New inventions, such as airplanes, submarines, automobiles, trucks, space vehicles, military tanks, weapons, and many others, began to be copied in toys.

Today, with the exception of a few special, handmade toys, almost all toys are produced in factories. Toys are made from a wide variety of materials—wood, rubber, metal, cloth, paper, and plastics. By walking through a toy store, you can see today's world in miniature.

Toy Safety The U.S. government, toy companies, and many parents' organizations have become interested in the safety of toys. The Product Safety Division of the Food and Drug Administration sets up rules for toy

▼ *Modern toys use the latest technology. This photon laser gun fires at an electronically sensitive target on a TV (much as a TV remote control unit switches channels) and produces flashing lights if it scores a hit.*

▲ *These Victorian china dolls were rediscovered in a drawer at Chalke Abbey, England. Their age makes them very valuable.*

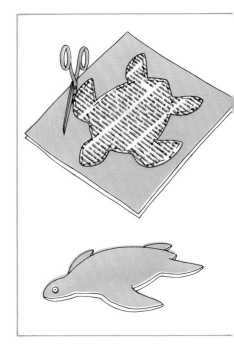

manufacture. Electrical toys must have safe wiring. Toys cannot be made of materials that burn easily. Toys must be nonpoisonous and made of materials that do not splinter or break easily.

Parents' organizations investigate new toys, checking them for all possible safety hazards. They test toys to make sure they are well designed and sturdily built. These parent groups send their suggestions to the toy manufacturers, who usually cooperate in altering toys that may be unsafe.

■ LEARN BY DOING

A Toy You Can Make Toys do not have to be expensive to be fun. Some of the best toys are the ones you make yourself. Any kind of sturdy fabric can be used to make a beanbag or stuffed toy. First decide what shape you want your beanbag to be and draw the outline on a piece of newspaper. A turtle pattern is easy to draw, or perhaps you prefer a bear, a horse, a giraffe, or an elephant. Funny beanbags can be made by using your own or someone else's hand or foot as the pattern. Be sure to make the pattern large.

Once your pattern is drawn, cut it out and pin it to a double layer of fabric. Then cut the fabric along the edges of your pattern. You should now have two pieces of fabric the same shape as the pattern. Put the two pieces together evenly so that the surfaces you will want on the outside are facing each other. Sew the beanbag tightly all around the edges, leaving an opening. Turn the beanbag inside out so your stitching will be on the inside. Now stuff your beanbag. You can use dried lima beans (from the grocery store) or small pebbles. If you are making a stuffed toy, use cotton or old rags that have been cut into small pieces. After you have sewn up the opening, decide how you want to decorate your beanbag. Buttons make good eyes and yarn makes good hair. If your beanbag is a hand or a foot, you can make fingernails and toenails from pieces of red cloth. ■

ALSO READ: DOLL, MODEL MAKING, PUPPET.

TRACK AND FIELD The athletic events that include running races, jumping contests, and weight-throwing contests are called track and field sports. These events may be held either indoors or out.

Races are run on an oval-shaped track. Outdoor tracks are usually made of earth with a hard-packed

▼ *The pole vault is one of the most demanding events in the athletics program. The athlete must be strong, fast, and supple and possess stamina and concentration.*

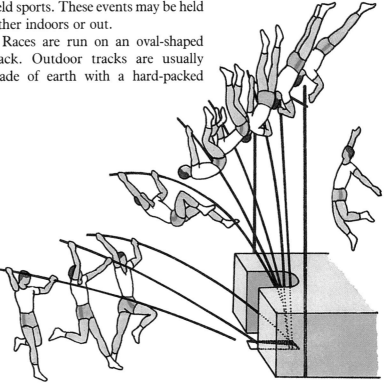

▲ *In Olympic relay races, runners must pass the baton to their teammates in special takeover zones.*

Probably the greatest track and field athlete of all time was the black American, Jesse Owens. On May 25, 1935, he set three world records and tied another. He achieved world records in the 220-yard dash, 220-yard low hurdles, and the long jump. He tied the 100-yard dash record. He accomplished all this despite the fact that he was suffering from a sore back at the time.

cinder surface. Indoor tracks are often made of wood. An outdoor track is a quarter of a mile, or 440 yards, around. To run a mile, you would have to go around the track four times. An indoor track is usually much smaller. To run a mile on most indoor tracks, you would have to go around ten times.

Jumping and weight-throwing contests are held on the field inside or surrounding the oval track. That is why they are called field events. Sometimes the weight-throwing events are held on fields away from the track to avoid hitting runners and jumpers with the weights.

Track events are timed for speed. Field events are measured for distance. The fastest times and the greatest distances are called *records*. There are world records, Olympic records, records for each country, intercollegiate records, interscholastic records, meet records, and records for each school and college. Perhaps your school has a set of track records.

During a college meet in 1935, the famous American athlete, Jesse Owens, set three world records. These records for the 220-yard dash, the 220-yard low hurdles, and the broad jump (now called the *long jump*) have since been broken. But Owens's record for the broad jump—26 feet, 8¼ inches (8.13 m)—was not broken until 1968, when another American, Robert Beamon, jumped 29 feet, 2 inches (8.90 m). Beamon's record remains the world record today.

All international track and field events, such as those in the Olympic Games, are measured by the metric system. Races are held at 100 meters, 200 meters, and so on.

Track Events DASHES. The shortest and swiftest running events are called "dashes," or "sprints." Some indoor dashes are run over distances of 40, 50, or 60 yards. Other dashes, run indoors and outdoors, are 100 yards or 100 meters, and 220 yards or

200 meters. The runners crouch at the starting line with their feet against starting blocks. At a starter's signal, they push off, straighten up, and run at full speed to the finish line.

MIDDLE DISTANCES. Races ranging from 440 yards to two miles are called middle-distance races. They include the 880-yard and one-mile races, the 400, 800, 1,500, and 3,000 meter races. The 440-yard and 400-meter races are run as dashes almost all the way. In these events, the runners go at top speed for about 200 yards, they "coast," or relax a bit for 150 yards, and finish the race with final bursts of speed. Champions run these distances in less than 44 seconds. In the other middle-distance races, the runners do not go at top speed until they are about 150 yards from the finish line. The mile run is one of the most popular track events. For many years, the world record for this race was over four minutes. In 1954, Roger Bannister of Britain ran

▼ *World record-breaker and Olympic gold medalist for the decathlon, Daley Thompson throws the discus.*

the mile in 3 minutes, 59.4 seconds. Since that time, the record has been broken many times. In 1985, Steve Cram of Britain set a world record of 3 minutes, 46.31 seconds.

DISTANCE RUNS. Races longer than one mile or 1,500 meters are considered distance events. They include 2,000-meter, 3,000-meter, 5,000-meter, and 10,000-meter runs. All of these races are held on a track. Some races are called cross-country races and are run over fields and hills for a distance of six miles. The longest race is the *marathon*, which is usually run on roads. The marathon distance is 26 miles, 385 yards. This is approximately the distance run by a Greek messenger in bringing the news of a Greek victory from the battlefield of Marathon to Athens.

HURDLES. Hurdling events are races in which the runner must jump over a series of obstacles called hurdles. The hurdles are evenly spaced between the start and finish of a race. Indoors, races are run at 50, 60 and 70-yard distances over high hurdles. High hurdles stand at 3 feet, 6 inches from the ground. Outdoor high-hurdle races are held at 120 yards or 110 meters. Races at 220 yards or 200 meters are over low hurdles that stand at 2 feet, 6 inches from the ground. The 440-yard or 400-meter races are run over intermediate hurdles that are 3 feet high. In all hurdle races, a runner must clear the hurdles without breaking the rhythm of his or her stride. A longer type of hurdle race is called the *steeplechase*. This event is run over a 3,000-meter course in which the runners must jump over hurdles, and pools of water.

RELAY RACES. Team events in track are called relay races. In these events, teams of four runners compete against other teams. Each person runs a given distance, called a *leg*, then passes a *baton* (stick) to the next person. The most popular relay races are 4 × 100 meters, 4 × 200 meters,

4 × 400 meters, 4 × 800 meters, and 4 × 1500 meters.

WALKING RACES. The walking events in a track meet are held at various distances from one mile or 1,500 meters to as long as 30 miles or 50,000 meters Olympic walking races are the 20-kilometer and 50-kilometer. Walking races are fun to watch because the contestants seem to shuffle along in an awkward manner. The rules state that the heel of a walker's forward foot must touch the ground before the toe of his rear foot leaves the ground.

Field Events The distances in the field events are measured either in feet and inches or in the metric system (meters and centimeters). Each contestant in these events gets three tries. Jumpers need speed, springy legs, and very good muscular coordination. Weight throwers must be heavy and powerful.

LONG JUMP. In the long jump (formerly called the broad jump), the contestants dash along a marked path, spring into the air from a take-off board, and try to jump as far as they can. While still in the air, the jumpers do a bicycle kick and then try to stretch their legs out in front of them without losing their balance. The jump is not good if they fall backward after landing.

TRIPLE JUMP. This event was once called the *hop, step, and jump*. The jumpers dash down the path as they would for a long jump. They hop into the air from the take-off board and come down on their take-off foot. They then step or "spring" forward on that foot, land on the other foot, jump into the air once more, and land in the sand pit as long jumpers do.

HIGH JUMP. In this jump, the contestants have to leap over a crossbar resting on two upright supports that stand about 12 feet (3.5 m) apart. There are two main jumping styles—the *straddle* and the *Fosbury flop*. In the straddle, the jumper rolls across

▲ *The javelin demands great strength and good balance. Top throwers can now reach over 280 feet (85 m).*

▲ *In the shot put, the shot may not be taken away from the neck, so it is pushed, rather than thrown. The world record is over 75 feet (23 m).*

2441

▲ There are judges at each flight of hurdles. A hurdler is disqualified for trailing a foot alongside the hurdle or deliberately knocking down a hurdle with hand or foot.

Training for long-distance running events is considered to be among the most rigorous of all sports. The South African champion, Arthur Newton, maintained that he ran an average of 20 miles (32 km) every day for 14 years.

the bar face down. In the Fosbury flop the athlete approaches the bar almost straight on, then twists his or her body so that the back is facing the bar before landing in the foam-rubber pit. Improved high-jumping techniques have enormously increased the heights jumped. In 1896, the Olympic high jump was won by Ellery Clark of the U.S. at a height of 5 ft. 11¼ inches. In 1989, Javier Sotomayer of Cuba cleared 8 ft.

THE VAULT. In the pole vault, the crossbar is set in the same way as it is for the high jump, but at much greater heights. The vaulters hold the pole, with one hand a few feet from the top of the pole and the other hand a few feet lower down. They race down the runway, dig the top of the pole into a slot in the ground, and swing upward toward the bar. As their feet near the bar, the vaulters are almost doing a handstand on the pole. They push the pole away from them and drop feet first over the bar into a padded pit. The body may just graze the bar, but if the bar is knocked off the uprights, the vault is not good. A vaulter must have speed, powerful arm and shoulder muscles, and acrobatic ability. Until about 40 years ago, bamboo poles were used and the best vaulters cleared the bar at about 13 feet (4 m). Then aluminum poles

were used, and vaulters were able to go over 15 feet (4.5 m). In the late 1950's, fiberglass poles were introduced. These poles bend and "whip" the vaulter much higher than the old poles. With fiberglass poles, vaulters now clear 19 feet (5.8 m).

SHOT PUT. In this weight-throwing event, a round metal ball (called a *shot*) is used. The standard shot weighs 16 pounds (7 kg). The one used in high school events weighs 12 pounds (5.4 kg), and an 8-pound (3.6 kg) shot may be used by younger athletes and women. The shot putters stand at the back of a 7-foot (2-m) circle. They hold the shot in the palm and fingers of the throwing hand and rest the hand against the shoulder. They then hop across the circle in a half-crouch. When they reach the front edge of the circle, they straighten up suddenly and push the shot away from their shoulder. The whole body acts like a coiled spring to release the shot. Shot puts are measured from the front edge of the circle to the point where the shot hits the ground. The world record in this event is now over 75 feet (23 m).

DISCUS THROW. A discus is a metal-rimmed wooden platter. Some are made entirely of metal. If you put two Frisbees together, you would have an object that looks like a discus. The standard discus weighs 4 pounds, 6⅔ ounces (2 kg) and measures 8½ inches (21.5 cm) across. The discus throwers stand at the back of a circle about 8 feet (2.4 m) across. They hold the discus flat against the palm and wrist, whirl rapidly around, reach the front of the circle, and hurl the discus forward with a whipping motion of the arm. A throw is measured from the front edge of the circle to the point where the discus lands on the ground.

HAMMER THROW. In the hammer throw, the contestants hurl a metal ball attached to a wire that has a triangular metal handle. The ball, wire, and handle weigh 16 pounds

(7.3 kg) and form a unit that is 4 feet (1.2 m) long. The throwers stand at the back of a 7-foot (2-m) circle, grip the handle with both hands, and start whirling the hammer around the head. They then spin around three times, reach the front edge of the circle, and release the grip on the handle. The hammer flies outward and upward. The best throws may be over 280 feet (85 m). A variation of the hammer throw is the weight throw in which the handle is attached directly to the ball without a wire in between. The weight may be either 35 pounds (16 kg) or 56 pounds (25 kg). The throw with the weight is made in the same way as with the hammer. But, because it is heavier than the hammer, athletes cannot reach the same distances possible with a hammer throw.

DECATHLON. The decathlon is a two-day contest in which each contestant competes in ten events. Five events are held on one day and the other five on the next day. The events are the 100-meter dash, long jump, shot put, high jump, 400-meter run, 110-meter high hurdles, discus throw, pole vault, javelin throw, and 1,500-meter run. An athlete's score in each event is rated against an ideal score of 1,000. The ideal score for all 10 events is 10,000 points. Nobody has yet scored 10,000 points in the decathlon. The best scores are over 8,000 points. Decathlon contestants must be big and husky. They must have speed, and above all they must have strength and stamina (endurance). A shorter form of the decathlon is the pentathlon, which has only five events. Men compete in the long jump, javelin throw, 200-meter dash, discus throw, and 1,500-meter run in one day. Women compete in the 100-meter high hurdles, shot put, high jump, long jump, and 800-meter run over two days.

ALSO READ: BANNISTER, ROGER; MARATHON RACE; OLYMPIC GAMES; OWENS, JESSE; SPORTS.

TRADE   Long before people learned to write, they were taking part in trade. Perhaps a tribe heard about a distant land where a strong, gray-black stone for axes could be found. The tribal people had an abundant supply of furs, so they loaded the furs on their backs and set off for the distant land where people had the gray-black stone (which we call flint). The people with the flint were happy to exchange some of the stones for furs. This kind of action was the beginning of commerce—trade with distant lands. The tribal people with their new supply of flint returned to their own country the same way they had come. They remembered the mountains they had crossed and the rivers they had gone through, so they could use the same path again to go back for more flint. That may have been the way trade routes started.

Old Trade Routes   In many parts of the world, archeologists have found evidence of trade routes that go back thousands of years. Some early routes dealt in gemstones. On one early route, a black stone called obsidian was carried from central Europe to Africa. The obsidian was mined in what is now Czechoslovakia and Hungary.

▲ *Steeplechasers have to negotiate the water jump seven times during the race. It is the fourth jump in each lap.*

▼ *Western sailing ships, of the kind known as East Indiamen, on the Canton River in southern China in 1835. Shortly after this picture was painted, Chinese efforts to stop the profitable opium trade led to war with Britain.*

TRADE

▼ *A caravan of camels laden with salt prepares to leave Bilma, Niger. In the Middle Ages, trade in northwest Africa depended entirely on camels, which were able to cross the desert from one oasis to another.*

The Phoenicians on the eastern shore of the Mediterranean Sea were the first people to develop seaborne trade routes that connected with overland routes. They became great sailors and traded all around the Mediterranean Sea and along the Atlantic Coast up to the British Isles. There, they headed for the ancient tin mines on the shore of Cornwall on Great Britian's southwest tip. These enterprising traders needed tin for mixing with copper to make the alloy, bronze.

The ancient Greeks introduced the use of money into commerce. Before this, trade was conducted by barter. When Rome became a great city, much commerce was needed to keep it supplied with food. The Egyptians, for instance, supplied Rome with 20 million bushels of grain a year.

Following the decline of Rome, Constantinople became the chief trade center of the Mediterranean world. Constantinople had a good money and banking system. It manufactured textiles, armor, leatherwork, metalware, and pottery. Its imports consisted of grain and raw materials for its industries. Goods came in from all directions. One trade route ran from the Black Sea up the Dneiper River into Russia, with goods being shipped overland at Novgorod into the Scandinavian territory. The furs and hides of the Scandinavians were desired by the Byzantines at Constantinople, while the Vikings took in trade the gold and silver of the Byzantines.

The Middle Ages Little international trade took place during the European Middle Ages until the Crusades (around the A.D. 1100's). The Italian town of Venice on the Adriatic Sea built up trade with the Byzantine city of Constantinople in the East. This trade made Venice a rich city-state by the year 1200.

The wondrous tales told by Marco Polo, the Italian traveler to China, and reports from thousands of Europeans who went to the Holy Land on Crusades created a great desire for the silks, spices, well-made steel, and other fine things from the rich cultures of the East.

Trade in silks and spices was cut off from northern Europe when the Ottoman Turks conquered Constantinople in 1453. Venice and Genoa then became the trade centers of Europe. Many traders and sailors began searching for new trade routes to the East. With the invention of the astrolabe and the compass, navigators no longer needed to stay within sight of land. The age of discovery had begun. The Portuguese gradually worked their way down the west coast of Africa and then sailed around the Cape of Good Hope. Christopher Columbus headed westward in search of new trade routes to India and ran into the Americas instead. Magellan's voyage around the world brought a whole new view of the globe.

World trade developed from explorers' discoveries. England, Holland, and France realized great wealth from world trade.

The Beginning of Modern Trade A great increase in world trade took place in the 1800's. Trade changed because of great inventions—steam vessels, railroads, and communication by telegraph and telephone. Thousands of people migrated from the countries of Europe to new homes all over the world. Commerce increased so that new settlers in North and South America, Africa, Asia, and Australia could have the European goods they were used to.

Trade Changes After World War II
World War II affected world trade in many ways. Before the war, the British, French, Germans, Japanese, and Americans had dominated world trade. After the war, Germany, Italy, and Japan were out of the trading markets for several years because their factories were shattered by the fighting. The United States replaced Britain as the leader in world trade. However, Japan and Germany gradually came back from defeat to strong trading positions in the world.

Modern Trade Agreements Since World War II, various groups of nations have entered into trade agreements for their mutual benefit. The best known of these groups is the association of European nations called the European Economic Community (EEC), or Common Market. *Tariffs* (taxes placed on the goods imported from another nation) have been eliminated by some nations to encourage two-way trade.

■ **LEARN BY DOING**
Look at a globe of the world and pick a very large city at random. Study its location, looking for rivers, harbors, nearby seas, and oceans. Where would the trade routes be? You can easily see why trade centers become large cities. They are connected with trade routes and have become places where goods from all over the world are imported and distributed. ■

ALSO READ: COLONY; COLUMBUS, CHRISTOPHER; EAST INDIA COMPANY; ECONOMICS; EXPLORATION; INDUSTRIAL REVOLUTION; INTERNATIONAL TRADE; MONEY; PHOENICIA; TRANSPORTATION.

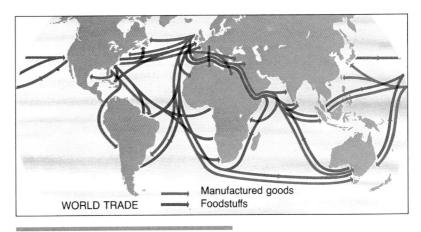

WORLD TRADE

→ Manufactured goods
⇒ Foodstuffs

TRADEMARKS see PATENTS AND COPYRIGHTS.

TRAFFIC PLANNING If you have ever been caught in a traffic jam, you know what a maddening experience it is. Cars and trucks stand bumper-to-bumper. Drivers lose their tempers, engines overheat, and the whole situation becomes very annoying. It is especially troublesome in large cities where there are so many motor vehicles crowding the streets that the air becomes polluted.

Traffic is especially bad during certain peak periods—at *rush hours* (from about 7:00 to 9:00 a.m. and 4:00 to 7:00 p.m.) when people are going to and from work, and on holidays when many people "take to the road" on trips. The growth of the suburbs has also added to city traffic problems. Every day, suburbanites by the thousands travel by car to their jobs in the city. Most city streets are not designed to handle such numbers of vehicles.

City planners and traffic experts are trying to find ways to ease the traffic problem. One of the best solutions is to establish inexpensive but efficient means of rapid public transporation, both within the city and from the city to the suburbs. But until such systems can be built, traffic planners must try to ease the present congestion on the streets. To do this, planners have set up combinations of regulation, routing, and physical and

▲ *Nations that produce more than they need of a product sell the excess to other countries and buy the things they lack.*

▼ *Many traffic lights are controlled by computers linked to detectors in the road as well as to a central traffic control computer.*

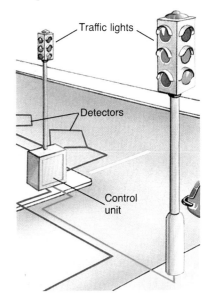

Traffic lights

Detectors

Control unit

It is believed that traffic in ancient Rome was required to keep to the left. The custom of keeping to the right, now recognized in most countries, began in France during the Revolution of 1789. The United States kept to the left-hand side of the street until 1792. In that year a "keep right" law was passed, which applied to the Pennsylvania turnpike between Lancaster and Philadelphia. New York (in 1804) and New Jersey (in 1813) also passed "keep right" laws. Canadians drove on the left until 1920.

▼ *Traffic planners have to take into account peak periods when commuters travel to work in the mornings and leave their work in the evenings. Such flows of traffic will affect expressways, like this one in Toronto, and cause jams if not properly regulated.*

mechanical devices to ease traffic.

Regulation is the job of traffic police. It involves strict enforcement of traffic laws. If traffic laws (such as no double parking, no blocking of intersections, and so on) are not enforced, then traffic jams will result no matter what else is done. Pedestrian laws must also be enforced to keep people on foot from blocking traffic at intersections.

Routing involves a number of things. A road may be made into a permanent one-way street when traffic on it is always heavy in one direction. A street may be one-way into the center of the city in the morning, and one-way going out of the city in the evening. Left or right turns may be prohibited at certain hours to speed up the flow of traffic. Slower trucks and buses may be restricted to certain streets where traffic is less heavy. Many cities are now setting up separate paths at the road's edge for bicycles. On-street parking is being eliminated as cities begin to provide off-street parking facilities. The vacated parking lanes are then used for traffic. Some cities are considering banning all auto traffic from downtown areas. Suggestions have even been made to route all auto traffic onto underground streets, leaving the surface for pedestrians and delivery trucks.

Physical and mechanical ways of controlling traffic involve everything from new road construction to better

traffic lights. Most traffic planners have concluded that building bigger and wider roads does not solve city traffic problems. When a bigger road is built, even more cars start coming into the city. The new roads soon become as badly congested as the old narrow streets.

Various systems of traffic lights have been tried. One is called the *synchronized block system*, in which all traffic lights on one street turn red at the same time, while the signals for the cross streets turn green. All traffic on a street is halted, which leads to congestion and delay. The *progressive light system* is somewhat better. Lights at intersections along the street turn green at certain intervals one after the other. This permits a vehicle moving at about 25 miles (40 km) per hour to proceed along the street without a stop. In heavily jammed traffic, however, this system rarely works.

Traffic signs are another device for regulating traffic. The United States has been gradually using the international traffic signs found in Europe and other parts of the world. These signs give the driver information about highway regulations and conditions through pictures using various colors and designs. With these picture signs, you can drive in almost any country of the world without having to know the language.

ALSO READ: AUTOMOBILE, CITY, POLICE, SIGN LANGUAGE, STREETS AND ROADS, SUBURB, TRANSPORTATION.

TRAIN   see RAILROAD.

TRANQUILIZER   see DRUGS.

TRANSFORMER   see ELECTRIC POWER.

TRANSFUSION   see BLOOD.

TRANSISTOR Do you have a transistor radio? Do you know how it works? Until 1948, when transistors were invented by William Shockley and his team, all radios used vacuum tubes as *rectifiers* (devices to change an alternating current into a direct current) and *amplifiers* (devices to increase the current or voltage of a signal). Now all radios and most television sets use transistors in place of vacuum tubes. This is because transistors are much smaller, less fragile, and cheaper, and work at a lower voltage. It is because transistors are so small that you can put a transistor radio in your pocket.

There are various types of transistors, each used for a special purpose. All of them are made of materials called *semiconductors*. Germanium and silicon are the commonest semiconductors. Metals such as copper or iron are called *conductors* because they have many free electrons floating around the atoms in the metal crystals. These free electrons carry the current when a voltage is applied across the ends of a wire made of metal. The opposite of a conductor is an *insulator*, such as mica, rubber, or plastic. Insulators do not allow a current to pass through them, as the electrons are held tightly by the atoms. Therefore the electrons are not free to move and cannot act as *current carriers*.

Semiconductors, as the word suggests, are halfway between conductors and insulators. They can be made to pass a current under certain conditions. One way of making germanium pass a current is to *dope* it with arsenic while its crystals are being formed. Arsenic atoms have one more outer electron than germanium atoms, and these electrons are free to act as current carriers. This type of conduction is called an *n-type* because the electrons are negatively charged.

If the germanium is doped with boron atoms, which have one less

outer electron than germanium has, there are electrons missing from the crystals. Gaps called *holes* are created. They can behave as positive current carriers. Electrons jump in and out of the holes. They move one way when a voltage is applied to a crystal, while the holes move the other way. This type of conduction is called a *p-type* because the current carriers appear to have a positive charge.

A simple transistor consists of three layers of semiconductor that form a sandwich. It may be a sandwich of p-n-p type conductors or one of n-p-n type conductors. Tiny wires called *electrodes* are fixed into each layer. The p-n-p type of transistor operates on the same principle as the n-p-n type of transistor, except in one major respect. The main flow of current in the p-n-p type is controlled by changing the number of holes.

When a transistor is operating, electrons or holes carry the current through it. The electrode at which they start, on one of the outer layers of the sandwich, is called the *emitter*. This is the equivalent of the cathode in a vacuum tube (the electrode producing electrons). The other outer layer in a transistor is connected to the *collector* electrode. This is the electrode to which the electrons or holes

▲ *William Shockley, John Bardeen, and Walter Brattain, the three American scientists who invented the transistor in 1948.*

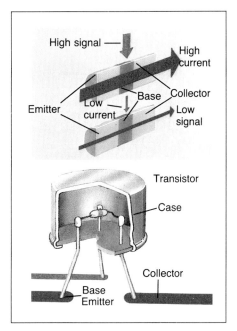

High signal — High current
Emitter — Low current — Base — Collector — Low signal

Transistor
Case
Collector
Base
Emitter

◀ *A transistor is made up of three layers of a material called a semiconductor. The middle of this "sandwich" is called the base. A low electric signal is fed to the base to alter its electrical nature. If this signal increases, the base lets through a high current. If it decreases, the base restricts the flow of current.*

▲ *The ancient Greeks were among the first people to use the chariot for transportation. This low-relief sculpture was made over 2,500 years ago.*

flow. It is equivalent to the plate of a tube. The electrode on the middle layer is called the *base*. If a voltage is supplied to this, it can control the flow of current between emitter and collector. It is the equivalent of a grid in a vacuum tube. Transistors can be used in electronic circuits as *rectifiers*. This means that they allow current to pass only one way and thus change alternating current into direct current. Another important use is as *amplifiers*. The current or voltage in the circuit can be increased in size (amplified). Transistors can now be made very small. Thousands of them can be made on a single piece of semiconductor *chip*, all connected up to each other and to other components. These tiny *integrated* circuits are used in computers and, because they are so small, also in watches and spacecraft.

ALSO READ: COMPUTERS, ELECTRONICS, RADIO, SILICON, TELEVISION.

TRANSLATING   see LANGUAGES.

TRANSPORTATION   For thousands of years, people have moved from one place to another. They have traveled on foot, on the backs of animals, and in various mechanical vehicles. They have transported themselves and their goods over land, on the water, through the air, under the ground, under water, and even into outer space. Whether carrying something on foot to a neighboring village or rocketing to the moon, people need transportation.

Uses of Transportation   People have traveled and used transportation for a wide variety of reasons. The earliest and most basic reason was for survival. Primitive people hunted for their food. When food ran out in a certain area, they picked up their belongings and moved to a location where food was plentiful. Survival also meant moving to escape dangers, such as enemy attacks, floods, and fires.

People use transportation in order to trade and do business with one another. Thousands of years ago in the Middle East, long trade and caravan routes were already being used by people to carry goods over great distances. Today, people still transport goods and produce to places where they will be sold.

Transportation has always been the main tool of exploration. Marco Polo traveled by ship and overland by caravan from Italy to China in the A.D. 1200's. Columbus and later explorers sailed across the Atlantic to explore the New World. Modern-day explorers set out in spacecraft to find out more about our solar system.

People use transportation for purposes of communication. In ancient times, there was no way to talk to an individual except by being in his or her presence. This might involve going on a long journey or sending a communication by messenger. Postal systems later developed as a means of transporting messages. Communications transport is still used in modern-day postal systems and messenger services. But the actual carrying of

▼ *Early forms of transportation: left to right, a Babylonian sled for transporting loads over rough ground, 2000 B.C.; a two-wheeled cart, in existence since 2000 B.C.; and a Chinese sedan chair, A.D. 125. The first wheel was probably a section cut off a log with a hole drilled in the middle for an axle.*

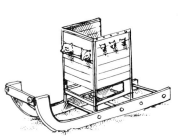

messages has been eliminated by such devices as the telephone and telegraph.

Kinds of Transportation Various kinds of transportation have developed with people's need to travel longer distances in shorter lengths of time. A person living in India 8,000 years ago didn't need to travel to England in a few hours. His or her whole life was taken up with farming and the problems of survival. The person had no time and no reason to travel halfway around the globe as many people do today.

WALKING. Walking was the first transportation. People who walk from place to place must carry their belongings with them. Then people discovered that they could move more weight if they dragged it rather than carried it. The American Indians and other peoples pulled flat wooden frames, or *litters*, on which they piled their belongings. Wooden platforms with runners, called *sledges*, were also built. These sledges were pulled over dry land as well as through snow.

BEASTS OF BURDEN. As people began to domesticate animals, they trained them to pull the litters and sledges. Animals used as beasts of burden are stronger than human beings and can pull heavier loads for longer distances. Dogs were probably first used, then oxen. Throughout the world, animals such as the water buffalo, elephant, camel, donkey or burro, reindeer, and yak are still used to transport people and goods. The horse was domesticated about 4,000 years ago in what is now the central part of the Soviet Union.

THE WHEEL. Logs used as rollers were probably forerunners of the wheel. People discovered that a very heavy load could be transported by rolling it over a series of logs. As the load was rolled along, the last logs were pulled out and placed at the front of the load. This process was repeated over and over until the load

reached its destination. True wheels were first used about 5,000 years ago in the Middle East.

As wheeled transportation became more and more common, more and better roads were needed. Animals can cross over almost any kind of terrain, but for wheels to work well, they must travel over relatively flat ground. Wooden wheels can break easily on a rough, bumpy surface. Wheels of all kinds easily get stuck in deep mud and loose sand. The ancient Romans constructed the first lengthy network of roads paved with stone. The Incas of South America also built a complex road system.

Roman roads fell into disrepair and disuse during the Middle Ages, when the primary means of long-distance transportation was walking, horseback riding, or ox riding. Heavy farm carts were used, but mostly for hauling things short distances. In the 1500's and 1600's, with the development of faster coaches and gigs, new road systems were established. Highways are now designed to handle wheeled vehicles traveling 70 miles per hour (112 km/hr) and more.

ON RAILS. In 1825, a British engineer named George Stephenson designed the first steam-powered locomotive. Railroads developed rapidly. By 1840, there were 2,800 miles (4,500 km) of track in the United States. The first U.S. transcontinental railroad was completed in 1869. Rail transportation was the first great ad-

▲ *Until the coming of the railroads, transportation on land depended almost entirely on the horse. Even today, draft horses such as this one in Finland are used for hauling heavy loads.*

▼ *This early railroad engine, designed by the British engineer John Blenkinsop, had a toothed driving wheel running along a racked rail.*

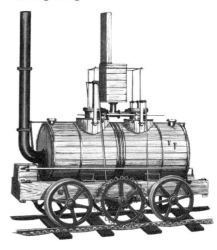

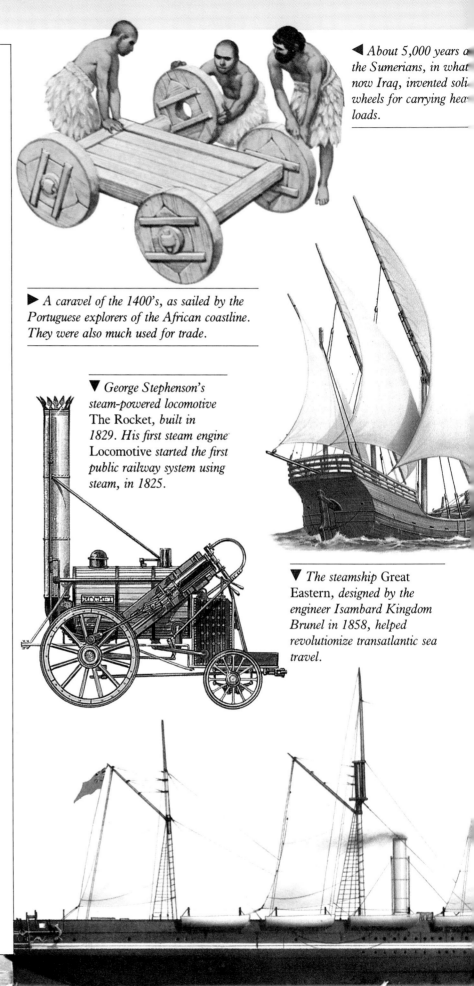

MILESTONES IN TRANSPORTATION

BC

c. 3500	First wheeled vehicles used in Mesopotamia.
1800	War chariots developed by the Hittites.
312	Romans construct the Appian Way, which ran 260 km from Rome to Capua.

AD

c. 1100	Magnetic compass developed.
1400's	Advent of versatile three-masted ship.
1662	First omnibus (horse-drawn), invented by Blaise Pascal.
1769	First steam-powered road vehicles, by Nicolas Cugnot.
1783	First balloon ascent by Montgolfier brothers.
1783	First successful experiment with steamboats.
1804	Invention of the first successful steam locomotive by Richard Trevithick.
1815	Macadam paving for roads.
1819	First ship employing steam power crossed the Atlantic.
1822	First iron steamship.
1825	Stockton and Darlington Railway opened.
1839	First pedal-driven bicycle, invented by Kirkpatrick Macmillan (Great Britain).
1852	First airship (France).
1862	First gas engine made by Alphonse Beau de Rochas.
1863	First underground railway opened in London.
1869	Opening of the Suez Canal. Completion of the first transcontinental railroad in the U.S.
1885	Gottlieb Daimler and Carl Benz make the first gas engine motor cars.
1890	First electric subway.
1894	First ships driven by steam turbine.
1897	First diesel engine built.
1903	First successful powered airplane flight by Wilbur and Orville Wright.
1908	First Model-T Ford.
1914	Completion of Panama Canal.
1919	First nonstop transatlantic flight made by John Alcock and Arthur Brown.
1925	First diesel locomotive in regular service (U.S.).
1930	Design for a jet aircraft patented by Frank Whittle.
1936	Prototype helicopter successfully tested.
1939	Construction and flight of the first jet aircraft by the Heinkel Company of Germany.
1952	The De Havilland *Comet* was the first commercial jet airliner to enter service.
1954	The submarine *Nautilus*, the world's first atomic-powered ship, launched by the U.S. Navy.
1957	First artificial satellite in space.
1959	First hovercraft.
1961	First man in space.
1962	First nuclear-powered merchant ship.
1968	First supersonic airliner.
1970	First Jumbo jet.
1981	First Space Shuttle.
1986	First nonstop flight around the world, without refueling.

◀ *About 5,000 years a the Sumerians, in what now Iraq, invented soli wheels for carrying hea loads.*

▶ *A caravel of the 1400's, as sailed by the Portuguese explorers of the African coastline. They were also much used for trade.*

▼ *George Stephenson's steam-powered locomotive* The Rocket, *built in 1829. His first steam engine* Locomotive *started the first public railway system using steam, in 1825.*

▼ *The steamship* Great Eastern, *designed by the engineer Isambard Kingdom Brunel in 1858, helped revolutionize transatlantic sea travel.*

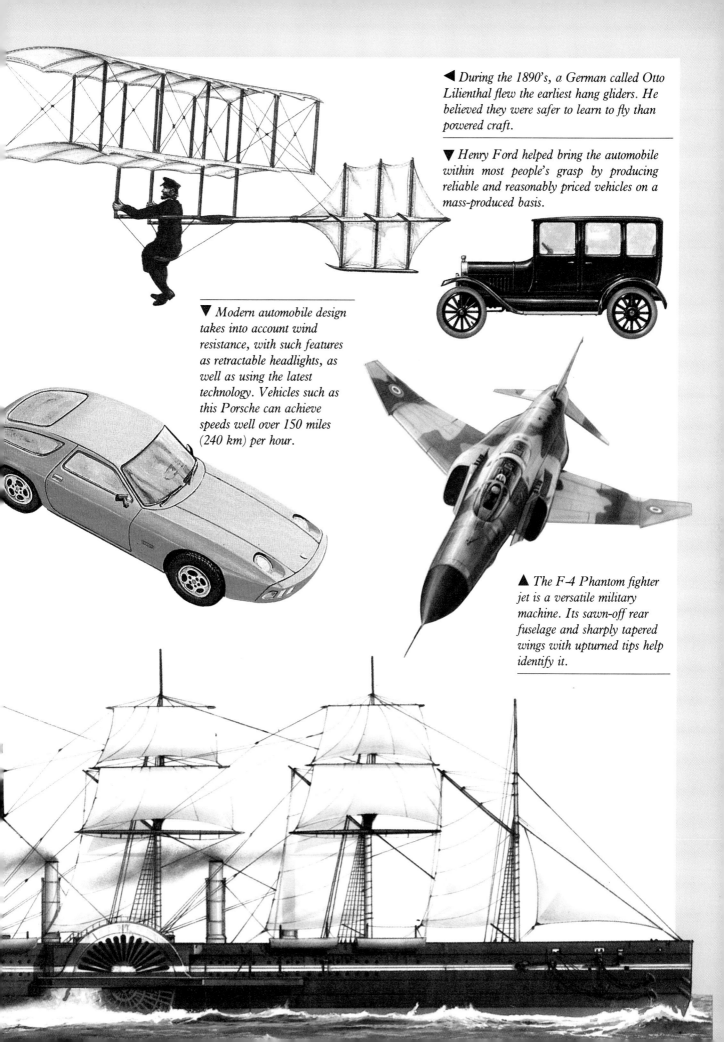

◀ During the 1890's, a German called Otto Lilienthal flew the earliest hang gliders. He believed they were safer to learn to fly than powered craft.

▼ Henry Ford helped bring the automobile within most people's grasp by producing reliable and reasonably priced vehicles on a mass-produced basis.

▼ Modern automobile design takes into account wind resistance, with such features as retractable headlights, as well as using the latest technology. Vehicles such as this Porsche can achieve speeds well over 150 miles (240 km) per hour.

▲ The F-4 Phantom fighter jet is a versatile military machine. Its sawn-off rear fuselage and sharply tapered wings with upturned tips help identify it.

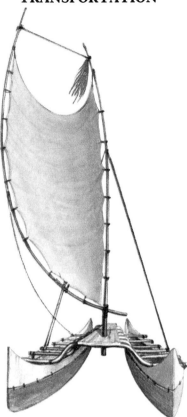

▲ *A Hawaiian double canoe. Fast and stable craft like this were common all over the South Pacific. Similar boats are still used by some Pacific islanders.*

▲ *In the early days of air transportation, the passengers rode in the open.*

vance in land transportation since the development of the wheel. For the first time, people could travel at significantly greater speeds and could haul heavy amounts of goods over great distances. The Industrial Revolution, which began in the early 1800's, was given a tremendous boost by the new railroads. Manufacturers had a fast way to transport their products over land to be sold in faraway places.

ON THE WATER. Water transportation developed much faster than land transportation. People have been using dugouts, canoes, and rafts since the earliest times. Early civilizations developed along rivers and other larger waterways. The water was used not only for irrigation of the land but also as a means of transportation to distant places. Boats and ships were built for use in commerce, warfare, and exploration. By the 1600's, people could transport themselves and their goods almost anywhere on the ocean by ship. Shipping also brought about the use of maps.

The world's first successful steamboat, the *Clermont*, was built in 1807 by the American inventor, Robert Fulton. As engines improved, so did the speed and capacity of the ships. Metal ships were in operation by the end of the 1800's. The construction of the Suez and Panama canals shortened considerably the routes from the Atlantic to the Indian and Pacific oceans. Shipping is now and always has been people's quickest way of transporting enormous loads of cargo.

IN THE AIR. In 1903, Orville and Wilbur Wright made the first successful powered airplane flight. Even though air travel is the newest form of human transportation, it enables people to travel longer distances at greater speeds than they ever dreamed possible. From propellers to jet propulsion to rocketry, people are now walking in outer space and exploring the moon.

Transportation for Tomorrow Modern transportation is separated into four categories—shipping, railroads, motor carriers, and air carriers. The transport of people is called *passenger service*, and the transport of goods is called *freight service*.

SHIPPING. In the future, more and more ships will be nuclear powered—cargo ships as well as military vessels. *Containerization* is used for both railroad and water transport. All goods to be shipped are packed in large metal containers of a standard size. These are transported by specially built trucks or railroad cars to the dock where the containers are tightly packed in the ship's hold.

Shipping is also being increased by the use of gigantic tankers to carry liquid cargo, such as oil. The largest tanker now afloat weighs more than 550,000 tons (560,000 metric tons) and is the longest ship ever built.

Automation is the future trend for all modes of transportation. Giant automated ships will be run by small crews of 20 people or less. The engine room operations, cargo loading and unloading, and many other activities

▼ *Otto Benz's three-wheeler of 1888, the first car to be advertised and sold as a standard model. Few were actually sold, but its production marks the start of the motor industry.*

will all be done automatically.

The *hydrofoil* ship will be in common use for future passenger service on water. The hydrofoil, once it reaches a certain speed, rises above the water on narrow, ski-like projections. Hydrofoils are now being used by the U.S. Navy and for ferry service in the United States and worldwide. The *hovercraft*, another passenger vessel, travels above the water on a cushion of air, reaching speeds of 100 miles per hour (160 km/hr) and more.

RAILROADS. Railroads will also become automated. Trains will be dispatched and eventually even run entirely by computer. Containerization, like that used on ships, is now being used by railroads.

At present, trains have reduced passenger service. People prefer cars and airplanes for traveling. But auto traffic has become too great in the cities, and airlines will not be able to handle enough of the future short-distance passenger transport. Experiments are being done into high-speed rail travel for trips of between 200 to 400 miles (320 to 650 km). Gas-turbine and jet engines have been successfully tested. *Monorails* are passenger vehicles riding on one rail, now being tested for commercial use in the United States. Another future project is the *aerotrain*, which has no wheels and travels over 250 miles per hour (400 km/hr). It will be supported over a single track on a cushion of air.

Plans are being made to combine auto and rail transport. One plan involves giant magnets that would clamp to the roofs of cars. The cars, with people in them, would be raised to elevated tracks and whisked away to their destinations. A fantastically fast subway is also being designed. Air forced through an underground tube would propel 100 passengers in a bullet-shaped capsule at speeds ranging from 500 to 2,000 miles per hour (800 to 3,200 km/hr).

MOTOR CARRIERS. Motor carriers

▲ *A modern passenger plane—the Boeing 767 in the livery of Ethiopian Airlines.*

are primarily automobiles and trucks. New and better safety devices for autos are constantly being developed—air bags to protect passengers in a crash, seat harnesses, no-glare windshields, and auto bodies that can absorb the force of a crash.

The amount of auto traffic keeps increasing, and congestion has already become uncontrollable. New means of private transport and new ways of controlling the highways are being planned. Traffic control centers in each city will tell drivers what roads are best to travel on to reach their destinations. Superhighways of the future will be electronically controlled. Private cars will be equipped with devices that control the speed and even the direction of the car. A traveler will enter a superhighway by a special gate into which he or she puts a computer punch card. The car would then be automatically guided to its destination by an electronic beam that would also keep the car at a safe speed.

In the future, privately owned cars will probably not be allowed on the streets of crowded cities. Commuter transportation may be by small vehicles attached to conveyor belts. A passenger could drive one of these vehicles from his or her house to a station where the vehicle would be attached to a belt and transported into the city. The passenger would then leave the vehicle at the station. When

▲ *A Boeing 747 is loaded with cargo. Air transport is fast but expensive. As a result, most goods sent by air are either perishable or small but valuable.*

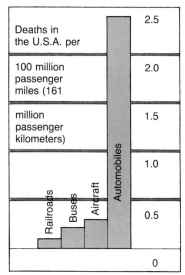

Deaths in the U.S.A. per 100 million passenger miles (161 million passenger kilometers)				
			Automobiles	2.5
				2.0
				1.5
				1.0
Railroads	Buses	Aircraft		0.5
				0

▲ *Traveling by train is very safe compared with other forms of transport.*

ready to go home, the passenger would get on another vehicle, which would be whisked by the conveyor belt to the passenger's home station. The passenger would then drive the vehicle to his or her house. The next morning, the passenger would repeat the process.

Trucks will travel in special lanes on highways of the future. Trucks will be faster and more powerful, using gas-turbine engines to pull several trailers. Trucks will not drive into the city but will unload their cargo at the outskirts onto conveyor belts. The belts will move the goods into the city and also bring loads to the outskirts for the trucks to pick up.

AIR CARRIERS. Future air transportation offers many possibilities. One of the most interesting is individual rocket packs that people would wear on their backs and with which they could travel through the air to their destinations. Experimenters have already flown at over 40 miles per hour (65 km/hr) using rocket packs.

New kinds of helicopters, or vertical take-off and landing (VTOL) craft, are also being tested. One VTOL craft can move straight up like a helicopter and then fly like a regular plane for faster and longer trips. Huge supersonic transport planes will carry an enormous quantity of goods and passengers over even longer distances in shorter amounts of time. Nuclear-powered freight and passenger airplanes are another possibility for the future, as are nuclear-powered, helium-filled *dirigibles*, or airships.

OUTER SPACE. Travel in outer space will become more and more common in the future. Many kinds of vehicles (from large tractors to buses) are being designed to transport people and equipment on the moon and on the other planets of the solar system. Larger and more powerful spacecraft will come into use and be able to land at airports on Earth, as the U.S.

Space Shuttle has already done. Manned and unmanned space stations will be built, where scientists can set up observatories and conduct experiments. Spaceships will stop at space stations for fuel, supplies, and repairs. Travelers will have to adapt to the weightless condition.

ALSO READ: AIR CUSHION VEHICLE, AIRPLANE, AIRSHIP, AUTOMOBILE, BALLOON, BOATS AND BOATING, BUS, CARRIAGE, HELICOPTER, MOTORCYCLE, RAILROAD, ROCKET, SHIPS AND SHIPPING, SLED, SPACE TRAVEL, SUBWAY, TRAFFIC PLANNING, TRAVEL, TRUCKS AND TRUCKING.

TRAVEL   Every year, many thousands of Americans travel to different parts of the United States and Canada or to other countries. They use airplanes, trains, automobiles, ships, and bikes. Airplanes carry most of the long-distance travelers. Buses and automobiles keep highways busy with short-distance passengers.

Why Do People Travel?   Until quite recently, most people stayed close to home for much of their lives. Those who lived near a lake or seashore made short trips to these places at holiday times. But few Americans saw both East and West coasts of the United States during their lifetime. People began to travel more after the first railroads were built. Automobiles gave travelers even greater independence. The bus companies followed, improving their services all the time. Airplanes made travel quick and easy.

Today, many people travel away from home for a holiday during the year. Airports, railroad stations, roads, and hotels and motels are most crowded during June, July, and August. Families with youngsters take their holidays during these months, when schools are closed. Many people plan winter vacations during Christmas holidays. They go south in search of warm sun, or they go to the mountains to ski. People travel for personal reasons, too. Many families are spread around the country, with children at college or in the armed services. Holidays draw them together again. Airports and train stations stay busy all year serving traveling salespeople and professional people. Business executives now travel from state to state as easily as from one town to another. They can be in Washington, D.C., in the morning and in Chicago after lunch.

The Travel Industry Travelers need meals, places to sleep, and other services. A whole new industry has grown up to provide these facilities. Hotels, motels, and restaurants earn millions of dollars every year through *tourism*, the business of serving travelers. People often travel to distant places after reading about them in *travel magazines*. When people travel, they shop for *souvenirs*, or things to remind them of their trip. They also take photographs of the places they have visited. Shopkeepers expect brisk business wherever travelers visit.

Some people have their trips planned by *travel agents*, who give out information about traveling. The agents talk with their clients, find out how they like to travel, what kinds of places they like to visit, and how much they plan to spend. They suggest places to stay and things to see and do. The agent will buy the necessary tickets and make reservations. This service is free to the traveler. The agent receives a commission, or fee, from the transportation and hotel companies with whom he or she does business.

Other travelers plan their trips themselves. If they are taking a train trip, they can obtain timetables from the railroad company. Airline personnel help passengers in any way possible. Their reservations clerks try to book the most convenient flight.

People on the Move. Many families travel on holidays in the United States, Canada, and elsewhere by automobile. This type of travel is usually less expensive. Passengers can see more of the countryside, and youngsters feel more at home in the family car. Families can obtain information about interesting sites to visit by writing ahead to the Visitors' Bureau or the Chamber of Commerce in the different cities and states. Road maps, which are provided free at some service stations, help the driver to plan the trip. Major hotel and motel companies provide folders about their inns in the area the family will visit. Some families pack tents and sleeping bags and stop overnight at campgrounds. Other people tow trailers, or mobile homes, behind their automobiles. These provide comfortable sleeping quarters.

Today, passenger ships are used mainly to take people on *cruises*, or shipboard holidays. In the wintertime, many cruise ships go to the warm Caribbean Sea. The passengers can usually land at various ports for shopping and sightseeing.

People such as business executives, who want to travel quickly, usually go by airplane. Many people fly abroad for their holidays. Those who travel to foreign countries usually carry *passports*, issued by their own governments, to prove who they are. Many

▲ *More people than ever now travel by air. They fly abroad or to other states in wide-bodied airplanes such as this.*

▼ *Many people, especially those in retirement, enjoy winter cruises on luxury liners such as this one.*

▲ *Trailer or camping vacations are ideal ways for families to travel and see many scenic landscapes. At night the family has an instant hotel. These travelers are beside a fiord in Norway.*

To become a member of the Los Angeles Travelers Century Club, a person must have visited 100 or more countries.

▲ *Ethel Rosenberg with her husband Julius. They were sentenced to death for treason which they committed by giving atom bomb secrets to the Russians. Their sons are still trying to prove their parents' innocence.*

countries require travelers to obtain *visas*, or special entry permits. Travelers often must have *vaccinations* to prevent them from catching or spreading certain diseases.

Students used to learn about distant places mostly from books. Today, they can travel to another city or country and learn for themselves. Travelers will meet people with a different way of life from their own. If the people they meet speak a different language, they will probably pick up a few words and phrases quite quickly. This will help them to travel around more easily and get to know the people. They will learn about history and art by visiting museums, art galleries, and historical sites. Many places have special music and drama festivals at certain times of the year. Travelers will taste new types of food, see new plants and animals, and even enjoy a different climate.

There are few things more exciting than entering a tropical rain forest for the first time, or standing in the clear, pure air of a mountain region. Some parts of the world offer special types of sports, such as deep-sea fishing off the coast of Florida, skiing in Switzerland, mountain climbing in the Himalayas, or safaris (expeditions) in Africa. The traveler will return with snapshots, souvenirs, and a much greater understanding and appreciation of other people in the world.

ALSO READ: AIRLINE, AIRPLANE, AIRPORT, BUS, CAMPING, HOTELS AND MOTELS, MAP, RESTAURANT, STREETS AND ROADS, SPACE TRAVEL, TRANSPORTATION.

TREASON A person who deliberately endangers the safety of his or her own country is usually said to have committed the crime of treason. The laws of some nations have ruled that any act of disloyalty to the government is treason. Other nations have allowed their people more freedom

and have stated that only certain acts should be called treason. A person who commits treason is called a *traitor*.

In most democratic countries today, people are allowed to speak out and demonstrate peacefully against their government. If people demonstrate against government policies, this is not usually considered treason. People are free to support a political leader who wishes to defeat the government in an election. According to the Constitution of the United States, "Treason against the United States shall consist only in levying war against them, or in adhering to [joining with] their enemies, giving them aid and comfort."

One of the best-known treason cases in U.S. history was that of Benedict Arnold, an American general in the American Revolution. In 1780, Arnold made plans to surrender the fort at West Point, New York, to the British. He was discovered, but he escaped and became a general in the British army. Another famous American treason case was that of Aaron Burr. In 1806, Burr supposedly helped plan an invasion of Mexico to free it from Spanish rule. Also, he reportedly wanted to seize western U.S. territory, join it to Mexico, and set up an independent country. Burr was arrested, tried for treason, but found not guilty.

In World War II, a Norwegian politician, Vidkun Quisling, helped the Germans take control of Norway. Quisling then became the leader of the Norwegian government. After the war, he was convicted of treason and shot. The word "quisling" now means "traitor." In 1953, Julius Rosenberg and his wife, Ethel, both convicted of supplying atomic military secrets to a Soviet spy, became the first American civilians to be executed for treason.

Spying against one's own country is a type of treason, as the secrets you are handing over to a foreign power endanger the safety of the home country. In the mid-1980's three members of the Walker family were convicted as spies for selling U.S. naval secrets. This greatly damaged the nation's defenses. In nations ruled by a monarch or an emperor, treason is usually any act that would harm the ruler or the heir to the throne. In the past, many such rulers have accused anyone who disagreed with them of treason. In a nation ruled by a dictator, any criticism of the government is often considered to be treason.

ALSO READ: CRIME, SPY.

TREATY Treaties are agreements made between the governments of two or more nations. One of the marks of an independent nation is its ability to make treaties with other nations. The state of California, for example, is not an independent nation. California cannot make treaties with a foreign government.

Treaties are the result of negotiations in which representatives of each government discuss their needs and come to an agreement. The agreements are written down and copies are prepared for each of the negotiators to sign. The treaty does not go into effect, however, until it has been *ratified* (accepted), usually by the chief lawmaking body of each participating nation. In the United States, the President ratifies a treaty, with the consent of two-thirds of the Senate. If the Senate rejects the treaty, it does not go into effect.

There are three main categories of treaties. *Political* treaties may deal with the terms of peace after a war. Political treaties establish military and

Three radio broadcasters who urged Allied troops to surrender during World War II were accused of treason. "Lord Haw-Haw" (William Joyce) was hanged by the British after the war. "Axis Sally" (Mildred Gillars of Oregon) served a prison sentence. "Tokyo Rose"(Iva Toguri of California) was also imprisoned.

SOME IMPORTANT TREATIES

Name	Date	Signers	Terms
Convention of 1818	1818	U.S., Great Britain	Fixed the boundary between Canada and the U.S. along the 49th parallel.
Conventional Forces in Europe, Treaty on	1990	Nato and Warsaw Pact	Officially ended the Cold War and drastically reduced arms.
Ghent, Treaty of	1814	U.S., Great Britain	Ended the War of 1812. Each party agreed to restore captured territory.
Japanese Peace Treaty	1951	Japan, U.S., and her World War II allies, except Czechoslovakia, Poland, and the U.S.S.R.	Formally ended World War II with the Japanese. There has never been a peace treaty ending World War II with Germany, although peace came in 1945.
Kanagawa, Treaty of	1854	U.S., Japan	Opened Japanese ports to U.S. trade. Ended Japanese isolation. Commodore Matthew Perry represented U.S. government.
Lateran Treaty	1929	Italy, Papal State	Established the Vatican State as a sovereign, or independent, nation.
Louisiana Purchase	1803	U.S., France	Purchase of the Louisiana Territory for 15 million dollars.
Nuclear Test Ban Treaty	1963	105 nations, including U.S., U.S.S.R., and Great Britain	Banned nuclear weapons tests in air, outer space, and under water.
Panama Canal Treaties	1978	U.S., Panama	Provided for turning over the Panama Canal and the Canal Zone to Panama on Dec. 31, 1999. U.S. and Panama have the right to defend the canal against threats.
Paris, Treaty of	1763	France, Spain, Great Britain	Ended the Seven Years' War in Europe and the French and Indian War in America. France gave most of its American possessions to England. The Ohio Valley and neighboring areas were allotted to the Indians.
Paris, Treaty of	1783	Great Britain, U.S., and allies	Ended the American Revolution. Britain acknowledged the independence of the U.S.
Peace of Paris, Second	1815	France, Britain, Russia, Prussia, Austria	Ended the Napoleonic Wars. European boundaries returned to where they were in 1790.
Rome, Treaty of	1957	Belgium, France, Italy, Luxembourg, The Netherlands, West Germany	Created the European Community (Common Market).
United Nations, Charter of the	1945	51 charter nations, including U.S. and U.S.S.R.	Established the organization of the United Nations.
Versailles, Treaty of	1919	U.S., Great Britain, France, Italy, and Germany	The chief among five peace treaties that ended World War I. Separate treaties were signed between the victors and Germany's allies. The League of Nations was established as a result of this treaty.
Westphalia, Treaty of	1648	France, Sweden, Spain, Holy Roman Empire, The Netherlands	Ended Thirty Years' War. Established a measure of religious tolerance. Peace that followed ushered in the modern era.

▲ *A glade of redwoods in California reach high into the sky. Redwoods and Sequoias are the giants of the tree world.*

"General Sherman" the giant sequoia tree, contains enough wood to make 500 million pencils. It has been alive for more than 4,000 years.

The timber of the balsa tree is lighter than cork. Balsa grows in the tropics at the astonishing rate of 15 feet (4.5 m) per year.

political alliances, such as the treaties that formed the North Atlantic Treaty Organization (NATO), the Association of South East Asian Nations (ASEAN) and the Warsaw Pact (alliance of five nations in eastern Europe with the Soviet Union). Political treaties also deal with territorial boundary lines between countries. The Treaty of Guadalupe Hidalgo, signed by the United States and Mexico after the Mexican War, established the boundary between these two countries.

Since 1963 there have been several treaties between the Western nations and the Eastern bloc limiting arms, especially nuclear ones. The most important was the Treaty on Conventional Forces in Europe, signed in 1990 by 22 countries of NATO and the Warsaw Pact. It formally ended the cold war and drastically cut the two sides' conventional weapons.

Commercial treaties set up rules for a nation's foreign trade and deal with fishing rights, tariffs, and other economic concerns. A good example of a commercial treaty is the Treaty of Rome, signed in 1957. This treaty established the European Community, or Common Market.

Legal treaties deal with agreements on copyrights and patents. A legal treaty may also be an agreement to help return criminals who have fled to other countries. The International Postal Union was set up by another type of legal treaty to regulate international postal rates and services among nations of the world. Legal treaties also establish international law, such as the rules of warfare established by the Hague Conferences of 1899 and 1907 and the Geneva Accords of 1864, 1906, 1929, and 1949.

Some treaties end by agreement, others because one party breaks them.

ALSO READ: EUROPEAN ECONOMIC COMMUNITY, INTERNATIONAL LAW, INTERNATIONAL RELATIONS, NORTH ATLANTIC TREATY ORGANIZATION.

TREE A tree is a tall, woody plant that usually has one main stem, or trunk. Some trees grow over 200 feet (60 m) tall. The largest living thing on earth is a California sequoia tree called the "General Sherman," 272 feet (82.9 m) tall with a trunk 32 feet (10 m) thick. The oldest known living thing is a California bristlecone pine tree about 4,600 years old.

Trees can be divided into two groups by the shapes of their leaves. The needle-leaf trees include pines, spruces, firs, hemlocks, and cedars. These trees are also called *conifers* because they bear cones. The cones produce the seeds. The seeds are "naked," or unprotected by a fruit, so these trees are given the scientific name *gymnosperm*, meaning "naked seed." Most conifers are evergreens. They keep their leaves throughout the year. But not all conifers have needle leaves and not all are evergreen.

The broadleaf trees are members of a large group of flowering plants called *angiosperm*, meaning "covered seed." These include the oaks, elms, maples, birches, beeches, hickories, sycamores, and almost all trees with fairly wide, flat leaves. All of these trees, like all angiosperms, bear fruits and flowers, though the flowers of some trees are too small to see and the fruit may not look much like fruit. The acorn is the fruit of an oak, and the small, winged seed casing is the fruit of a maple. Many angiosperms are *deciduous*—their leaves fall off in the winter and grow back in the spring. But some, such as the hollies and live oaks, are evergreen.

When used as lumber, the conifers are often called "softwood" and the broadleaf trees "hardwood." But this is not always accurate. Some conifers have harder wood than some broadleaf trees have.

The Growth and Anatomy of a Tree
A tree grows from a seed. If you were

to break open the seed, you would find inside, in miniature, a little tree that will later grow to full size.

The seeds normally drop from trees in winter. A seed may be carried for some distance by the wind, a bird, or an animal. With luck, it falls on fertile ground.

The seed lies dormant through the winter. In the warmth and wetness of spring, it begins to sprout. The root emerges first, poking through the seed coat and digging down into the soil. Then the first shoot appears, pushing up into the air and sunlight.

The taproot grows straight down to anchor the tree and reach for deep water. Other roots grow outward in search of surface water. At the same time, the shoot develops into the stem, branches, and leaves. The roots and the leaves must grow at about the same rate. The leaves, through a chemical process called *photosynthesis*, make food so the tree can live and grow. The roots provide the water and minerals that the leaves need to make the food.

The flow of food and water be-

▲ *Many old trees are historic. This Osage orange tree, which stands in front of Patrick Henry's home near Brookneal, Virginia, is approximately 300 years old. The American patriot once played the violin for his grandchildren in the shade of this great tree.*

tween the roots and leaves is accomplished by layers of cells formed by the *cambium*. The cambium lies between the wood and the bark. As the cells of the cambium divide, they form an inner layer of tubelike cells called the *xylem* and an outer layer of cells called the *phloem*. The xylem carries water from the roots to the leaves, and the phloem carries food from the leaves back down to the roots. As the phloem and xylem age, they harden and die. The dead xylem forms the wood of the tree. The dead phloem forms part of the bark. The cambium produces new layers of xylem and phloem to carry on the flow of fluids and the growth of the tree.

Forest Regions The trees growing in a particular place vary with the soil and the *climate*—the temperature, sunlight, wind, and rain. North America, with its wide range of climate and soil, is especially rich in trees, having more than 1,000 different species (kinds).

The United States can be divided into six forest regions—Northern, Central, Southern, Pacific, Rocky Mountain, and Tropical.

The Northern forest runs across New England and the Great Lakes from Maine to Minnesota. A thin finger of this forest follows the ridges of the Appalachian Mountains down

▼ *The ancient Eastern tradition of* bonsai *has produced this miniature* Pinus thunbergii *tree.*

▼ *A cross section of a tree trunk.*

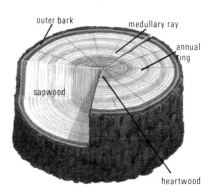

outer bark
medullary ray
annual ring
sapwood
heartwood

▲ *Part of a great forest of evergreen, cone-bearing trees. Coniferous forests ring the world's cool lands near the tundra.*

A banyan tree is a kind of fig tree that grows in India and Sri Lanka. It is possible for one banyan tree to be the size of a small wood! There is one tree in Sri Lanka that is said to have 350 large trunks and more than 3,000 smaller ones!

into Georgia. The Northern forest is a mixture of conifers and broadleaf trees. The conifers include pine, fir, cedar, hemlock, and spruce. The most common broadleaf trees are the yellow birch and the sugar maple.

The Central forest stretches across the middle of the eastern United States from Cape Cod to Texas. This is the largest forest region, and it includes mostly broadleaf trees—oaks, ashes, poplars, gums, beeches, and walnuts.

The Southern region runs from Virginia across the coastal southern states to Texas. The most important trees are pines—loblolly, slash, and longleaf. But broadleaf trees also grow here—oaks, elms, red maples, and cottonwoods.

The three eastern forest regions are separated from the two western regions by the vast, almost treeless plains of the Midwest. Beyond the plains lies the Rocky Mountain region, an area with scattered forests of tall conifers—ponderosa pine, lodgepole pine, Douglas fir, and others.

West of the Rockies is the Pacific region, the home of the largest trees in the world—sequoias, redwoods, Douglas firs, Sitka spruce, and other great conifers. This land, running from Canada to Mexico, provides one-third of America's lumber.

Small tropical forests are located at the southern tips of Florida and Texas. Mahogany, mangrove, and bay trees grow there. Every American state has its official state tree. (See the individual state articles.)

Over half of the forest land in North America is located in Canada. In the East, along the Great Lakes and the St. Lawrence River, the forest is a mixture of conifers and broadleaf trees. To the north and west are almost all conifers—great stands of fir, pine, spruce, and hemlock stretching to the treeless tundra of the Arctic. Canada's forests provide the pulpwood used to make over half the newsprint in the world.

Tree Identification How can you tell one kind of tree from another? The first step is to decide whether the tree is a conifer or a broadleaf tree.

Look at the leaves. Are they thin, like needles? If they are, you are looking at a conifer. Each needle is a separate leaf. Each scale of the cone has a flat seed at its base. These seeds are not covered.

If the needles are long and arranged in small bundles, the tree is probably a pine. If the needles are short and grow on all sides of a twig, the tree may be a spruce. If the needles are short and flat and grow side by side on opposite sides of the twig, the tree may be a balsam fir or a hemlock. Most conifers have a single trunk running from the root to the tree top in a straight line.

Suppose the tree has a broad leaf. How can you tell what kind of broadleaf tree it is? There are almost 700 kinds of broadleaf trees, so this is a little harder than separating the varieties of conifer. You will want to narrow the selection. First, see if the leaf is *simple* or *compound*. A simple leaf is one leaf growing alone on a stem. Oak and maple leaves are simple. A compound leaf has many leaflets growing on one stem. Hickory and walnut leaves are compound. Some compound leaves are confusing because their leaflets may be as large as simple leaves. There is an easy way to decide which one you are looking at. A simple leaf usually has a bud growing on the twig right under the stem. The leaflet of a compound leaf does not.

The next clue you will need for identification is the shape of the leaf and the leaf edges. Leaves may be almost round, heart-shaped, or long and narrow. The edges may be smooth, lobed, or toothed. A maple leaf is lobed, which means that the edges are deeply divided into sections. Toothed edges have many small points. Leaves can be both lobed and toothed. One large group

TREE SPOTTING

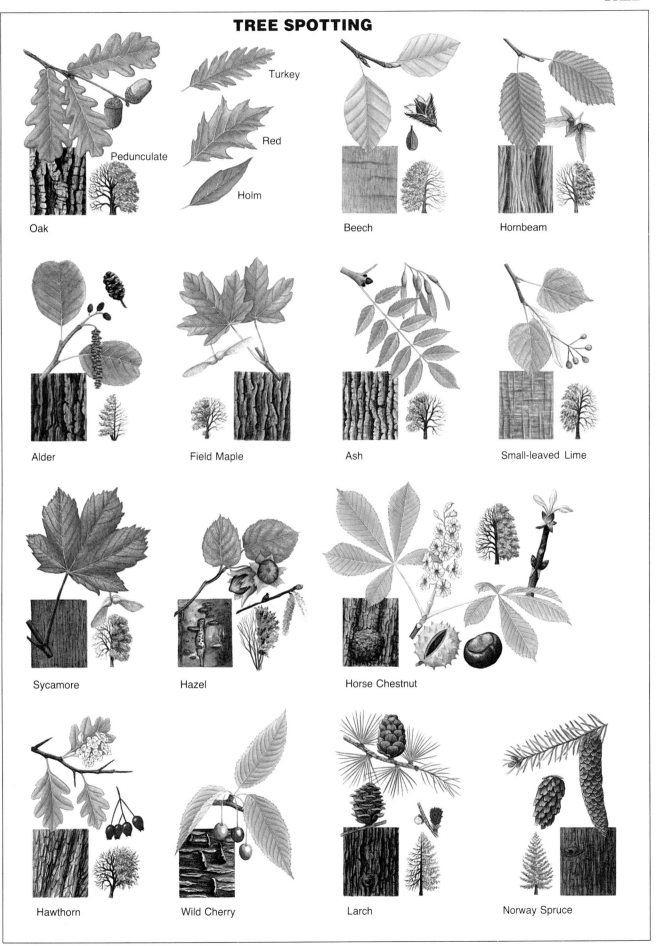

Oak
Pedunculate
Turkey
Red
Holm

Beech

Hornbeam

Alder

Field Maple

Ash

Small-leaved Lime

Sycamore

Hazel

Horse Chestnut

Hawthorn

Wild Cherry

Larch

Norway Spruce

▲ *A deciduous forest of oak. Such forests grew in many temperate lands near coniferous forests. But most of the world's deciduous forests have been cut down.*

▼ *The divi-divi trees, on the island of Aruba in the Netherlands Antilles, are shaped by trade winds that blow constantly from the northeast.*

of trees, the oaks, includes smooth, lobed, and toothed leaves. But oaks are not hard to identify, because they all bear acorns.

Leaves are usually the easiest way to identify a tree. But perhaps you have looked carefully at the leaves of a tree, and you are still not sure what kind it is. You may have decided, for example, that it is a maple. But which maple is it? Silver maple? Norway maple? Sugar maple? If you are just beginning, it may be enough simply to say, "It is a maple tree." As you become more familiar with trees, you will want to be more specific. You will learn how to look for the identifying leaf scars on winter twigs. Buds have distinctive shapes, too. Tree bark is as individual as skin is. Oaks and elms have thick, rough bark. Beeches have smooth, gray bark that looks like stretched metal. Many birches have bark that peels off like paper.

You can often tell the kind of tree by the shape of its bare branches. Some trees can be identified by their fruit. Some trees bear nuts that are easy to identify. Nuts are tree seeds enclosed in a shell.

When you are able to identify trees, you can begin to observe how and where different trees grow. What trees grow in wet areas? In dry areas? You may notice that certain trees usually grow in groups, while others, such as the tulip tree, usually grow alone. Which trees grow fast and which grow slowly? If you find a cut

stump, you can count the rings to see how old the tree was when it was cut down.

Trees and People   Trees have long been useful to people. Early people used wood to make tools and build fires. Later, they cut trees to build shelters. They probably never thought about protecting trees because the supply seemed to be endless. But they were wrong. There are now deserts where there were once thick forests.

Today, millions of acres of trees are grown for lumber. Houses and furniture are built of wood. The paper in this book is a product of trees. We eat the fruits and nuts from trees. Birds and wildlife need trees for food and shelter. The changing beauty of trees delights us. Trees flower in spring. Their summer green provides welcome shade. Autumn brings glorious color to trees, and in winter, their branches are like lace against the sky.

Ecology is the relationship among plants, animals (including human beings), and the rest of the environment. Trees are an irreplaceable part of the Earth's ecology. The oxygen we breathe is produced by plants through photosynthesis. Trees are the largest plants, so they make the most oxygen. When trees are cut down and more roads are built, fewer and fewer trees are left to make oxygen. More roads carry more cars, buses, and trucks. The exhaust from these vehicles pollutes the air. Many varieties of trees cannot live in heavily polluted air. They sicken and die. Sycamores and ginkgo trees are often planted in city streets and in parks because they are sturdy enough to grow in the unfavorable environment.

Trees also absorb sound and control noise pollution. Trees keep moisture in the ground by holding the soil in place to prevent erosion.

For further information on:
Ecology and Forestry,   *see* CONSER-

VATION, ECOLOGY, EVOLUTION, FOREST FIRE, FORESTRY, PLANTS OF THE PAST.

Kinds of Trees, *see* CONIFER, EVERGREEN, FRUIT, PALM.

Tree Anatomy and Growth, *see* BARK, BUD, CELL, FLOWER, GROWTH, LEAF, PHOTOSYNTHESIS, PLANT, PLANT BREEDING, SEEDS AND FRUITS, SHRUB.

Tree Products, *see* CITRUS FRUIT, LUMBER AND LUMBERING, NUT, PLANT PRODUCTS, WOOD.

TRIAL A trial is a legal procedure that gives people a chance to go to a court and present facts before a judge or jury in order to seek justice in a dispute. A dispute brought before a court is called a *case*.

Cases brought before a court are of two types—civil and criminal. A *civil case* is any legal dispute between two private individuals or between two states, organizations, or businesses. Divorce cases, cases concerning property or business disputes, and many others are civil cases.

A *criminal case* is a dispute between the state and a private individual, business, or other organization. The individual or organization is accused of having broken the criminal laws of the state. The state tries to prove the individual guilty of having committed a crime (of having broken the criminal laws of the state). Murder, drunk or reckless driving, theft, kidnaping, and illegal business practices are a few examples of criminal cases.

Bringing a Case to Trial In a civil case, one party (the *plaintiff*) files charges with the court against another party (the *defendant*). The charges are a written document outlining the matter under dispute and the accusations of wrongdoing against the defendant. The charges also list any civil laws the defendant is accused of breaking. The case is then entered in the court *docket* (schedule), and a date is set for the trial. Cases are always

referred to by the names of the contesting individuals, with the plaintiff's name first—*Jasper* versus *Diddybump* or *Logan* v. *The Rattletrap Automobile Company*.

Bringing a criminal case to trial is more complicated. The state must file charges against an individual or group suspected of committing a crime. In the case of felonies (very serious crimes), the state's attorneys must submit evidence of a crime to a *grand jury*, made up of between 6 and 23 people. If the jury decides that the evidence against a suspect is sufficient, it hands down an *indictment*. An indictment is a written statement charging an individual with committing a crime. The indictment is filed with the court, and the accused person is *arraigned*—summoned before a judge to answer the charges in the indictment.

At arraignment, the accused usually pleads *guilty* or *not guilty*. If he or she pleads guilty, no trial is held because there is nothing to argue over. The judge merely *declares sentence* (decides the punishment that the person must undergo). If the accused pleads not guilty, a trial must be held. The case is entered on the docket, and a trial date is set. In criminal cases, the state is always the plaintiff and the case is listed in writing as *The State of Illinois* v. *Herman Kickabout* or *The Commonwealth of Virginia* v. *John Slugger*.

Trial Procedure For a civil or criminal jury trial, people eligible for jury duty are summoned to the court. In the United States, any citizen between the ages of 18 or 21 and 70 who is able to read and write is eligible for jury duty. The clerk of the court calls the names of prospective jurors. If the persons have good reasons for being unable to serve on the jury, they state their reasons, and the judge decides whether to dismiss them or order them to serve. The attorneys for each side are allowed to question the jurors

▲ *Anne Hutchinson was put on trial in Massachusetts in 1637 for speaking out against officials of the church. She was found guilty and banished from the colony.*

▲ *An FBI technician prepares a scale model of the locale in which a crime was committed. The model will help the judge and the jury in a trial to understand the facts surrounding the case.*

▲ *Congressional leaders conduct open hearings to find out whether certain government officials who have acted wrongly should be sent for trial in the criminal courts.*

The longest criminal trial on record began in California in November 1981. It was the murder trial of Angelo Buono and lasted for just over two years. There were more than 400 witnesses.

to find out if they will make fair jurors for their side.

The trial begins with the attorneys' opening remarks to the jury. The plaintiff or *prosecution* then sets out to prove the various charges made against the defendant. Witnesses are called by the prosecution, sworn in by the clerk, and questioned. After *direct examination* of a witness by the attorney who called him or her, the opposing attorney may choose to *cross-examine* the witness. In cross-examination, the opposing attorney tries to discredit the witness's *testimony* or prove that the witness's evidence is inadequate.

The defendant's attorney then calls witnesses to prove the defendant's innocence. At the conclusion of the defendant's case, both attorneys make closing remarks to the jury. They try to show the jury how the testimony and evidence does or does not prove the defendant's guilt. After the closing remarks, the judge explains to the jury the laws that apply.

The jury then leaves the court to decide on a *verdict* (a decision as to whether or not the charges against the defendant have been proved). Throughout the trial, jurors are not allowed to discuss the case with anyone. In reaching a verdict, they must talk about the trial with each other, but they are not allowed to have contact with anyone but the court's bailiff and the guards.

If the jury reaches a verdict of "not guilty," the defendant is *acquitted* (allowed to go free with the charges dropped). If the verdict is "guilty," the defendant is *convicted* and the judge hands down a sentence within the limits set by law. If the jury cannot reach a verdict, it is called a *hung jury*. The case must then be tried again with a new jury and judge. In civil cases, the jury decides who is at fault and what damages (usually money) shall be paid to the plaintiff. All verdicts are read in court by the *foreman* of the jury. In trials conducted before a judge only, the judge decides both the verdict and the sentence.

If a defendant and his or her attorneys feel that the verdict is wrong or in some way unfair, they may *appeal* their case to a higher court. Appeal procedures are very complicated and usually take a long time, but they are one way of making sure justice is done by giving suspects a second chance for acquittal.

Throughout a jury trial, the judge acts as an umpire. The rules for conduct of a trial are very strict. The judge must enforce those rules and make sure the trial is completely fair to both sides. If a judge fails, even in the smallest way, to enforce the trial rules or to keep the trial fair, the defendant's attorneys can try to force a *mistrial*. The case must then be retried with an entirely new jury and judge.

Many civil cases are heard in *closed court*. The general public is not allowed to be present. Criminal cases are almost always conducted in *open court*, where spectators are allowed to watch the proceedings. During all trials, a *court stenographer* takes down the entire proceedings word for word. All participants in the trial receive written copies of the proceedings.

News reporters often attend criminal trials, but no photographs are allowed to be taken in a U.S. court of law. The press usually sends artists to sketch the people and proceedings in important trials. Sometimes a case gets a great deal of publicity before or during the trial. If the publicity is bad for the defendant, his or her attorney may ask that the trial be held in a different city or state. This is called *change of venue*, and it is done to make sure that an impartial or fair jury can be selected and a fair trial held.

ALSO READ: COURT SYSTEM, CRIME, JUVENILE DELINQUENCY, LAW, LAWYERS AND JUDGES, MURDER, POLICE, PRISON, SUPREME COURT.

TRIGONOMETRY see GEOMETRY, MATHEMATICS.

TRINIDAD and TOBAGO see WEST INDIES.

TROJAN WAR The legends of ancient Greece tell of a ten-year war between the Greeks and the Trojans. The Trojans lived in a city called Troy, located in Asia Minor (now Turkey). Homer tells of the Trojan War in his story-poem, the *Iliad*. (Ilium was the Greek name for Troy.) The area that has traditionally been considered the site of Troy was actually the location of several ancient cities. Archeologists have unearthed several cities, each one built on top of the ruins of another, dating back to about 3000 B.C. The Troy of legend probably exists in the 1200's B.C. Historians believe that the Greeks may have attacked Troy for its goods or to destroy its power.

According to legend, the Trojan War began when three goddesses, Hera, Athena, and Aphrodite, all wanted a golden apple that was to be given to the most beautiful of the three. Paris, son of King Priam of Troy, was chosen to judge their beauty. He awarded the apple to Aphrodite, who promised to give him

the most beautiful woman in the world. She presented him with Helen, wife of King Menelaus of Sparta, Greece. Paris and Helen ran off to Troy together. All the Greek princes, heroes, and kings gathered in anger and sailed for Troy to bring Helen back. Different gods and goddesses backed each side. The Greek armies surrounded the city of Troy for nine years, but the Trojans would not surrender.

During the war, the bravest Greek warrior, Achilles, killed the Trojan leader, Hector. Achilles was later killed by Paris. In the tenth year of the war, the Greek hero, Odysseus, thought of a masterful trick. He had the Greeks build an enormous hollow wooden horse, fill it with soldiers, and leave it outside the city gates. The Trojans thought the horse was a gift and dragged it into the city. That night, the Greek soldiers climbed out of the horse and opened the city gates. The Greek armies captured Troy and burned it.

The romantic story of Paris and Helen has appealed to the imagination of people for centuries. Numerous stories, plays, paintings, and sculptures have been based on the Trojan War.

ALSO READ: GREECE, ANCIENT; GREEK LITERATURE; HOMER; MYTHOLOGY.

TROPICAL FISH Tropical fish are small, brightly colored fish that come from the warm waters of the tropics. Some of these fish live in fresh water, and some live in salt water. Tropical fish are popular as pets. Until fairly recently, most people kept only freshwater tropical fish. Today, many enjoy recreating the beauties of a coral reef in saltwater tanks. The temperature and *salinity* (amount of salt) in these tanks is carefully controlled.

Tropical fish can be divided into two groups—those that give birth to

▲ *It was thought that this was the gold death mask of Agamemnon, king of Mycenae.*

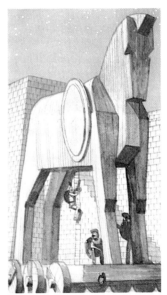

▲ *The wooden horse in which Greek soldiers managed to enter the city of Troy.*

bubblenest

Male

Female

▲ *The colorful male Siamese fighting fish is known for its aggressiveness. Its native waters are around Thailand. The female does not have such elongated fins and is not aggressive.*

▼ *Two types of angelfish and a Rock beauty, all exotic additions to a tropical fish aquarium.*

live young and those that lay eggs. The live bearers include guppies, mollies, and swordtails. Egg layers include angelfish, tetras, Siamese fighting fish, and gouramis.

Live bearers are easier to care for and breed than egg layers. If a male and a female guppy are kept in the same aquarium, the female will almost certainly become pregnant in a short time. She should then be moved to a separate aquarium that is full of plants. Fish often eat their offspring, and the plants will provide hiding places for the young. After she has given birth, the mother should be returned to her original tank.

Egg-laying fish are more finicky breeders. If the water and the food are not just right, they are unlikely to produce offspring. Each fish has its own special requirements, so that what is right for one fish may not suit another one at all.

Tropical fish are of many different shapes, colors, and personalities. The guppy is probably the most popular tropical fish. It is a small, colorful, peaceful fish. It will eat almost any food, and it can live in water at temperatures from 60° to 90° F. Mollies, moonfish, and zebra fish are also peaceful and easy to care for. These fish can live happily with other fish.

Some fish are dangerous to other fish, need a special diet, or can live only in water at a certain temperature.

The kissing gourami is a fairly large tropical fish from Asia. Kissing gouramis kiss each other, but they attack and eat smaller fish. Kissing gouramis should be kept alone or with fish of their own size, in a tank with a water temperature of 75° to 80° F. They like to eat oatmeal, Pablum, and dried shrimp.

Tropical fish are easy to care for and interesting to watch. If they have clean, fresh water and good food they rarely become sick. The only real danger to them is overeating. They should be fed only enough to keep them healthy, because they will literally eat themselves to death.

ALSO READ: AQUARIUM, FISH, PET.

TROPICS   The tropics are a generally warm zone encircling the Earth about 1,600 miles (2,575 km) north and south of the equator. The equator is an imaginary line exactly halfway between the North and South poles. It divides the world into two halves, or *hemispheres*.

The tropics are bordered by two other imaginary lines—the Tropic of Cancer in the Northern Hemisphere and the Tropic of Capricorn in the Southern Hemisphere. The Tropic of Cancer is 23 degrees and 27 minutes north of the equator (0 degrees latitude), while the Tropic of Capricorn is 23 degrees and 27 minutes south of the equator. These two lines are the northernmost and southernmost places where the sun can be directly overhead on one day a year—on June 21 at the Tropic of Cancer and on December 23 at the Tropic of Capricorn. This is because the Earth's axis (an imaginary line joining the North Pole, the center of the Earth, and the South Pole) is tilted by about 23½ degrees. As a result, as the Earth travels around the sun, the Northern and Southern hemispheres alternately tilt towards the sun for half of the year and away from it for the other half.

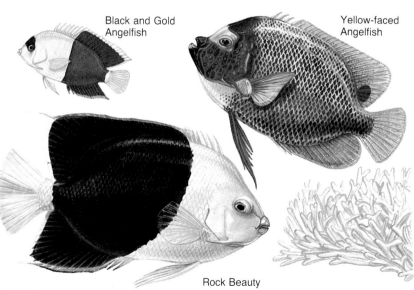

Black and Gold Angelfish

Yellow-faced Angelfish

Rock Beauty

This is why many parts of the Earth have four seasons.

The tropics get more intense sunlight than any other zone on earth. This explains why they are always warm. But different climates are found in the tropics. Most places near the equator are very rainy. Because of the high temperatures and the heavy rain, dense forests grow in such places. Farther away from the equator, however, the rain occurs in one or two rainy seasons, with dry seasons between them. Here the forests thin out and merge into tropical grasslands with scattered trees, called *savanna*.

TROTSKY, LEON (1879–1940)
One of the Communist leaders who brought about the 1917 Russian Revolution was Leon Trotsky.

Born Lev Davidovich Bronstein, he became a revolutionary as a youth, and took a new "revolutionary" name, Leon Trotsky. He was often on the run from the government in the dangerous years before the Revolution. He fled abroad and for a time lived in the United States. He returned to Russia in 1917, joined the Bolsheviks, and became second in importance to the new Communist leader, Vladimir Lenin.

Trotsky was given the task of reorganizing the army. He created the Red Army, recruiting professional officers from the old imperial army to lead the untrained peasants and workers. The Red Army became a formidable force.

Trotsky did not always agree with Lenin, and after Lenin's death in 1924, he was ousted by rivals. In 1929, he was expelled from Russia. Trotsky criticized the brutal rule of Joseph Stalin and was accused of being a spy and a traitor. In 1940, while living in Mexico City, he was murdered, probably on Stalin's orders.

ALSO READ: LENIN, VLADIMIR; STALIN, JOSEPH.

TRUCK FARMING
Truck farming is growing fruits and vegetables for market—to sell to individuals or to supermarkets and grocery stores. The term "truck farming" originated when growers began transporting their produce by truck to cities and other places to be sold. Truck farming increased as cities grew. (When most people lived in rural areas, they could grow the vegetables they needed. But city residents must buy the food they need.) Until railroad lines were built, most truck farms were located near large cities. Now many large truck farms are located far from many of their markets, but railroads, trucks, and airplanes, using refrigeration, can bring produce to market while it is still fresh.

Several kinds of vegetables can be grown on a single truck farm. Farmers often plant and harvest several crops from a given area during one year. For example, they may harvest an early crop of radishes and later plant carrots or beans. Truck farmers water, fertilize, and usually spray their crops to kill insects so that their land will produce good crops.

Truck farms vary in size from large gardens to farms of several hundred acres. Small truck farms are usually located near cities. These farmers raise many kinds of fruits and vegetables—cabbage, lettuce, squash, carrots, celery, radishes, peaches, strawberries, blueberries, mushrooms, and many others. They may set up roadside stands to sell their crops or take them into the city to sell to stores. Larger truck farms usually specialize in growing one or two crops. Many of the largest farms quick-freeze their crops, package them, and send them to market. Some of the largest truck farms are in Florida and California.

Harvesting is done by machine as frequently as possible. But many crops, such as tomatoes, lettuce, and cabbages, would be damaged by harvesting machines and must be picked

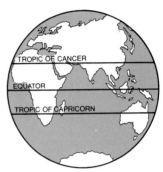

▲ *Leon Trotsky, Russian agitator and revolutionary who supported Lenin.*

▲ *A sanitation truck dumps its load of garbage and refuse at a waste disposal plant. The truck body is tilted by hydraulic pistons.*

▼ *This powerful truck is an "off-the-road" truck. High ground clearance, long-travel suspension, and heavy tread tires are special design features for traveling over dirt tracks or desert sand.*

by hand. Since they need extra "hands" at harvesting time, farmers hire *migrant workers*, people who travel around the country working on truck farms.

Small farmers often join together in *cooperatives* to market their crops. In a cooperative, the participating farmers arrange to ship their crops together so that they can get reduced freight prices.

ALSO READ: AGRICULTURE, FRUIT, VEGETABLES.

TRUCKS AND TRUCKING
Whether moving furniture to a new house or hauling giant logs to a lumber mill, trucks are an essential part of a nation's economy. Trucks are motor vehicles that transport freight and sometimes people. They carry raw materials to factories. They carry goods from factories to stores, and they deliver products from stores to homes. Trucks are used to haul cargo to and from other forms of transport, such as trains, planes, and ships. Trucks are used in the construction of new buildings and roads. And trucks are used in performing community services, such as garbage pickup, fire fighting, and telephone and electrical repair.

Trucks are much more versatile than airplanes, trains, and ships. Trains and ships can travel only on rails and water. Planes, trains and ships can do most of their loading and unloading only at airports, rail terminals, and docks. The cargo carried by these forms of transport almost always has to be taken to its final destination by truck. Trucks can pick up a great variety of cargo and make deliveries right to the doors of factories, stores, and individual homes.

Kinds of Trucks Trucks come in a great variety of sizes, shapes, and weights and are designed for many different uses. Trucks are usually classified according to weight—light, medium, light-heavy, and heavy. A truck's weight includes the weight of the truck itself and the weight of the maximum load it can carry. Most modern truck bodies are made of strong, lightweight metals, such as aluminum. The less the truck itself weighs, the more cargo it can carry, if the truck is constructed of strong materials.

Lightweight and mediumweight trucks are usually of the *single-unit* type. In single-unit trucks, the driver's cab and the cargo-carrying space are both built on the same *chassis*, or body frame. They generally have two axles and four to six wheels. The familiar pickup, panel, and delivery trucks are examples of single-unit vehicles. They have been adapted for many different uses, such as mail delivery, bookmobiles, campers, single horse vans, and police vans.

The big heavyweight trucks are usually of the *combination* type, made up of tractors and trailers. The *tractor* houses the driver's cab and the engine. The *trailer* is the large cargo-carrying part that is hooked onto and pulled by the tractor. A combination truck in which the trailer has one or more forward axles is called a *full trailer* or *tractor-trailer*. Many combination trucks have trailers with no forward axles. These are called *semi-*

trailers. When not attached to a tractor, the semitrailer's front end is supported by metal struts and wheels, called *dollies.* When being pulled, the trailer's front end is coupled to a disk at the back of the tractor. Beneath the disk, the tractor has a number of wheels that act as the semitrailer's front axle. A full trailer, with wheels at both ends, is often coupled to the end of a semitrailer. The tractor can then pull two loads of cargo. This largest type of truck is called a *double bottom.*

All trucks, even the single-unit, lightweight ones, are more ruggedly built than automobiles are. Their engines are more powerful and most operate on diesel or very low-octane fuels, rather than on standard-octane gasoline. Most trucks have four-wheel drive. The engine is connected to all four wheels. In an automobile, the engine is usually connected only to the rear or front wheels.

Truck bodies have to withstand extremely heavy loads. For this reason, most trucks have more than four wheels. The biggest ones have as many as five axles carrying 10 to 18 wheels. Double wheels are located under areas of greatest weight.

Driving Trucks Engines of heavy-weight trucks have up to 12 forward gears. Automobiles have usually only three or four gears. The first gear is slowest but most powerful. It is used to move out from a dead stop and to climb steep hills. The twelfth gear is for cruising on flat, open highway. A truck's gears are usually shifted by hand, but automatic transmissions are being used more and more.

There are always two drivers for cross-country hauls of longer than ten hours. No driver is allowed to operate his or her truck for more than ten hours at a time. When one driver tires, the other takes over. Cabs are often equipped with bedding, located behind the driver's seat, so one person can rest while the other one

▲ *The long distance cargo truck, a familiar sight on interstate highways, carries anything from refrigerated foods to furniture.*

drives. Some very modern trucks are equipped with refrigerators, showers, and all the conveniences of a tiny apartment.

In order to drive a truck in the United States, a person must pass a series of very difficult tests. A driver must demonstrate the ability to handle the type of truck he or she wants to drive. All states require truck drivers to obtain a special license, called a *chauffeur's license.* You cannot operate a truck of three or more axles with only an automobile license.

Trucks in Use Today A large variety of trucks are now in use for all kinds of special jobs. You have probably seen many of them yourself. *Tanker trucks* are rounded, completely enclosed tanks for carrying oil, milk, or any other kind of liquid cargo. *Cement-mixers* transport, mix, and dump cement at construction sites.

Some trucks are produced specially for use in the desert. They have special tires that help them "float" over the loose surface, and special seals and filters to keep out the dust. They also have four- or sometimes six-wheel drive, and special radiators with large fans to keep the engine temperature at a reasonable level.

▼ *A modern dump truck has big, heavy tires for working on construction sites.*

▲ *This heavyweight crash tender has to carry bulky equipment including a crane (to deal with fires). At the front is a high-powered foam canon.*

▲ *Canadian Prime Minister Trudeau meets President Nixon on the U.S.—Canadian border in June 1969.*

Flatbed trucks are open on three sides and are used for hauling logs, steel girders, bulldozers, or anything large, solid, and carried in one piece. *Dump trucks* are used to haul coal, dirt, or anything spillable. Their carrying space raises up at the front on pneumatic lifts so the load can be dumped out through the tailgate at the back. Some have machinery for compressing loads, such as garbage. *Auto haulers* are large trailers that can carry six cars or more. *Mobile homes* are trucks whose carrying space in the back has been made into living quarters with rooms, furniture, appliances, and all the comforts of home. *Tow trucks* have equipment, such as jacks and hoists, with which they can lift and pull disabled cars and trucks. The cargo space in *refrigerator trucks* is a gigantic freezer for frozen fruit, vegetables, and meat.

There are hundreds of other kinds of trucks equipped to do special kinds of work, from cleaning streets to carrying glass bottles. An unusual new truck that will be used in the future is the *walking truck*. It has several legs, each with three joints. The driver controls the legs by means of cables and hydraulic fluid, much as the arms of cranes and steam shovels work. The truck can walk over exceedingly rough terrain.

ALSO READ: AUTOMOBILE, DIESEL ENGINE, TRANSPORTATION.

TRUDEAU, PIERRE (born 1919)

Pierre Elliott Trudeau was prime minister of Canada from 1968 to 1979 and again from 1980 to 1984.

He was born in Montreal, Quebec. His mother was of British descent, and his father was French Canadian. Trudeau studied law at the University of Montreal and later attended Harvard University. As a student, he traveled around the world by hitchhiking and by riding a motorbike. On his return to Canada, he became a lawyer in Montreal.

Trudeau was elected a Liberal member of parliament in 1965. Two years later, he was appointed minister of justice and attorney general. Trudeau succeeded Lester Pearson in 1968 as leader of the Liberal Party and prime minister. Despite calls by French Canadians in Quebec for a separate state, Trudeau spoke out for a united Canada and a "just society" for all Canadians. He supported programs to make Canada economically stronger. Under his leadership, Canada established diplomatic relations with China. Trudeau served three terms as prime minister until 1979, when the Progressive Conservative Party took control of the government. In 1980, the Liberal Party won a majority of seats in parliament, and Trudeau became prime minister again. In June 1984, Trudeau resigned and stepped down as Liberal leader and prime minister.

ALSO READ: CANADA; MULRONEY, BRIAN; PEARSON, LESTER.

TRUMAN, HARRY S. (1884–1972)

Harry S. Truman served as Vice-President during the three months of President Franklin Roosevelt's fourth term. President Roosevelt was one of the best-known world leaders, and when he died in 1945, Truman filled his position.

Harry S. Truman was born in

Lamar, Missouri, on May 8, 1884, and grew up on a farm near Independence, Missouri. His father could not afford to send him to college, but Truman educated himself by reading widely on his own.

During World War I, Truman served in the United States Army and was promoted to the rank of major. Truman and the unit he commanded fought bravely in France. After the war, Truman held several public offices in Missouri and attended the Kansas City Law School. He was elected to the U.S. Senate in 1934. As a senator (1935–1945), he was appointed head of a committee to investigate defense production during World War II. "The Truman Committee," by careful supervision of war production plants, was able to save the country billions of dollars.

During Truman's three months as Vice-President (January 20–April 12, 1945), President Roosevelt was out of the country for part of the time. It was not until Truman became the chief executive that he learned about the existence of the atomic bomb. Leading scientists, working for the American government, had been experimenting on a new kind of weapon. President Truman made the decision to use the atomic bomb in order to end the war in the Far East as soon as possible. Two atomic bombs were dropped, three days apart, over two Japanese cities, Hiroshima and Nagasaki. The destruction was so terrible that Japan surrendered on August 15, 1945.

The end of the war did not bring real peace. A nonviolent conflict known as the "Cold War" developed with a former ally, the Soviet Union. During the war, Nazi forces had been driven out of several countries in eastern Europe by Soviet armies. But Soviet leaders, instead of permitting free elections as they had agreed, set up Communist governments backed by Soviet arms in those countries. Armed pressure was used in Greece and Turkey to try to establish communism there.

In response to this challenge, the President announced the Truman Doctrine—official U.S. foreign policy that gave support to "free peoples who are resisting attempted subjugation by armed minorities or by outside pressures." Among other measures supported by the President to aid foreign countries was the European Recovery Program, or Marshall Plan, suggested by Secretary of State George C. Marshall. With the aid of money and materials voted by the U.S. Congress, 16 countries in Europe rebuilt the factories, railroads, and docks that had been bombed during the war. Millions of Europeans were given work, and their countries began to prosper.

▲ *When North Korea invaded South Korea on June 25, 1950, President Truman quickly sent U.S. soldiers into action to aid South Korea. The soldiers soon discovered that they had to cope with severe winter weather as well as with the enemy.*

HARRY S. TRUMAN
THIRTY-THIRD PRESIDENT   APRIL 12, 1945—JANUARY 20, 1953

Born: May 8, 1884, Lamar, Missouri
Parents: John Anderson and Martha Young Truman
Education: Kansas City Law School
Religion: Baptist
Occupation: Bank clerk, farmer, merchant, government official
Political Party: Democratic
State Represented: Missouri
Married: 1919 to Elizabeth ("Bess") Virginia Wallace (born 1885)
Children: One daughter
Died: December 26, 1972, Kansas City, Missouri
Buried: Truman Library Grounds, Independence, Missouri

The *Chicago Daily Tribune* was so certain that Harry Truman would lose the election of 1948 to Thomas Dewey that an edition with the headline "Dewey Defeats Truman" was actually printed before all the votes had been counted.

▲ *Harriet Tubman, a black heroine who helped to free many slaves.*

Truman was less successful with domestic issues. He tried to extend Roosevelt's New Deal with his own Fair Deal. Truman asked Congress for increased social security benefits, national health insurance, and public housing, among other things. Truman also wanted to establish a commission to help black people gain fairer treatment. But a conservative Congress refused to cooperate with most of his plans. Even some Democrats, especially those from Southern states, began to turn against Truman and his programs. Over Truman's veto, Congress passed the Taft-Hartley Act, which lessened the power of labor unions.

In the Presidential election of 1948, most people expected Truman to be beaten by the Republican nominee, Thomas E. Dewey. The split within the Democratic Party was so great that a group of Southern Democrats broke away and formed their own party. In addition, Henry Wallace, who was Vice-President before Truman, ran on the Progressive ticket. Truman surprised nearly everyone by winning the election. After the election, Congress passed Truman's programs for social security and public housing but did not approve his ideas on civil rights.

In 1950, Communist North Koreans supplied with Russian weapons invaded the Republic of Korea to the south. The President ordered U.S. military forces to go to the aid of South Koreans, and the invasion was condemned as an act of aggression by the United Nations Security Council. This was the start of the Korean War.

Also in 1950, Senator Joseph McCarthy began a search for Communists in government and elsewhere in the country. Many people were unjustly accused, including members of the Truman administration.

Truman refused to run in the election of 1952. He returned to Independence, Missouri, in 1953. After his retirement, Truman published two

volumes of memoirs and several volumes of his speeches.

ALSO READ: COMMUNISM; KOREAN WAR; ROOSEVELT, FRANKLIN D.

TRUTH, SOJOURNER (about 1797–1883)

Sojourner Truth spent much of her life working for the freedom of other black people in the United States. She was born a slave in Ulster County, New York. Her original name was Isabella Van Wagener. In 1827, New York State passed a law freeing all slaves. Isabella then traveled to New York City, where she took a job as a household servant.

In 1843, she had a vision in which she believed she heard voices from God. She changed her name to Sojourner Truth and joined the abolitionist movement, organized by people who wanted to put an end to slavery. But in the Southern states, slavery remained legal. Sojourner Truth traveled through several states preaching against slavery. She also spoke out for the emancipation (freedom) of women.

Although Sojourner Truth never learned to read or write, she was a convincing speaker. She spent the last years of her life in Washington, D.C., working to bring a better standard of living to black people in the city.

ALSO READ: ABOLITION, SLAVERY.

TUBMAN, HARRIET (about 1821–1913)

Harriet Tubman was an active worker in the abolitionist movement that was organized to put an end to slavery in the United States. Harriet Tubman was born a slave on a plantation near Cambridge, Maryland. As a young girl, she was forced to work in the fields. About 1849, Harriet escaped from the plantation. She traveled to the Northern states, where most of the slaves had already been freed. She became a "conductor" on the Underground Railroad. The "railroad" was a secret route by which slaves escaping from Southern plantations could travel to the North. Harriet traveled up and down the route, helping the runaway slaves and encouraging them to complete the journey. She was nearly captured herself several times. She was immensely strong and courageous and was often called "General" Tubman or the "Negro Moses."

After the Civil War broke out, Harriet worked as a nurse and cook for the Union Army. She also traveled behind enemy lines as a spy. After the war, she built a house in Auburn, New York, which was open to any black person who needed help. Harriet could not read or write, but she told her life story to her friend, Sarah Bradford, who published it in the book, *Scenes from the Life of Harriet Tubman*.

ALSO READ: ABOLITION, SLAVERY, UNDERGROUND RAILROAD.

TUNDRA The tundra is a flat, treeless area that extends across the Arctic lowlands in North America, Europe, and Asia. Much of Lapland in the northern part of Scandinavia is tundra.

The tundra is mostly snow-covered for about ten months of the year. Most of the soil under the snow, except for a thin top layer that is only 4 to 24 inches (10 to 60 cm) deep, stays frozen all year long. This frozen soil is called *permafrost*. When the snow and ice melt in June, the water cannot seep into the permafrost, so it forms lakes and ponds of all sizes.

Summer on the tundra, where the temperature never rises above 50° F (10° C), lasts from about mid-June to mid-August. During those two months, the tundra brightens with color. Red poppies, blue lupines, and other flowers mingle with mosses, lichens, and other vegetation. Subarctic animals drift up to join their

Arctic neighbors during the short summer. In North America, the hardy musk ox shares grazing space with the caribou. Hungry wolves roam the tundra, seeking food. The king of the tundra, the mighty polar bear, hunts seals and walruses. Tundra animals also include white Arctic hares, lemmings, and Arctic foxes. Birds are numerous and include ptarmigans, ducks, and owls.

The sun never sets in the Arctic Circle in summer. With the coming of autumn, birds and other animals wander south. Twilight ushers in winter, with its snow and darkness.

The Arctic tundra holds vast amounts of mineral resources, such as oil, natural gas, lead, and iron ore. Because of the cold, permafrost, and the extreme weather conditions, it has been only recently that these minerals have been extracted. Special roads, buildings, and equipment have been designed to withstand the tundra environment. Long pipelines have been built to transport oil to refineries in southern locations.

Though it may be hard to realize, the tundra environment is one of the most fragile on Earth. Any change or destruction of plant and animal life on the tundra may take many thousands of years to repair itself. Therefore, strict environmental laws have been passed to protect the tundra.

ALSO READ: ARCTIC, POLAR LIFE.

TUNISIA The Republic of Tunisia, North Africa's smallest country, lies between Algeria and Libya on the Mediterranean coast. It is slightly smaller than the state of Washington. (See the map with the article on AFRICA.) The Atlas Mountains separate the fertile northern part of Tunisia from the dry southern area.

Tunis, the capital city, is a port and a university center. The modern city exists with the old part, with its *souks* (marketplaces) on narrow streets.

▲ *Tundra landscape in northern Norway.*

▲ *Tunisian women wear long, loose, cotton clothes to protect them from the desert sun.*

TUNISIA

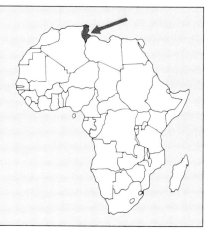

Capital City: Tunis (1,000,000 people).
Area: 63,175 square miles (163,610 sq. km).
Population: 7,900,000.
Government: Republic.
Natural Resources: Phosphates, iron ore, oil and natural gas.
Export Products: Oil, phosphates, olive oil.
Unit of Money: Tunisian dinar.
Official Language: Arabic.

The Bedouin people of the southern desert region raise sheep, goats, and camels. Cattle graze on land near the coast. Fishing and mining of phosphates and iron ore are major industries. Oil is refined at Bizerte. Olive trees, date palms, grapevines, fruit trees, and wheat fields bring some agricultural wealth to Tunisia. The people of Tunis are mainly Arab and Berber, with some Europeans.

The ancient city-state of Carthage was founded by the Phoenicians as a trading center near the site of present-day Tunis. It became a possession of the Roman Empire in 136 B.C. Visitors to Tunis can see the ruins of Carthage and a beautiful collection of Roman mosaics in the Bardo Museum. Near El Djem stands a Roman colosseum built about 100 B.C. Tunisia was controlled by a succession of powers. The last was France, which took over in 1881.

Several World War II battles in North Africa between the Allied forces and the Germans were fought in Tunisia. France recognized Tunisian independence on July 20, 1956, and the next year the old monarchy was abolished. The republic's first president was Habib Bourguiba.

ALSO READ: AFRICA, CARTHAGE.

TUNNEL A tunnel is a tube-shaped underground passageway. Tunnels are usually designed to go through or under some obstacle, such as a river, mountain, or busy city. Tunnels under rivers and through mountains are built to make shorter and easier traveling routes. Tunnels under cities are built to divert some of the traffic from the streets. Other tunnels allow pedestrians to get across busy intersections.

Tunnels may be built in many sizes for a variety of purposes. Small tunnels are built to carry the lines for electricity, petroleum, water, gas, telephone, telegraph, and sewers. These tunnels are rather small in diameter, but they may extend for many miles. *Vehicular* tunnels are designed as roads for vehicles, such as cars, trucks, and railroads. Railroad tunnels are special vehicular tunnels

▲ *These workers are performing caulking operations. They are filling in cracks in the walls of a tunnel in order to keep it watertight.*

▼ *Tunnels through mountains are built to provide shortcuts. This tunnel was blasted through the solid rock of Mont Blanc in the French Alps.*

that permit only rail traffic. Subways are commuter railroad tunnels located under cities that have heavy traffic.

Other vehicular tunnels permit only cars and trucks. Some underwater tunnels are combined with bridges. A vehicle travels part of the route *over* water on a bridge and part of the route *under* water in a tunnel. Many mines consist of networks of tunnels that allow miners and their equipment to get to the ore deposits.

Methods of construction depend on the material through which the tunnel is dug. To build a tunnel through solid rock, several large holes are drilled. Then explosives are placed in the holes, and the rock is blasted to pieces. Steel supports, called shoring, must be placed along the walls and top, especially in building through soft earth. These supports protect the tunnel workers.

In constructing *subaqueous tunnels* (tunnels in the soil under a river or bay), air pressure must be kept equal with the pressure of water outside so water will not enter the tunnel. A shield at the tunnel face is also used during construction to keep the water out. Tunnels are lined with iron or steel so the walls and roof will not cave in. Concrete or tiles give a neat surface finish. Tunnels are ventilated by large fans that force in fresh air and suck out exhaust fumes. The next time you travel through a tunnel, look for the air vents along the sides near the floor and on the roof.

ALSO READ: CAISSON, SUBWAY.

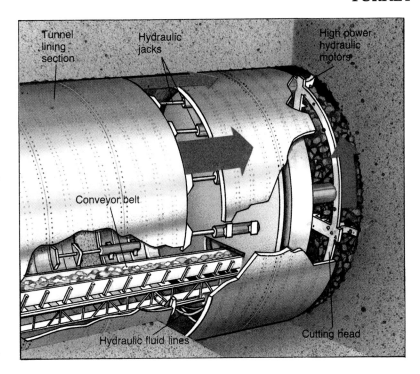

TURBINE   see ENGINE.

TURKEY   A visitor to the Middle Eastern city of Istanbul, Turkey, could travel from Asia to Europe on a ferry and still be in the same city! Located in Asia Minor, Turkey lies mostly in Asia but partly in Europe.

The Turkish Straits separate the continents and connect the Black Sea with the Aegean and Mediterranean seas. The straits (narrow passages of water) are made up of the Dardanelles, the Sea of Marmara, and the Bosporus Strait. (See the map with the article on the MIDDLE EAST.)

Central Turkey is mainly a high plain, called the *Anatolian Plateau*. It

▲ *Most tunnels are dug with tunneling machines called moles. They are like huge drills that cut a shaft through the ground. At the head of the mole, rotating cutters dig out the rock or soil, which is carried away along a conveyor belt. Powerful jacks act like springs to force the mole forward as it removes the rock and soil ahead.*

The West Delaware water supply tunnel in New York is the world's longest tunnel. It is 105 miles (170 km) long.

THE LONGEST TUNNELS IN THE WORLD

MOTOR TRAFFIC TUNNELS			RAIL TRAFFIC TUNNELS		
Tunnel	Location	Length (ml./km)	Tunnel	Location	Length (ml./km)
St. Gotthard	Alps (Switzerland)	10.2/16.4	**Seikan**	Japan	33.5/53.9
Arlberg	Alps (Austria)	8.7/14	**Oshimizu**	Japan	13.8/22.2
Mt. Blanc	Alps (France-Italy)	7.5/12.1	**Simplon**	Alps (Switzerland-Italy)	12.3/19.8
Mt. Ena	Japan	5.3/8.5	**Kanmon**	Japan	11.6/18.7
Great St. Bernard	Alps (Switzerland-Italy)	3.4/5.5	**Apennine**	Italy	11.5/18.5
Mount Royal	Montreal, Canada	3.2/5.1	**Rokko**	Japan	10.1/16.3

▲ *The University of Istanbul, which dates back to the 1400's, is Turkey's most respected center of learning. Notice the Turkish flag at the front of the building.*

According to the Book of Genesis in the Bible, Noah's Ark came to rest on "the mountains of Ararat" when the great flood ended. The highest mountain in Turkey is called Ararat. Some people think it is the Biblical peak.

is a land of salt lakes and hot springs. Earthquakes often take place. High mountains, some of them active volcanoes, almost completely surround the plateau. More than 20 peaks rise higher than 10,000 feet (3,000 m). Summers are hot and dry, and winters are cold.

The warm and sunny garden area by the Aegean Sea around Izmir (Smyrna) yields figs and other fruits. Turkish farmers also grow wheat, cotton, and tobacco. Turkey is the world's largest producer of *mohair*—fleece from the Angora goat. Chromite, coal, and iron are mined. State-owned factories produce steel, textiles, paper, and farm machinery. The people, who are mostly Muslims, speak Turkish. In eastern mountain villages, people called the *Kurds* have kept their own language and customs.

Istanbul, divided by the Bosporus Strait, has been an important city under several different names. The Roman emperor, Constantine, established the capital of the Eastern Roman Empire at Byzantium in A.D. 330 and called it New Rome. But it was soon known as Constantinople. The Turks captured Constantinople in 1453 and made it the capital of the Ottoman Empire. The city was officially renamed Istanbul in 1930. Today, it is the cultural and economic center of Turkey, although the capital is Ankara.

The rule of the Ottoman Empire collapsed after World War I (the Turks were allies of the Germans

during the war). In 1923, the Republic of Turkey was formed, with Mustafa Kemal, or Kemal Atatürk, as president. Turkey invaded Cyprus to protect Turkish Cypriots in 1974. Political violence and economic disorder helped military leaders seize control of Turkey's government in 1980. Power was transferred to an elected parliament in 1983.

ALSO READ: CYPRUS, OTTOMAN EMPIRE.

TURNER, JOSEPH MALLORD WILLIAM (1775–1851)

Can you imagine going to sea in a violent storm, so bad that you had to be lashed to the mast to keep from being washed overboard? That is what the artist Turner did, in order to be able to paint the storm scene as he wanted.

Turner was born in London, England. His father was a barber; the family was poor, and Turner's mother was mentally ill. He had little training in art, but his genius soon showed. As a teenager he painted and drew, selling drawings in the window of his father's barber shop. From these humble beginnings, Turner rose to be Britain's most celebrated painter.

He traveled around Britain on foot, and also in Europe, making sketches that he later made into oil or watercolor paintings. He showed that landscape pictures (or scenery) could be as great as portraits (pictures of people).

TURKEY

Capital City: Ankara (1,700,000 people).
Area: 301,404 square miles (780,576 sq. km).
Population: 55,380,000.
Government: Republic.
Natural Resources: Iron, coal, chromite, oil.
Export Products: Cotton, tobacco, fruit, nuts, textiles.
Unit of Money: Turkish lira.
Official Language: Turkish.

In particular, Turner was interested in light and color. Often he left out details in a picture, using instead marvelous effects of color. These make some of his pictures almost "abstract."

Turner became a very successful painter. He remained, however, a secretive person, and his friends thought him miserly. Sometimes, he refused to allow even his friends into his studio. Yet at other times, at London's Royal Academy of Art, Turner would hang a blank canvas on the wall and paint in full view of his fellow artists, astonishing them with the skill and freedom with which he worked.

ALSO READ: ABSTRACT ART, ART, ART HISTORY.

TURNER, NAT (1800–1831) A revolt by black slaves alerted the South to the discontent caused by slavery. The revolt was led by Nat Turner, a slave born on a plantation in Southampton County, Virginia.

Nat Turner's mother had been brought from Africa as a slave. Turner learned to read and became deeply religious. He believed God had chosen him to lead his fellow slaves to freedom.

In August 1831, Turner and seven other slaves killed their master, a white man named Joseph Travis. They set out for Jerusalem, the county seat, hoping to rally other slaves and to seize weapons before escaping into the swamps. But only 75 others joined their revolt, and their small band was quickly overwhelmed by the local white militia. Nat Turner evaded capture for six weeks, but was finally caught, tried, and hanged. Whites and blacks had died during an episode that showed slavery could not endure.

ALSO READ: BLACK AMERICANS, SLAVERY.

TURPENTINE see PLANT PRODUCTS.

TURTLE Turtles are reptiles with shells. The top shell and the bottom shell join at the sides. The head, legs, and tail can be pulled at least partly inside to protect the turtle from its enemies. Some turtles, such as the box turtle, have a hinged bottom shell that can be pulled up.

The turtle, like all reptiles, is cold-blooded. This means that its body tempertaure varies with that of its surroundings.

More than 200 different species (kinds) of turtles live in the warmer parts of the world. Turtles live in the ocean, in fresh water, and on land. Turtles that live on land are commonly called tortoises, and those that live in the ocean are called sea turtles. All turtles, even those that spend most of their lives in water, lay their eggs on land.

Turtles are of many different sizes. Tiny bog turtles average 3½ inches (9 cm) long. Giant Galápagos tortoises can grow to weigh more than 500 pounds (225 kg). The huge leatherback sea turtle is the heaviest of all reptiles. An adult may be 8 feet (2.4 m) long and can weigh over 1,200 pounds (540 kg). Turtles, large and small, are usually long-lived. Some have been known to live a hundred years and more. Some turtles add "growth rings" to their shells as they grow. A young turtle's growth rings can be counted, but it is not a very accurate way to tell the turtle's age. Not all turtles grow a new ring every year.

Turtles do not have teeth. The edges of their jaws are sharp, hard ridges, similar to a bird's beak. Some turtles eat fish and animals that live near water. Others eat insects and plants.

Land turtles, or tortoises, are slow-moving animals, so they usually have

▲ *A detail from* Snowstorm; Hannibal and his army crossing the Alps, *an oil painting by J.M.W. Turner. Here, the artist combines history with landscape to powerful effect.*

▲ Greenbacked turtles hatching. Most reptiles lay eggs with leathery skins.

▼ Tortoises are land dwellers. They have rounded shells and well-developed legs. The largest are Galapagos tortoises, which can grow to 5 feet (1.5 m) long. Sea turtles, on the other hand, only leave the sea to lay eggs.

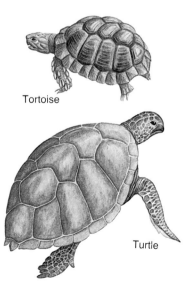

Tortoise

Turtle

especially strong, tight shells to protect them from enemies. The box turtle is a common tortoise. Gopher turtles are tortoises that dig burrows in the ground.

Freshwater turtles, like other turtles, can be beautiful or ugly. Their names often tell you which they are. Snapping turtles are the largest freshwater turtles in North America. They prefer muddy waters and often crawl on land. They get their name for their lunging snaps when they attack prey. They can also be quite dangerous to handle on land. All turtles have to put their heads out of water to breathe, but some pond turtles cannot swallow unless their heads are under the water.

"Terrapin" is an American Indian name sometimes given to turtles, also often called box or pond turtles. The diamondback terrapin is found in saltwater marshes. Box and pond turtles are found in the southern states.

Large sea turtles spend almost all their lives in the sea, but egg-laying is always on land. The female comes out on land only to lay her eggs. She digs a hole in the ground with her back feet, lays the eggs, and covers them with sand or debris. Turtles lay from 2 to 200 eggs at one time, depending on the variety of turtle. The female returns to the water and the eggs hatch under the sun's warmth. The

newly hatched turtles have to fend for themselves and are at risk from birds, raccoons and snakes.

ALSO READ: GALÁPAGOS ISLANDS, REPTILE.

TUTANKHAMEN see EGYPT, ANCIENT.

TUVALU see MICRONESIA AND PACIFIC ISLANDS.

TWAIN, MARK (1835–1910)
Mark Twain's real name was Samuel Langhorne Clemens, and he was one of America's most popular writers. He was born in Florida, Missouri, but grew up in Hannibal, Missouri, on the Mississippi River. Twain worked at many jobs. He was a printer, a steamboat pilot on the Mississippi River, a silver miner, and a reporter. The words "mark twain" mean "two fathoms" (a depth of 12 feet or 3.6 m). The phrase was used on Mississippi River steamboats in calling out the water's depth. When Clemens began writing, he adopted this phrase as his pen name, or pseudonym.

Twain went to California in 1864. The following year, his story about frontier life, "The Celebrated Jumping Frog of Calaveras County," made him famous. In the next few years, Twain traveled all around the world and began giving humorous lectures. Twain married in 1870 and moved to Hartford, Connecticut. In 1884, he became a partner in a publishing firm. The firm failed ten years later, and Twain had to begin lecturing again to pay his debts.

Twain wrote about his travels in *Innocents Abroad* and *Following the Equator*. *Life on the Mississippi* is an account of his experiences working on Mississippi River steamboats. Twain's most popular books are *The*

Adventures of Tom Sawyer and its sequel, *The Adventures of Huckleberry Finn. Tom Sawyer* is about a boy growing up in a small town on the Mississppi with his good friends, Becky Thatcher and the independent, mischievous Huck Finn. Twain modeled Tom, Becky, Huck, Aunt Polly, and even the villain, Injun Joe, on real people he had known. *Huckleberry Finn*, which carries Huck's story further, is considered Twain's best book. The book tells of the adventures of Huck and the runaway slave, Jim, as they travel down the Mississippi River on a raft.

ALSO READ: LITERATURE, NOVEL.

TYLER, JOHN (1790–1862)

"His Accidency," as John Tyler was called by some of his enemies, was the first Vice-President to succeed a President who had died in office. When President William Henry Harrison died on April 4, 1841, Vice-President Tyler decided to become President rather than serve as Acting President until new elections could be held. On April 6, Tyler took the Presidential oath of office, but some leaders in government did not believe he had the right to that title. Tyler insisted that he had both the responsibility and the privilege that went with the highest office in the land.

John Tyler, born on a large plantation in Charles City County, Virginia, was the son of a distinguished judge and former governor of Virginia of the same name. The younger Tyler graduated from the College of William and Mary at 17 and then studied law. At 21, he was elected to the state legislature. He served in the House of Representatives from 1817 to 1821 and as governor of Virginia from 1825 to 1827. Tyler was elected to the Senate in 1827, where he served until 1836. Although Tyler was elected to the Senate as a Democrat, he disagreed with some of President Andrew Jackson's policies. Tyler believed strongly in a very strict interpretation of the Constitution. He believed in states' rights as opposed to the power of the central (federal) government. Nationalism (pride in one's country and its destiny) was growing at this time and, as a result, the Federal Government was growing. So Tyler's views were not very popular. In 1840, the rival political party, the Whigs, hoped to gain the votes of dissatisfied Democrats. They nominated Tyler, a Democrat, for Vice-President. Harrison, known as "Old Tippecanoe," was their Presidential nominee. Their campaign slogan—which has since become famous—was "Tippecanoe and Tyler too."

As President, Tyler opposed bills introduced by Senator Henry Clay, a

▲ *Mark Twain, author of* Tom Sawyer *and* Huckleberry Finn.

Mark Twain protected his pseudonym (his writing name) by registering it as a trademark.

Twain was born in 1835, the same year that Halley's Comet appeared. He predicted that the comet would return the same year he died. He was right. Both happened in 1910.

JOHN TYLER
TENTH PRESIDENT   APRIL 6, 1841—MARCH 4, 1845

Born: March 29, 1790, Charles City County, Virginia

Parents: John and Mary Armistead Tyler

Education: College of William and Mary, Williamsburg, Virginia

Religion: Episcopalian

Occupation: Lawyer

Political Party: Democratic, then Whig

State Represented: Virginia

Married: 1813 to Letitia Christian (1790–1842); 1844 to Julia Gardiner (1820–1889)

Children: 3 sons and 5 daughters by first wife; 5 sons and 2 daughters by second wife

Died: January 18, 1862, Richmond, Virginia

Buried: Hollywood Cemetery, Richmond, Virginia

▲ *A key event in Tyler's Presidency was the invention of a reaping machine by Cyrus H. McCormick. It created a revolution in farming methods. The drawing shows the machine that McCormick patented in 1845.*

Whig leader. A split soon developed between Tyler and many Whigs. Tyler brought about an end to the Seminole War in Florida and settled the boundary dispute between Maine and Canada. During his administration, the nation signed a treaty with China, giving Americans the right to trade in China for the first time. At Tyler's urging, Congress passed a resolution admitting Texas as a state.

Tyler's first wife died in 1842. When he married his second wife two years later, he became the first President to be married while in office. In 1845, Tyler retired to Sherwood Forest, his Virginia estate. In 1861, he returned to Washington to preside over a peace conference to settle differences between the North and the South. When the conference failed, Tyler favored secession.

ALSO READ: CIVIL WAR; CLAY, HENRY; HARRISON, WILLIAM HENRY; TEXAS.

▲ *Modern typesetting methods now use the latest technology, such as lasers and fiber optics, with visual display units (VDUs) and computer keyboards, to produce photocompositon typesetting.*

TYPESETTING Have you ever looked at a book or magazine and wondered how the words and letters are put on the page? Type consists of *characters* (letters, numbers, and various marks) that are reproduced in printing. *Foundry type* is cast in individual *letterpress* (raised) metal characters that are used over and over again. *Hot-metal type* is cast for use on one job only and later is melted. *Cold type* is photographed and is reproduced chemically on a plate from which the printing is done.

Type is made in more than 30,000 different sizes and styles. Each style gives a different feeling to a page. The choice of type style depends on the purpose and kind of material being printed. The type used for advertisements often looks unusual and is chosen to draw attention to the ad. Newspaper headlines are printed in large, heavy, dark type to get you to read the article. Books are usually printed in clear, plain type that is easy on the eye and not difficult to read. Invitations and formal documents are often set in very fancy type to emphasize the importance or formality of the material.

Type styles are divided into four classes according to certain characteristics. *Roman type* is the class most used in modern-day printing. The type you are reading is a Roman type called "Plantin." The Roman types all have *serifs* (little finishing strokes) on the characters. You can see the very tiny serifs at the ends of the lines that form each letter.

Sans serif type has no serifs on the letters. The letters are straight, clean, and squared off at the ends. The tables and charts in this encyclopedia are printed in a sans serif type called "Helvetica."

Script type looks like fancy handwriting, and all the letters are connected. *Black letter type* has an old-fashioned look, similar to the handwriting used during Gutenberg's time.

A basic design for type is called a *face*. Most faces come in a number of sizes, which are called *fonts*. Most fonts include CAPITAL LETTERS, SMALL CAPITALS, and lower-case letters (each type of letter has just been printed). The word face can also refer to the relative darkness of type. **Boldface** is much darker than ordinary type. There is also an *italic* and a ***boldface italic.*** Showy type designs are called *display faces*.

Setting type is the process of assembling type pieces in words and lines. Up until the late 1800's, most typesetting was done by hand. Each piece had to be selected from a case and inserted into a frame. Blank spacer pieces were inserted to make spaces between words and to *justify the lines* (make them come out even on the right-hand side).

Typesetting Machines Typesetting by machine is usually divided into two methods—*hot metal typesetting* and *photocomposition* (also called *phototypesetting*, or *cold type typesetting*).

Most hot metal typesetting is done on the *Linotype* or *Monotype* machine. The Linotype machine, invented by Ottmar Mergenthaler in 1884, casts one line of type at a time. An operator strikes a key that releases a mold for a specific character. Each mold is automatically moved to its place in the line of type being set. The line is justified by *spacebands*. The machine's casting mechanism then pours molten metal into the molds. When the metal hardens, a line of raised type, called a *slug*, is formed. The *Intertype* is a similar slug-casting machine.

The Monotype machine, invented by Tolbert Lanston in 1887, casts individual characters instead of lines of type. It has two parts—a *compositor*, or *keyboard unit*, and a *typecasting unit*. An operator strikes the keys on the keyboard, automatically punching a set of holes on a paper tape. The holes are coded for all the characters, line lengths, word spacings, and line justifications. The tape operates the typecasting unit, which selects the molds, forces molten metal into

them, and assembles the molds in correct order to form lines.

Photocomposition is the newest method of typesetting. It is widely used today in the production of books, magazines, newspapers, and other printed material. In photocomposition, the type characters are rapidly photographed by a high-speed camera, which is usually run by a computer. The computer is programmed for the size and style of type, the line length, and so on. The computer justifies the lines automatically, and the operator only needs to feed it the correct program. The photographed lines of type are prepared for printing through a chemical process that transfers their image onto a metal plate. This encyclopedia was set by photocomposition. A new typesetting method, *cathode-ray tube (CRT) photocomposition*, can reproduce images of type characters, stored in a *memory* (part of a computer), on a screen before transferring the images onto photosensitive paper or film. Recently, photocomposition has been changed by the introduction of *word processing*—composing characters and words on a computer that can show a whole page at a time.

ALSO READ: BOOK; GUTENBERG, JOHANNES; MAGAZINE; NEWSPAPER; PRINTING; PUBLISHING.

▲ *This is a laser typesetter, which produces images onto photosensitive paper or film.*

▼ *The first commercial "hot metal" linecasters were being used in the United States by the late 1800's. By 1892, over 1,000 of these Linotype machines had been produced, mostly for newspaper production.*

UGANDA Uganda is a country in the highlands of East Africa. It has no seacoast and is surrounded by other countries. (See the map with the article on AFRICA.)

Uganda lies on the equator. But because it is on a plateau about 4,000 feet (1,200 m) high, the climate is mild. Temperatures range from 60° to 90° F (15° to 32°C). The Ruwenzori Mountains, sometimes called the Mountains of the Moon, rise from the plateau along Uganda's border with Zaire in the west. Lake Victoria lies on Uganda's southeastern border with Tanzania and Kenya. The headwaters of the White Nile drain the country.

The Victoria Nile, which branches off from Lake Victoria, is the home of many hippopotamuses and crocodiles. Wildlife is also abundant in the plains. Uganda has two of the finest parks in all Africa. The Ruwenzori National Park is an animal sanctuary for waterbucks, lions, leopards, warthogs, and huge herds of buffaloes. Road markers read, "Elephants have the right-of-way." Kabalega Falls Na-

UGANDA

Capital City: Kampala (330,000 people).
Area: 91,141 square miles (236,036 sq. km).
Population: 16,800,000.
Government: Republic.
Natural Resources: Copper, phosphate.
Export Products: Coffee, cotton, tea.
Unit of Money: Ugandan shilling.
Official Language: English.

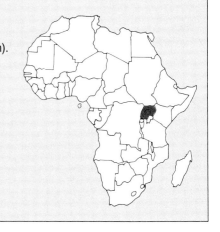

tional Park has giraffes, rhinoceroses, parrots, ostriches, and cranes.

Uganda is mainly an agricultural country. Coffee, cotton, tea, and plantain (a type of banana) are grown. A huge hydroelectric station on the Victoria Nile supplies power to some industries. Copper is mined.

The Baganda are the most numerous of the more than 30 tribes living in Uganda. For centuries, the Baganda had their own king, called the *kabaka*. The last kabaka became the first president of Uganda. The Bamba and the Bakonja, who live near the Ruwenzori Mountains, are small people related to the Pygmies of the Congo. Uganda's capital and chief commercial center is Kampala, located on Lake Victoria.

John Speke, a British explorer searching for the source of the Nile River, became the first European to reach Uganda. The year was 1862. In 1894, the British made the territory that is now Uganda a protectorate. Uganda became independent in 1962. Major General Idi Amin ruled as a dictator from 1971 until he was ousted in 1979. Inflation and public disorder are continuing problems. There is also an AIDS epidemic.

ALSO READ: AFRICA, EQUATOR, NILE RIVER, PYGMY.

UNCLE SAM Uncle Sam is a nickname for the United States government. It was first used during the War of 1812.

The name Uncle Sam may have come from the initials U.S. stamped on uniforms and government property during the War of 1812. According to one story, the name originated with Samuel Wilson, an upstate New York patriot and merchant during the War of 1812. He owned a meatpacking business that supplied provisions to U.S. troops. When the governor of the state visited the plant, he asked what the initials U.S. on barrels

in the factory stood for. He was told they stood for Uncle Sam Wilson. The hard-working, honest Sam Wilson seemed to symbolize the ideal American. Before the end of the war, the name Uncle Sam was commonly used to mean the United States itself. In 1961, the U.S. Congress made Uncle Sam the country's national symbol.

Uncle Sam is usually depicted with a beard, high hat, and tailed coat, as seen in the posters used to appeal for volunteers to join the armed forces in the two world wars.

ALSO READ: PROPAGANDA.

UNDERGROUND RAILROAD
The Underground Railroad was a secret system by which people helped runaway slaves flee from their masters to freedom in Canada in the days before the Civil War. As many as 75,000 slaves may have used the Underground Railroad to escape between 1830 and 1860.

The name Underground Railroad did not mean that an actual railroad was used. But railroad terms were used for many parts of the escape system. For example, the places where slaves were hidden along the way—usually the homes of abolitionists, Quakers, and other people who hated slavery—were called *stations*. The people who guided the slaves from station to station were called *conductors*, and the slaves themselves were sometimes referred to as *freight*. Because many people were against helping runaway slaves, and rewards were offered for the capture of slaves, the system was kept "underground," or secret.

Underground Railroad lines extended from Kentucky, Maryland, and Virginia up into Ohio, Pennsylvania, New York, and New England. Moving from station to station, usually at night, most slaves tried to escape over the Canadian border.

▲ *A member of the Karamojong tribe, a people who live in northeast Uganda.*

▲ *This poster by artist James Montgomery Flagg, showing that Uncle Sam needed volunteers, was widely displayed during World Wars I and II.*

▲ *One of the many "genuine" photographs said to show a UFO of classic saucer shape. Often the UFO is a speck of dust on the film or an unusual cloud formation.*

Both black and white people helped the slaves to use the Underground Railroad. One of the best-known conductors was a black woman named Harriet Tubman. She made many daring trips into the South to bring slaves north. She became known as "Moses" to her fellow blacks because, like the character from the Bible, she helped her people find the "Promised Land." Thomas Garrett, a Pennsylvania Quaker, is said to have helped more than 2,500 blacks escape.

ALSO READ: ABOLITION; CIVIL WAR; SLAVERY; TUBMAN, HARRIET.

UNICORN   see ANIMALS OF MYTH AND LEGEND.

UNIDENTIFIED FLYING OBJECT   Objects frequently fly across the sky—airplanes, dirigibles, helicopters, stars, planets, satellites, and clouds. Most of these objects can be easily identified. But occasionally someone sees an unidentified flying object, or UFO.

The first written report of a UFO was made in Egypt in 1500 B.C. A few hundred more UFOs were seen over the next few thousand years. A rash of UFOs was reported in 1896 and 1897. These were often described as cigar-shaped silver airships. Some passengers were even observed. The most

dramatic UFO of 1897 was that which landed in a Kansas farmer's field, carried off his heifer, and dropped it a few miles away.

UFOs are sometimes called "flying saucers." This name was first used in 1947 when an American pilot reported sighting ten saucers flying in formation near Mount Rainier in Washington. Shortly afterward more sightings were reported, and the Air Force began a study of UFOs. Over the next 22 years, the Air Force investigated more than 12,000 reports of UFOs.

Most of the reported UFOs were eventually identified as known objects—airplanes flying in the vicinity, weather balloons, peculiar cloud formations, satellites, or meteors. Those few that could not be explained had not usually been very carefully described by the observers.

ALSO READ: MIRAGE, SPACE TRAVEL.

UNIFORM   see CLOTHING.

UNION OF SOVIET SOCIALIST REPUBLICS   see SOVIET UNION.

UNITED KINGDOM   The United Kingdom of Great Britain and Northern Ireland is a nation made up of four regions—England, Scotland, Wales, and Northern Ireland. The

UNITED KINGDOM

Capital City: London (6,700,000 people).
Area: 94,535 square miles (24,828 sq. km).
Population: 56,600,000.
Government: Monarchy.
Natural Resources: Coal, iron ore, oil, natural gas.
Export Products: Aircraft, chemicals, clothing, coal, electrical goods, iron and steel, machinery, metals and metal products, motor vehicles, ships, textiles.
Unit of Money: Pound.
Official Language: English.

name of the kingdom is usually shortened to "Great Britain," "United Kingdom," or just "U.K." The United Kingdom covers all of the British Isles except for the southern part of Ireland, which is the Republic of Ireland. (See the map with the article on BRITISH ISLES.)

Wales was united with England by an Act of Union in 1536. In 1603, the king of Scotland, James VI, also became king of England and Wales, as James I. His successors ruled both kingdoms during the 1600's. In 1707, an Act of Union joined Scotland with England and Wales as the Kingdom of Great Britain. Ireland became part of Great Britain in 1801 by an Act of Union, and the whole nation became known as the United Kingdom of Great Britain and Ireland. In 1922, The Irish Free State was formed. Later it broke all ties with Britain and became an independent republic. Six counties in the north of Ireland voted to remain a part of the United Kingdom. In 1927, the name of the kingdom was changed to the United Kingdom of Great Britain and Northern Ireland.

The capital of the United Kingdom is London, England, and the official language is English. But Scotland, Wales, and Northern Ireland have their own capitals. The three areas have kept their own traditions, religious faiths, and local languages, although English is spoken throughout the United Kingdom. Each region sends representatives to the British Parliament.

ALSO READ: BRITISH ISLES, ENGLAND, ENGLISH HISTORY, IRELAND, NORTHERN IRELAND, SCOTLAND, WALES.

UNITED NATIONS On October 24, 1945, 51 nations created the international peace organization called the United Nations. By 1990, the organization had a total membership of 158

nations. The U.N. was first proposed by Franklin D. Roosevelt and Winston Churchill in the Atlantic Charter, issued in 1941. The first plans for the U.N. were made at a conference at Dumbarton Oaks in Washington, D.C., in 1944. Plans for the United Nations were based on the League of Nations, a peace organization formed after World War I. But the United States had refused to join the League of Nations, which had never been successful in forcing nations to keep the peace.

The U.N. has five major goals: to promote peace and security; to bring about friendly relations among all nations; to encourage respect for the rights and freedoms of others; to improve living conditions, education, and health; and to develop an effective system of international law. To accomplish these goals, the U.N. works through six major bodies.

The *Security Council* has 15 member countries. Ten are elected for two-year terms, and five are permanent. The ten temporary members are chosen from all areas of the world in an effort to assure fair geographical representation on the council. The five permanent members are the People's Republic of China, France, the Soviet Union, the United Kingdom, and the United States. If just one permanent member votes against a Security Council resolution, the measure is automatically defeated.

The Security Council studies aggression and disagreements that might lead to war and recommends ways to solve them. It may set up a fact-finding commission or try to per-

▲ *One of the finest medieval cathedrals in the United Kingdom is Lincoln Cathedral in England. The city of Lincoln has been occupied since it was the site of a camp in Roman times.*

▼*Representatives of the member countries of the United Nations meet in the General Assembly at U.N. headquarters in New York City.*

▲ *The modern buildings of the U.N. headquarters in New York City gleam in the late afternoon sun. The low building houses the General Assembly and other meeting rooms. The glass-faced skyscraper contains the offices of the U.N. Secretariat.*

▲ *A UNICEF worker in Uganda teaches mothers to prepare nourishing food.*

suade quarreling nations to submit their dispute to the International Court of Justice (World Court). If these measures fail, the Security Council may ask the U.N. to impose some kind of sanction (economic punishment) to try to force the offending nation to cooperate. The U.N. has sometimes deployed peacekeeping forces.

The largest body of the U.N., the *General Assembly*, is made up of the delegates from every member nation. Each nation has one vote. The General Assembly discusses and makes recommendations on any problem relating to the welfare of member nations. But the General Assembly cannot discuss matters that are under discussion in the Security Council, unless the Security Council is unable to agree upon a course of action. A new president of the assembly is elected each year.

In the U.N., the 54-member *Economic and Social Council*, supervised by the General Assembly, studies living conditions in many lands and sends experts to teach people the skills they need to survive. Eighteen agencies are attached to the U.N. by treaties or agreements. They work through the Economic and Social Council to help people everywhere. The International Atomic Energy Agency works for the peaceful use of atomic energy. The Food and Agriculture Organization helps to improve nutrition and farming methods.

Other U.N. agencies include the World Health Organization (WHO), which coordinates health work throughout the world; the Universal Postal Union (established as long ago as 1874), which makes it possible for countries to exchange letters; the International Labor Organization, which tries to ensure that working conditions are fair everywhere; and two organizations that control air and sea traffic.

One special branch of the U.N. is devoted to children—the United Na-

tions Children's Fund (UNICEF). UNICEF helps to combat disease by vaccinating children and improving nutrition-scarce diets in underdeveloped nations. It also tries to brighten the future of poor children everywhere by teaching them valuable work skills.

The day-to-day work of the U.N. is done by the fourth major body, the *Secretariat*, the administrative branch of the U.N. The Secretariat, which employs more than 6,000 people, is headed by the Secretary-General, a delegate appointed for a five-year term by the General Assembly.

The *International Court of Justice* is the main judicial body of the U.N. Its 15 judges, who serve for nine years, are elected by the General Assembly and the Security Council. The court is at The Hague in the Netherlands.

The *Trusteeship Council*, also supervised by the General Assembly, is the least active of the U.N. bodies today. It was set up to guide eleven *trust territories* (former colonies) to independence. Ten of the eleven original trust territories have now gained independence.

U.N. headquarters are located in New York City. The U.N. has its own post office that issues stamps, its own police, fire department, and school. U.N. headquarters are a popular international tourist attraction. If possible, visitors are given tours by guides who speak their native languages.

There are five official languages at the U.N.—English, French, Russian, Spanish, and Chinese. Each seat is provided with earphones and a dial. Whenever a delegate speaks, his or her words are immediately translated into the five languages. A listener can listen in the language of the speaker or in one of these languages.

ALSO READ: BUNCHE, RALPH; HAMMARSKJÖLD, DAG; INTERNATIONAL LAW; INTERNATIONAL RELATIONS; LEAGUE OF NATIONS; SANCTIONS; WAR.